TRANSCEND

Transcend

A GUIDE TO THE
PERENNIAL SPIRITUAL QUEST

MORTON T. KELSEY

Rockport, Massachusetts • Shaftesbury, Dorset

© 1981 Morton T. Kelsey

Published in the U.S.A. in 1991 by
Element, Inc.
42 Broadway, Rockport, MA 01966

Published in Great Britain in 1991 by
Element Books Limited
Longmead, Shaftesbury, Dorset

Cover design by Max Fairbrother
Cover illustration The Persian Sybil by Michelangelo
courtesy SCALA
Printed and bound in the U.S.A. by
Edwards Brothers, Inc.

Library of Congress Catalog Card Number available

ISBN 1–85230–259–3

To our friend and collaborator
Caroline Whiting

Contents

Introduction

If we get a safe distance from Western Europe and those cultures that have sprung from these roots, we find that religious practice and belief are central in the daily life of most men, women and children. Three quarters of the human race can't imagine a universe that is not in part spiritual. In his penetrating, best-selling book, *The Religions of Man*, Huston Smith demonstrates the perennial and world-wide quest for spiritual life and experience. Indeed, the only place in the world where human religious experience and religious practice are viewed as meaningless is in that tiny peninsula of Asia known as Europe and in those cultures which originated there. Materialism is the view that the only true reality is objectively verifiable physical reality. This view has never dominated any other culture in history.

Western Christianity has in many ways accommodated itself to materialism and has laid little emphasis on the spiritual quest or the individual's experience of the Holy. The New Age movement, diverse as it is, is a reaction in our Western ethos to its dominant materialism. Men and Women want experience of the Divine and few churches provide guides, directions, and/or classes for leading Western people to that experience. If we do not have a view of reality that allows for both a spiritual and a material realm of experience, then the spiritual quest is nonsense. In a recent lecturing tour to Singapore and Malaysia we came into close contact with the rapidly expanding Chinese church there. Because these people can hardly imagine a world that is only material, they are totally open to the message of the risen Jesus and the Gospel that flows from that event. The Church in Singapore has quadrupled in twenty-five years just as it has in Korea where a similar view of reality is dominant. Dr. Peter Wagner, a professor of Christian missions at Fuller Theological Seminary, told me that most churches have been more interested in Westernizing third-world countries then in Christianizing them.

Few people today have much confidence in authority or involved rational arguments. Many authority figures, both secular and religious, have been found to be self-serving and to misrepresent the facts. Recent developments in mathematics and physics have shown that rational inferences about the nature of reality have often been very wrong. Today's men and women usually require evidence and experience to undergird authority and verify conclusions reached through rational speculation.

The same concern for evidence and experience is found among people interested in religion as well as those involved in science. Few people in this present age are drawn to vital religious practice unless they can experience a religious reality which makes a genuine difference in their lives. Is it possible for critical modern men and women to find such experiences as a base for religious belief and practice?

For forty years I have been wrestling with this very problem. In 1950 I came into a religious dead-end street. My training as a Christian pastor had been in the liberal theology which had been in vogue since World War I. God was known only by inference and through his/her participation in the historical process. Having an experience of a Divine Lover was not even considered a possibility and seldom suggested.

A God known only by inference cannot sustain us human beings when we face darkness and evil in the world and within ourselves. In my own inner turmoil it was my good fortune to find a group of people who believed that God still encountered men and women directly. Through listening to my dreams I discovered a wisdom greater than my own trying to communicate with me and show me a way out of my dead-end street. My friend Max Zeller suggested that God still speaks to us as he did to Samuel and that we can have a fellowship with God and converse with the Holy One. I found that keeping a journal of these conversations and dreams provided a foundation for a new religious attitude of hope and confidence in a saving God.

As I spoke in lectures and sermons I found that many people were open and ready to receive just such a hopeful message and start such practices. I realized that it was necessary to provide a world view for these practices since current theology provided little or no base from which to consider the subject of God's direct action in the lives of people in our time. The late Dr. James Kirsch pointed out to me that the philosophical thinking of Dr. C. G. Jung provides a view of reality which is spiritual as well as material. I studied Jung's work and went to see Jung in Zurich. I then went back to study in depth both the Bible and Christian tradition. In both of them I found the conviction that we human beings live a real and important earthly life and also have access to a real and ultimately important spiritual world, to the Kingdom of Heaven.

Jung's philosophical thinking opened my eyes to the depth and power of the early Christian Church. Jung did not provide ultimate answers for me, but rather a key to unlock the treasures of vital Christianity. The direct experience of God is as available to us now as it has ever been. The church could offer this transforming gift to people today. Hilde Kirsch's statement put it well: there is no reason that there cannot be healing of body, mind and soul in the church as well as in the psychiatrist's office.

The many implications of this point of view began to dawn on me and I began to write. First of all I wrote on the subject of tongue speaking which my Jungian friends suggested that I take very seriously. For years I worked on the subject of dreams and discovered that throughout the early Church they were seen as the way par excellence that God is revealed to human beings. Then I tackled the subject of Christian healing and discovered its rich tradition within the church. Subsequently, while teaching at the University of Notre Dame, I wrote books on theology, journal writing and the life of prayer. My writing has continued in the years that followed.

Many of these books are technical studies of the philosophical and theological framework needed to make sense of mystical experience. Several years ago I decided to make this material available to a wider audience. With the help of Caroline Whiting we produced a series of news letters. We summarized and edited many of the books that I had written with my longtime friend and line editor, Paisley Roach. The popular response to the news letters prompted my editor, Richard Payne to publish this material in book form. I am grateful to Mr. Payne and Element Books for making available this new edition of suggestions on the perennial spiritual quest.

Friends, parishioners and students far too numerous to mention have helped me formulate many of the ideas in this book. Leo Froke MD, John Sandford, Andy Canale, Abbot David Geraets and Jim Scully of Pecos Benedictine Monastery, and Ollie Backus have sifted and tested these ideas and experiences in hundreds of hours of discussion and conversation.

Most of all I am deeply grateful to my wife, Barbara, for her help on the books that form the basis of the material and for her journeying with me on her own spiritual quest. In addition to this she has proof read and checked sources as well as making sure that my writing was clear and simple.

Morton Kelsey
Gualala, California
Easter 1991

Transcend

I

Paranormal Experiences and Christian Belief

Approximately one-fifth of the population of the United States reports having paranormal experiences frequently. This astounding fact, cited by Andrew Greeley in his monograph *The Sociology of the Paranormal: A Reconnaissance,* was discovered in a study of belief systems commissioned by the Henry Luce Foundation. Let's take a look at some of the other findings of the Greeley study.

Greeley defines paranormal as psychic, mystic and contact-with-the-dead experiences. The first such experience for which Greeley reports research data is déjà vu, the feeling that one has been in the same situation previously, even though the precise incident could not possibly have occurred. Three-fifths of the persons responding to the Luce Foundation survey said they had experienced this déjà vu sensation.

Another paranormal experience, extrasensory perception, is defined as communication between persons without using usual means of perception. According to the survey, 58 percent of all Americans have had an ESP experience.

A third phenomenon, clairvoyance, is described as the ability to see an event occurring far away. Twenty-five percent of the American population reported experiencing this form of the paranormal. Altogether, the Luce study showed that 30 million Americans frequently experience one of the three forms of psychic experience mentioned.

A fourth type of paranormal experience—contact with the dead—reportedly occurred to 27 percent of the United States population. Twenty-one percent of these respondents were widows or widowers, but they constitute only 7 percent of the population at large.

The mystical branch of paranormal experience is more difficult to define and deal with than are the psychic or contact-with-the-dead experiences. Little research has been done on mysticism, but William James, in his *Varieties of Religious Experience,* notes four characteristics. The mystical experience cannot be adequately described; it must be experienced. It gives knowledge: it is noetic. The mystical experience brings a feeling of oneness with the universe and a sense of insight. The experience is brief, usually only a few minutes. And the experience is passive, bringing the feeling that one has been taken over by another power.

The Luce Foundation researchers concluded that mystical experiences can be defined as religious, that these experiences are affected by childhood family relationships and religious life, and that such experiences have long-term effects. Thirty-five percent of all Americans have had at least one mystical experience. Of these 70 million Americans, a sizeable percentage were male, college educated, black, and earning over $10,000 a year. Many were over forty and Protestant (but nonfundamentalist). Evidence also indicated that persons having mystical experiences came from religious homes with close family ties. The research further showed that mystics tended to be better educated, more successful economically, more psychologically well off, more optimistic and confident of survival, and less racist.

Greeley concluded that the contention that psychics and mystics are out of touch with normal reality and are social deviants is false and that persons who experience the paranormal may well be experiencing greater emotional and psychological well-being than the rest of the population. He noted that no other sociologist had made such a study. His research has been replicated in both Great Britain and Germany.

Certainly Greeley's findings are important, for they document the existence of nonrational experiences in the lives of millions of Americans and show the high correlation between mental health and mysticism. They provide the data and statistics which make serious discussion of the paranormal intellectually and psychologically respectable. (There is no other serious sociological study of these subjects.) And they lead us to reexamine our worldview, a view that maintains that there is only one way of knowing—through reason and sense experience. For if we believe that paranormal experiences do happen, we need a framework which allows belief in a nonrational, nonmaterial reality.

For centuries humankind has believed that our senses provide the primary source of our information about the world. But the recent explosion of interest in "psi" phenomena indicates that human beings have the ability to gather information without using the normal input channels of the senses and nervous system. This ability enables people to make contact with "psychic" beings and to influence physical matter. Until recently no serious scientist considered the possibility of such a thing as ESP. Rather, exploration of the paranormal was left to people involved in the occult.

Such isolation of psi experiences to a small group of people has not always existed, however, for until early in the sixteenth century almost everyone was interested in these strange abilities. The change in outlook began to occur with the development of a scientific point of view which was concerned with showing that physical things work in an orderly manner. Thus scientists became so engrossed in spelling out facts based on sense experience and reason that they forgot that there was any other way of knowing.

We have learned a great deal about the physical world, but the more we learn about its order and regularity, the more things we find that don't fit with the ordinary ways we perceive and experience this world of matter, space and time. Today's scientists admit that the universe seems to operate in more than one way and that the idea that everything is determined by one set of laws gives us only part of the picture. In the last ten years physicists in particular have become deeply interested in the meaning of extrasensory perception for their own study.

The first serious investigation of ESP in modern times was begun in the late nineteenth century by a group of men, several at Oxford, who organized the Society for Psychical Research in England. Early in the 1900s a similar society was founded in the United States, and by 1930 J. B. Rhine at Duke University had established the study of parapsychology as a science.

Certainly initial ESP research created an uproar in the scientific community, but in 1969 the Parapsychological Association, after years of rejection, was accepted into the distinguished American Association for the Advancement of Sciences and psi had achieved scientific respectability.

During the years when the scientific view of the world perpetuated the belief that reason and sense experience were humankind's only way of knowing, Christian theology arrived at the conclusion that God was immanent in the processes of the physical world and could be known in history, but not through direct experience. But with the discoveries of people like Marie Curie, Albert Einstein and Loren Eiseley, the props of the old order were knocked down, for these scientists demonstrated that the laws of the universe are not so simple as we thought. Although many theologians, along with behavioral psychologists and some other social scientists, are still caught in the materialist point of view, they need to update their thinking if they are to minister to a world in which experiences of the paranormal are becoming increasingly important.

As strange as it may seem to us who have been taught to use only one kind of experience, this understanding of another way of knowing has had a long and honorable history. Almost all pre-modern religions have held this view. Certainly the early Church Fathers believed in a direct experience of God. It was only when Aristotle's thinking was adapted to Christianity by Thomas Aquinas and further refined by Descartes that the church abandoned its belief in two ways of knowing. The understanding of another realm of reality is found in nearly all Oriental religions and in the Chinese scripture known as the *I Ching,* the idea that human beings can reach out in two ways to two different realities is fully expressed.

In our time the basic point of view which acknowledges two realities has been revived by psychiatry, largely through the work of Sigmund Freud, Carl Jung and their followers.

Modern Christians have varying attitudes about the ways of knowing reality. Some biblical critics ignore all parts of the Bible that tell about experiences which could be called paranormal—like prophecy, healing, miracles, dreams and visions.

Other Christians, including most modern theologians, maintain that any significant knowledge comes to us only through our five senses. This viewpoint means that we have to strip the New Testament of a good share of its contents, including all mythological elements, thus reducing biblical riches to poverty level.

A third attitude contends that all kinds of miraculous things happened in New Testament times but that once the world knew about the revelation of Jesus Christ, parapsychological events were no longer needed. We are to believe that God has the power to make these events happen, but they do not happen any more.

A fourth point of view, that of conservative Christians, believes that paranormal experiences are either directly from God or from Satanic powers. Thus when psi events occur outside the circle of orthodox belief, they can only be the work of the Evil One, damaging to anyone who comes into contact with them. Thus even scientific study of ESP is considered unwise, if not catastrophic.

Finally, there is the view that extrasensory perception is a natural part of human knowing which the modern world gradually forgot in its effort to develop as much objective understanding as possible. From this point of view the paranormal is understood as natural and morally neutral and may be used either for good or for evil. Thus, psi experiences can point the way to an understanding of classical Christianity and help modern Christians grasp the power of that Christianity and share in it. This last view is the one we shall consider, especially as it relates to Christian thought and practice today.

The Bible and Paranormal Phenomena

The Bible is a mine of information on psi phenomena. Nearly every book of the Bible shows the belief that human beings have contact with more than just the physical world and that there are other ways of influencing the world and people besides physical means. Because the Bible is a practical book, the main point of both the Old and the New Testaments is how to get on in a world which is everywhere touched by God's meaning and purpose. The biblical writers showed little interest in science as the Greeks perceived it.

Frequently in the Old Testament paranormal practices such as "augury" or divination were condemned as dangerous because they were thought to lead one away from dependence on Yahweh and toward the pagan temples where they were practiced.

The New Testament, however, has a different tone. While the Old Testament Yahweh was often seen as a harsh judge who administered both healing and sickness, Jesus maintained that God is a loving father who does not send sickness. Rather, disease is a result of Evil Forces let loose in the world.

Therefore to the early Christian, healing was good in itself because it was one of the best ways of turning back the works of Evil. In the Old Testament, on the other hand, healings sometimes happened, but they were not a central concern.

There was also a change in the attitude about evil and a new understanding that evil forces, the demonic, are abroad and doing men and women in. The Old Testament in its concern for monotheism described angels as messengers of God, but avoided saying much about demonic powers. It also said little about a realm with which we could communicate in addition to the physical one. The Old Testament stressed the idea that one must look only to Yahweh. Foreign deities were considered evil and

Hebrews were warned not to deal with them. There was, therefore, little possibility of a theoretical discussion of psi in the Old Testament, even though the book is full of experiences of it.

The New Testament is not so restrained. It is full of the idea that we are in touch with a spiritual world containing *both* good and evil forces, and that we had better know them and know how to deal with them.

Now let's take a look at some biblical psi experiences.

Divination and Power

The Old Testament reveals a number of different ways to get knowledge of the future or of the will of God—through the casting of lots, the use of household gods to ask information from God, and through dreams and visions.

In the story of Balaam an omen was used to reveal the presence of an angel and several references are made to stars as omens of destiny. Direct conversations with God also take place. From the call of Abraham to the final vision of the book of Revelation, the Bible is a record of contacts like these with another realm of reality.

There is a basic difference, of course, between magic and religion. Magic is an attempt to use the powers of the spiritual world for one's own ego purposes, while in religious actions like prayer, meditation, and healing, one attempts to be in tune with God's power to be used as an agent of his loving will. But religion and magic both use the same psi experiences.

Gifted Heroes

Although the practice of soothsaying is condemned in certain passages of the Old Testament, the narrative parts show how common and apparently quite accepted these practices were. The history of Israel began when Abraham listened to a voice speaking within him telling him to leave Ur of the Chaldees and go to a new land. The young Jacob received a pledge from God through his dream of the ladder ascending to heaven. The meaning of Joseph's life revolved around his remembering and interpreting dreams. Moses met God face to face and was surrounded by such manifestations of power as the burning bush. For Samuel, who had clairvoyant abilities, the voice of God came in the night.

Later, Elijah and Elisha performed such "magical" acts as bringing down an omen of fire from heaven and healing a leper. Amos, Hosea, Isaiah, Jeremiah and Ezekiel all had visions and were seers.

Jesus as Healer

One reason why so few people in modern times actually look to Jesus of Nazareth for help and guidance is that he is regarded as no more than a great moral teacher, when in fact he is much more than that.

The Gospels report that Jesus walked on water, healed the sick and exorcised demons. He knew the future, calmed the storm, read minds, practiced clairvoyance and finally arose from the dead. He was in mortal combat with the Evil One, and if we do not understand this fact, we cannot understand his ministry. Jesus not only used these powers himself, but he passed them on to his followers.

Paul wrote one of the clearest outlines of the kind of power Jesus gives to his disciples and agents through the Spirit. In Corinthians, Romans and Ephesians he describes these gifts which include such abilities as healing, discerning spirits, receiving revelations, speaking in tongues, interpretation and prophecy.

Acts of the Apostles and Later Christians

The results of contact with the living Christ were set down in the book of Acts, which shows that almost every major decision of Christianity was made because of a dream, a vision, a prophecy, a supernatural visitation, or some kind of divination. For example, Paul was struck down by a vision and then healed and converted. Through the experience of an angel and later a vision and telepathic information, Peter's attitudes were changed.

The overwhelming experience of Pentecost, with the gift of supernatural languages, was followed almost immediately by a series of healings, casting out demons, and raisings of the dead. Over and over the actions of the apostles depended on clairvoyant or precognitive information, prophecies, supernatural visitations, and omens and visions.

Later on every one of the apologists who stood against the Empire and fought the battle to gain acceptance of Christianity believed in healing and dreams. Such men as Irenaeus, Athanasius, and Sulpicius Severus all wrote about paranormal happenings like those in the Gospels. Such Church Fathers as Basil and Gregory of Nyssa in the East and Ambrose and Augustine in the West emphasized dreams and visions and healing miracles.

In the West the lives of saints in every period have been touched by miraculous events and psi happenings. St. John of the Cross, St. Teresa of Avila, St. Ignatius of Loyola all had direct experience with the realm of spiritual reality.

In recent years the same kind of experiences have occurred in the charismatic movement which stresses the understanding that God breaks into human life directly and gives these gifts. But most of the mainline churches have departed from the belief that these experiences can happen.

The Christian Framework and Psi Events

As we have seen, all of the experiences which students of ESP are investigating today are found in Jewish and Christian sources and throughout most of Christian history. In addition to experiencing the paranormal spontaneously or through being "in the Spirit," one may also encounter it through participation in such traditional religious rituals as Holy Communion or by engaging in meditation.

Christianity offers no sanction for the use of drugs to alter consciousness and bring contact with the divine, as do some religions. Fasting, however, which can have some of the same effects as drugs, has been used in many Christian groups.

For the most part, psi events simply occur where there is vital Christianity. The *experiences are not to be valued in themselves* but as tools to be used in expressing and furthering the will of God. If these phenomena are sought for personal gain or power, they become evil. It is not the gifts or experiences of ESP in themselves which are then evil, but the purpose for which they are sought and the way of seeking them. This understanding is important in both the Bible and later tradition. Evil does not seem to be connected with any particular practice or experience, but rather with the method of obtaining it and the way of making use of it.

ESP, Theology and Christian Living

The first and most obvious task of the intelligent Christian is to be informed about the area of paranormal experiences. People today show a legitimate longing for spiritual experiences, as demonstrated by interest in Eastern ways of meditation, in mystical experiences, use of drugs and practices like the *I Ching*. But the church cannot touch this longing until it is equipped to open up ways of finding such experiences.

First, the church needs to change its worldview to include honest belief in two levels of reality—the spiritual as well as the material. Once people realize that there is good reason to believe in the reality of the New Testament experience, we may find it easier to change our familiar ways of theologizing and philosophizing. The Platonic view of the world, with which Christianity grew up and became triumphant, is still available. If we are willing to interpret such a view with the one that parapsychological facts suggest, Christianity will again be in a position of central influence in modern culture.

We have seen that there are various ways of opening oneself to parapsychological experiences, some of which present real dangers. These phenomena need to be experienced within a religious group where men and women respect them but are not afraid to explore them. The safest approaches are through dreams and spontaneous visions that open this area up naturally, and through meditation and religious ritual.

No inner journey should be undertaken without guidelines from those who have traveled that way before and returned in a better state than they were before they undertook the journey. The wisdom of the church can offer valuable guidance in this realm.

Psi Theology

The implications of psi phenomena for theology are many. They suggest a new view of experiences of God and so of the value of meditation. They reaffirm the validity of the New Testament narrative. Christian healing again becomes sensible. Factual reasons can be shown for believing in immortality, and for taking Christian morality seriously. Altogether, a new thrust is given to the idea of ministry and to the training of those who are to minister.

If ESP can bring knowledge of physical events that can be verified, we need not deny people's statements about experiences of a nonphysical world. These experiences, described in every culture, must then be considered. It is up to serious students of religion to study them and see if any consistent pattern emerges from the descriptions. Statements about religious experiences become necessary data for understanding our religion. It becomes almost absurd to decide what religion is, or ought to be, only by working with concepts and ideas about it on the basis of rational reflection.

The task of trying to make sense of the complex data of experience is not an easy one. It has been the task of all the great historical religions and most philosophies. Christianity has also tried to provide a view of reality in this way, particularly during the first four or five centuries of its life. Dr. C. G. Jung has tried to perform the same task in modern times.

As we begin to take inner experiences seriously and learn about the reality of the psychic world, we find facts about the world and ourselves that give a different picture of the universe from the familiar one most people believe is true. These inner experiences help us to realize that the psychic world is a real world which is not totally tied to the physical one, and that we live in an open universe. They show that human personality has direct and observable, although finite, effects on the physical world. Once this is accepted, it is easier to realize that there is a psychic or spiritual reality beyond the human which also has such effects. We then have good reason to believe that we can be in touch with a reality like ourselves, but infinitely greater than we human beings, from which the image of the human being was struck. This reality appears to be the organizing principle of the world.

Indeed, the experience of those who have known most deeply the realities of the Christian gospel, speak of meeting this principle as the risen Christ. They describe encountering a love which will go to any length to reach and touch and transform human life. These individuals have also described how they were then filled with a new understanding of their destiny and purpose, and were given new power to put that kind of love into action. This encounter is still available to men and women who seek it. ESP reminds us that such experience is real and that it may be one's most important experience.

Christians can understand ESP and see it as a natural capacity that can happen spontaneously and often becomes alive within deeply religious people. When ESP is seen in this light, religious people need not fear it. These experiences can be integrated into the fabric of our religious lives, giving them more depth and completeness and excitement and also making it harder for unwise separatist groups to spring up.

ESP is a natural phenomenon of the human psyche. It can be used for the glory of God and the enrichment of human life when it is understood and placed in the service of divine love, the love expressed in and through Jesus Christ. Religion shorn of these psi experiences becomes far more dull, and instead of attracting people, turns many of them away from the creative wholeness which is possible as God's people.

FOR FURTHER READING

Kelsey, Morton T., *The Christian and the Supernatural,* Minneapolis: Augsburg Publishing House, 1976.

2

Finding a Worldview that Permits Belief in a Spiritual Reality

It was said of Thomas Kelly, author of *A Testament of Devotion,* "He seemed to be expounding less as one possessed of 'knowledge about' and more as one who had unmistakable 'acquaintance with'." The Christian gospel maintains that individuals are not limited to a mere intellectual knowledge *about* God, but can personally experience a relationship *with* God. The modern church, however, has generally ceased to be a channel for persons to experience the power of Christ. The rationalism and materialism which has permeated Western civilization, including the church, is based on a worldview which precludes the existence of a nonmaterial, or spiritual, reality. If the modern person is to really encounter God, he or she must have a worldview which allows belief in a spiritual reality.

How did we arrive at such a thoroughly secularized worldview and how can we find a new one that will permit us honestly to set about being acquainted with, not merely knowledgeable about, God?

The Schism Between Science and Religion

In 1543 the ideas of Nicolaus Copernicus fell into the neatly ordered medieval cosmology like an explosion. Copernicus' well-supported hypothesis simply stated that the sun, not the earth, was the center of the solar system.

For those of us who have not struggled with doubts about our place in the universe, it is difficult to imagine the impact this theory had upon the entire Christian world. It shook the religious foundations of the medieval conception of the universe, for if the earth were no longer its center, then the whole schema would collapse.

Understanding the implications of Copernicus' hypothesis, the church reacted violently, declaring him a heretic after his death and exhuming and burning his body. Giordano Bruno, burned at the stake in 1600 for views similar to Copernicus', spoke the truth in his last statement: "Ye who pass judgment over me feel, maybe, greater fear than I upon whom it is passed." On June 22, 1633 Galileo either had to deny his belief in the sun's centrality to the solar system or suffer the same fate as Bruno.

That the philosophical foundations of the church were shaken by Copernicus' hypothesis and subsequent scientific ideas clearly demonstrates that the church feared its beliefs could be disproven. The furor caused by the intrusion of scientific discovery exposed the fact that the church was based on a rationalistic theology. To understand how this rationalistic basis for belief occurred, it is necessary to take a look at the ideas of Plato and Aristotle and briefly trace the development of Western philosophical thought.

Platonic Thought in the Early Church

Plato believed that human beings are not limited to experiencing a merely physical reality, but have access to a spiritual reality as well. He also maintained that there are four ways of knowing—that the source of humankind's knowledge is not reason and sense experience alone, but rather includes prophecy, healing (cleansing), artistic inspiration and love. Plato believed that an individual's psyche has a spiritual element and thus he or she can have experiences which transcend logical thought and sense experience alone. It is important to note that if we accept Plato's methods of knowing, we must realize that knowledge is never certain or final; rather, our conclusions are always tentative and subject to new revelation.

One of the early Church Fathers, Justin Martyr (150 A.D.), realized that Plato's philosophical ideas gave an intellectual expression to what Christ lived and taught. Since Plato gave the clearest, most systematic account of how man could know both the spiritual and the physical worlds, Justin began a great theological tradition joining the essential categories of Platonic thinking and Christian experience. This Platonic point of view was expressed by all of the major Church Fathers, including Irenaeus, Tertullian and Cyprian in the West, and Clement, Origen and Athanasius in Alexandria. In the Eastern and Greek side of the empire, Basil the Great, Gregory of Nyssa, Gregory Nazianzen and John Chrysostom based their works on Platonic thinking. Ambrose, Augustine, Jerome and Gregory the Great laid the foundation for thinking in the West for almost a thousand years upon a Platonic basis.

How Aristotle's Worldview Affected the Church

With the beginning of Western Christianity and a new culture, Platonic thought was displaced, for men and women in the West were cut off from the center of life in Byzantium. Roman law was adopted, Latin became the language of scholarship, and the Greek spirit, including Plato's understanding of human experience, was lost.

Instead, the thinking of Aristotle, revived by the Arabs, was brought west soon after 1000. Thomas Aquinas became convinced of the truth of Aristotle's worldview, particularly that individuals receive direct knowledge *only* through sense experience and reason, not by divine inspiration. Aquinas concluded that Christians ought to accept this view, so he wrote the *Summa Theologica,* attempting to show that Aristotle's worldview was compatible with Christian tradition. Toward the end of his life Aquinas did have a powerful experience of God, but his writings, prior to this experience, were instrumental in shaping the official doctrines of the church.

Thus the ideal of certainty based on logic rather than experience became the chief cornerstone of theology and the church. And it was this attitude of certainty that could not tolerate priest-philosopher Copernicus' scientific inquiries.

Naturalistic Science and the Western Worldview

The eventual result of the scientific inquiry started by Copernicus was the conclusion that the ultimate nature of the universe was materialistic and mechanistic. Kepler perfected Copernicus' theories, showing that heavenly bodies act as any physical thing and need no heavenly beings to account for their movements. Then Newton theorized that the entire universe acted as a machine working according to precise mechanical laws. Next, Darwin's evolutionary theory of natural selection seemed to indicate that humankind was simply the result of chance interaction, and thus human life had no ultimate meaning or significance.

These theories were systematized by such thinkers as Karl Marx in Germany, August Comte in France, Herbert Spencer in England and B. F. Skinner and other behaviorists in the United States. The idea common to these systems was that human beings were only intricate combinations of physical atoms and thus the idea of a spiritual reality and of a divine-human encounter became absurd.

Because of the variance between the dogmas of the church and the theories of science, the average Christian has been caught in a terrible dilemma. He or she has had to maintain a divided mind—with religion in one compartment and science in the other. This split makes it difficult to hold an integrated worldview and frequently results in one's buying into the claims of a fundamentalist type of religion and ignoring the reasoning of science.

On the other hand, the modern person may dismiss the realm of the spirit as complete nonsense and adopt the hypotheses of science as the cornerstone of his or her belief system. It is interesting to note how few people have ever thought that this religious/scientific division could be solved with a new worldview, a new hypothesis of reality that allows belief in both a material and a nonmaterial reality, room for sense experience and logic on one hand, and an encounter with the numinous on the other.

Unable to ignore the impact that scientific discovery made upon human thinking, the church eventually attempted to update its thinking. This attempt, however, resulted in merely fitting the Christian faith into the rationalistic framework provided by the secular world. Such Protestant theologians as Rudolf Bultmann, Dietrich Bonhoeffer and Karl Barth believed that God does not break into the modern world in a personal way, and Catholic philosophers like Jean Danielou and Bernard J. F. Lonergan hedge on the subject of a direct encounter with God.

A Worldview that Permits Belief in a Spiritual Reality

Ironically, it is twentieth century scientific thought which has begun to point the way toward belief in a spiritual reality once again. Madame Curie's discovery that the 92 atoms break apart into innumerable pieces demonstrated to even the best scientists that their theories and discoveries were limited and there was yet much to learn.

The great modern mathematician, Kurt Godel, ascertained that discovery does not come through sharp, well-defined reason, but through intuition. Laws formerly believed to be infallible and indisputable have been shown to be merely roadmaps to find a way through the world.

Teilhard de Chardin has shown that the seemingly unwarranted mutations which occur in the evolutionary process prepare for adaptation, rather than result from it, allowing the hypothesis that some spiritual purpose is working in and through the physical world.

Psychosomatic medicine has provided us with the realization that the body cannot be described merely as a mechanism which reacts to various stimuli from the physical world. Dr. Flanders Dunbar, in a study at a large New York City hospital, demonstrated that all parts of the body are affected by emotions.

Psychiatrist Jerome Frank states in his *Persuasion and Healing* that there are some diseases for which faith is as specific a remedy as penicillin is for pneumonia. Such noted persons as Robert Oppenheimer, Loren Eiseley, T. S. Kuhn and Werner Heisenberg all attest to the importance of a non-material reality in our lives.

Another viewpoint demonstrating the reality of the spiritual world in our lives is the thinking of Swiss psychiatrist C. G. Jung, who maintained that modern persons' mental problems can only be touched and healed as they are brought into meaningful contact with the living God. Jung believed that there is a depth in humankind called the unconscious through which one experiences the spiritual world.

In both the Old and the New Testaments we encounter the same type of belief in another reality that Plato, the early Church Fathers, insightful modern scientists, C. G. Jung and others have spoken of. Most theologians today, however, still hold beliefs based on an Aristotelian worldview which prohibits belief in direct encounter with God. These theologians must now update their thinking so that the church may once again minister a gospel of power to the whole person—a gospel that can speak to our need for acquaintance *with* God, not mere *knowledge about* God.

The church can begin to update its thinking and enliven its ministry if it will follow Dr. Jung's lead in exploring the nonrational, or spiritual, world. Jung believed that through dreams, symbols, archetypes, visions, intuitions, we can encounter that realm of the numinous where the divine and the human intersect and relate. How did Jung arrive at his theories and what empirical evidence does he offer for support? In order to understand Jung, we need to first look at the contributions of Sigmund Freud to our knowledge of the unconscious.

Freud's Contributions

With the publication of *The Interpretation of Dreams* in 1900, Sigmund Freud became the first scientist to write convincingly about the significance of the unconscious and dreams. Although he had done lengthy empirical studies, his initial response from the scientific community was one of contempt.

Other prominent medical men, beginning with Hippocrates, had regarded the dream as significant; however, they had seldom viewed it as a psychic reality. They had merely considered it a part of the brain's physical functioning. Many great literary artists, such as Shakespeare and Goethe, had recognized the existence of the unconscious, but Freud was the first person to discover that the meaning of dreams could have a practical application.

Primarily Freud was a physician who had been trained in neurology. In Paris he had learned to use hypnotism. Disappointed with the ineffectiveness of the hypnotic method in helping his patients' neuroses, he started using dreams to show people what was going on in the unconscious parts of their personalities. He believed that if dreams could be adequately interpreted, the conflict between conscious and unconscious attitudes producing neurosis could be healed.

Thus Freud started his method of psychoanalysis to enable his patients to regain their health. Because many of the dream contents are objectionable to the conscious personality, Freud thought that a censor existed within the human personality to conceal the meaning of the dream from the ego. The dream images, then, resembled a code that needed deciphering because they were disguising the primitive sexual roots of our personalities. Thus the dream images were not really alive or autonomous in their own right.

As members of the medical profession started taking Freud seriously, some adhered completely to his theories and others began to doubt that it was valid to reduce the unconscious primarily to sexuality, or to the pleasure principle and the death wish.

Jung's Approach to the Unconscious

One of the men who had learned much from Freud but could not accept what he considered a dogmatic system was Carl Jung. Although Jung disagreed with Freud's emphasis on sexuality, the primary reason for the disciple's split from his mentor was that Freud was a rationalist while Jung was an empiricist.

Contrary to Freud, Jung maintained that the unconscious communicates symbolically—through images, not rationally—through concepts. Thus he believed that rather than being purposeful distortions, dreams are clear communications in the same way that art, literature, mythology and folklore are. The modern person's problem is that for the most part he or she has forgotten how to think in symbols. In his work Jung discovered that the dream images of his patients appeared repeatedly in the myths, art work and religious stories of peoples the world around.

As a result of paying attention to his own unconscious, Jung found that "there are things in the psyche which I do not produce, but which produce themselves and have their own life." The work he did with his own

symbolic images led Jung to believe that this level of reality he had encountered fostered the development of a religious attitude toward life.
Through the unconscious, then, individuals could contact their religious
depths and cultivate a meditative and imaginative, rather than merely logical and analytical, attitude toward the numinous, permitting an actual encounter with God.

Jung maintained that the only way the contents of the unconscious can
benefit an individual is for them to be "brought into serious relationship
with the conscious mind." Because dreams do speak in images they sig-
nify, as do parables and cartoons, meanings that frequently challenge our
understanding. A single dream image may evoke a wealth of memories and
feelings just as a single cartoon character may arouse a charged emotional
reaction in us. How are we to deal with these images so that we may, in
fact, establish a beneficial relationship between the unconscious and the
conscious aspects of our personalities?

First, we need to realize that each figure appearing in our nightly dramas
represents some part of our *own* personality. As Jung wrote, "One should
never forget that one dreams in the first place, and almost to the exclusion
of all else, of oneself. . . . The 'other' person we dream of is not our friend
and neighbor, but the other in us, of whom we prefer to say: 'I thank thee,
Lord, that I am not as this publican and sinner'. "

In order to understand our ongoing inner drama, we must ask what part
of our personality resembles the figures in our dreams and what reaction
we have to these figures.

Frequently symbols from mythology and religion may appear in our
dreams, signifying the presence of some deeper, universal meaning. These
symbols, called archetypes, often occur in our more powerful or striking
dreams.

To deal effectively with our dreams, we need to recognize the key figures
that people them. Jung isolated and named the various types of images
that recur. Among them, the chief ones are called the shadow, the anima,
and the animus. The shadow image represents that part of our personality
that is undeveloped, uncivilized or primitive. We usually project this part
of ourselves upon other people, holding them responsible for the rejected
sides of ourselves. If we take the trouble to become acquainted with this
shadow side, however, it will contribute greatly toward our potential
wholeness.

The anima is the unconscious feminine side of a man's personality. It
usually seems to be the bearer of qualities foreign to the conscious person-

ality and may include moods and relationship to or belief in beauty, love and the divine.

The animus is the unconscious male side of a woman and may include her opinionated, argumentative side and her ability to relate to truth or to hard facts and to spiritual reality.

Because it is much easier to project the unconscious male or female side of our personalities onto another human being, we often find the sort of romantic love which results eventually collapses under the psychic burdens it must bear. By assuming responsibility for this unconscious side of ourselves, however, we will find greater personal wholeness as well as more authentic, real relationship to the living, outer male or female we choose to relate to.

Projection can also operate on a national level or some other collective level. Because they projected their negativity onto the Jews, the Germans were susceptible to Hitler's propaganda and became demonic destroyers in World War II. In our culture, black people often receive the projection of the primitive or the sexual side of whites. Only by dealing inwardly with the figures that are so easily projected outward can we avert disaster for others and come into our own birthright and wholeness.

Although the shadow, the anima, and the animus are, perhaps, the three major inner figures Jung delineated, there are many other important inner personages. The child archetype, the maiden, the Great Mother, the wise old man and the Self occur frequently in dreams.

There are also many nonhuman dream symbols we should enumerate. The sea may symbolize the unconscious; the house may be the totality of the psyche; the automobile may refer to ones' conscious life and ego adaptation; an animal may represent instinctuality. Journeys occurring in dreams may symbolize an inner spiritual quest; an earthquake often indicates a psychic change about to take place. Frequently a dream about one's childhood may represent one's psychological reorientation and growth.

We must be wary of easy, cheap methods of dream interpretation, however, for dreams must be viewed respectfully as living things, handled with care and understood in context. We should remember that dreams are parables of our inner lives.

Types of Dreams

Dreams express their meaning to us in several different ways. Compensatory dreams, for example, reveal hidden qualities in our personalities or draw our attention to aspects of our lives we have ignored or repressed.

One young woman, for example, dreamed that she was wearing a pair of shoes marked "holy." Upon dealing with the dream, she discovered that she unconsciously had a holier-than-thou attitude which she needed to change.

Because some of the early Christians had somewhat one-sided personalities, they often regarded some dreams as evil, for they did not undertstand that their dreams were compensating for their lopsided views of life. Thus an ascetic might dream of voluptuous women.

Another type of dream might emphasize that one's conscious attitude is currently compatible with or in balance with the unconscious attitude. Frequently these dreams are abstract, using figures to represent one's situation. Such a dream is Ezekiel's vision of the wheels in the Old Testament account. This type of dream may also reveal its own meaning through direct statements.

The "ordinary" dreams about people and places common in our everyday experiences may be much more profound and helpful than we could anticipate. As a result of our loving attention and faithfulness to their images, dreams eventually lead us to a new center of personality, and we may become what is known as *individuated.* Jung characterized individuation as that process "by which a man becomes at one with his own individuality, and at the same time with mankind, with the humanity of which he is a part."

Dreams may also express themselves in a clairvoyant or telepathic manner that shows us things beyond ordinary time and space boundaries. Thus we may know of future or long-distance occurrences in an almost uncanny way.

Numinous dreams, endowed with a powerful and radiant quality, place us in the presence of God and thus provide us with meaningful religious experiences. These dreams do not usually need any interpretation but stand just as they are, indicating to us "that a light has burst forth in the darkness which the dark cannot catch up with."

Because a great deal of skill is needed to interepret dreams sensitively and meaningfully, we need to be aware of certain rules for dealing with this nonrational world. One must approach the unconscious with an open mind—listening to see what it has to say. Through much practice, through learning about the dreamer's conscious life and attitudes, one can start to develop a feel for interpreting dreams. If one is to be effective in interpreting the dreams of others, one must pay attention to his or her own dreams. A broad life experience and a personal relationship with God are also indispensable to the person who would attempt to guide others in exploring their way in the spiritual kingdom.

Jung and the Inner Journey

We can now easily see why the thinking and the experiences of Carl Jung are so important to the Christian church. It is he who calls us to reestablish the religious view of life we have long since forfeited in favor of a rationalistic approach to understanding the meaning of the universe. Jung's approach to human experience gives us the opportunity to reclaim the lively meaning that is our Christian heritage by experiencing relationship with the numinous in this way.

Why has the church thus far paid little heed to Jung?

One reason why the clergy has not realized the immensity of Jung's contribution is that he is extremely difficult to read, and the clergy, already burdened with innumerable tasks, has little time to sift through volumes of weighty psychological writing.

Secondly, Jung's writings, based upon experience, virtually require that one investigate these experiences oneself in order to believe that they actually occur.

Thirdly, the path Jung followed is not easy or to be embarked upon lightly. Confrontation with the divine, whom Jung termed "an annihilating force and an indescribable grace," can be a painful and consuming experience as well as a joyful and radiant one.

Thus Jung has marked for us a very direct, personal and individual means for coming into contact with spiritual reality. If we embark on the spiritual journey to which he has introduced us, we will find it brings life-changing experiences.

FOR FURTHER READING

Kelsey, Morton T., *Encounter with God*, Minneapolis: Bethany Fellowship, 1972.
———, *Afterlife: The Other Side of Dying*, Ramsey, N.J.: Paulist Press, 1979.

3

How the Spiritual Breaks into Our Lives

W e live in a world of technology—of computers and robots, missiles and spaceships. Yet in the midst of all of the scientific advances and technological achievements of the outer world there is an ever-increasing expression of interest in the inner world of meditation, psychic phenomena, and religious experience. Thousands of people have learned to concentrate quietly on a mantra, while others have taken yoga classes or joined Eastern religious sects like Zen or Buddhism. The fastest growing groups among Protestantism are the charismatics, and the Catholic charismatics are also growing in numbers.

Many persons seek an inner experience through some form of drug experience, while others dabble in such psychic experiences as hypnosis and mediumship. Everywhere there is evidence that the material world alone cannot satisfy the deepest desires of men and women for transcendence and meaning. People are desperate to discover what it is that makes life worth living, and if they cannot find a healthy way to come into relationship with spiritual reality, then they may seek an unhealthy way to enter the inner world.

Our purpose in this chapter is to examine fourteen specific ways through which human beings can encounter psychic reality. Any of these ways may be used to gain entrance to the inner world, but some states of altered consciousness are more natural and safer than others. All fourteen ways testify to the reality of the spiritual world.

Dreams

One of the safest natural ways to encounter the unconscious is through dreams, a fact recognized by almost all world cultures with the exception of the Western world since Descartes. Dreams are a spontaneous altered state of consciousness; we do not have to seek them out.

In the 1950s William Dement started studying dreams from a physiological vantage point, discovering that they occur four to six times nightly and vary in length from a few minutes to an hour. Marked physiological characteristics accompany the various stages of dreaming. First, rapid eye movements are signs of vivid dreaming. Second, patterns in brain waves change during dreaming as demonstrated by the recordings on an electroencephalograph.

Since Dement's work, other researchers like Montague Ullman, Stanley Krippner and Charles Honorton have shown that dreams are capable of giving ESP information. Thus the dream puts us into direct contact with a world that cannot be known through a rational or sensory way.

Furthermore, as Dr. Carl Jung pointed out, dreams give us a means of discovering our unconscious viewpoints and unearthing repressed memories. Dreams also give us a way of becoming connected to rich archetypal symbols and myths. Although dreams provide encounters with creative forces and even enable us directly to experience the spirit of God, they may also be sources of negative experiences in which destructive forces are at work.

Visions, which are akin to dreams but spontaneously happen to us while we are awake, are also a means of experiencing the spiritual world. In fact, the Hebrew and Greek languages scarcely differentiate between the two words. Although many modern-day persons have had visions, as Andrew Greeley demonstrated in his monograph *The Sociology of the Paranormal: A Reconnaissance,* very few report them to anyone, least of all to their ministers or priests, for fear of ridicule or condemnation.

Meditation

Meditation is the second way we can experience spiritual reality, for it can help us develop a new state of consciousness and thus provide us direct access to the divine. The sort of meditation practiced by Easterners has as its purpose the loss of one's ego and absorption into cosmic consciousness. The purpose of Christian meditation, in contrast, is to allow one to *relate to* spiritual reality, particularly to the Christ.

Christian meditational practice requires a turning inward to concentrate on those images and symbols that arise from our depths if we will but provide the silence and time that are necessary for their cultivation. By using the creative imagination we can encounter the Risen Christ and even participate in New Testament stories that speak to our particular needs.

Concentrating on a specific symbol, like a crucifix or a religious icon, can produce an inner calm and repose which enables us to be receptive to the voice of the inner Christ. Or we may repeat the Jesus Prayer or some other meaningful religious lines that focus us on Christ. Whatever meditative means we choose to help us become still and gain entrance to spiritual reality, we need to keep in mind that our purpose is to relate to this reality, not be absorbed by it.

Religious Ritual Behavior

The third way of encountering spiritual reality, through religious ritual behavior, may be termed sacramental meditation. One way to experience an altered state of consciousness, for example, is by participating in a religious service based on a pattern and including such behaviors as chanting, music, and ritual acts like the Eucharist. Through these components of institutional religious observance, we enter a realm where myth is alive and can be mediated safely because it is contained by the church as a body. The presence of others also acts as a safeguard to help us be present to our earthly lives while engaging in moving spiritual experience.

Such time-honored Roman Catholic rituals as saying the rosary or following the stations of the cross can bring one into relationship with the spiritual world as one concentrates in prayer or participates symbolically in the last hours of Christ's life. The ritual celebrations of the religious year, such as Christmas, Easter, Pentecost, give us a sense of the numinous in relationship to the here and now as we see myth become concrete in our experience.

Because the spiritual world is dangerous and we should not attempt to traverse it unaided, we should remember to rely on the church, the body of Christ, to help us explore it. Certainly one way the church can help us is by providing us with the rituals that anchor us in material reality while allowing us communion with the divine nature.

Love

Surely love is one of the chief ways that the divine manifests its presence in humanlife. Love may be of two types. First is the romantic love that causes us to feel that we are on "cloud nine." This form of love is based primarily on some projection of ourselves that we see mirrored by another. A young man finds his own capacity for sensitivity and beauty embodied in a lovely young woman. Enchanted by this beautiful reflection, he falls in love. Certainly this type of love is real, but it is fraught with dangers, for as individuals get to know each other, they discover that the projections, the glamour, the image, does not coincide with the real person, and the relationship must either take a new form or be dissolved.

The other sort of love is based on authentic relationship so that one gets to know another person as he or she is and can see the reflection of the Divine in this individual's humanity. When we love another person, we participate in the mystical splendor of God. Only as we exemplify the love of God by allowing it to work in our lives do we translate the universal into the concrete and specific. If we refuse to love, then we betray life and allow evil to grow in our lives and in the lives of others.

In Paul's writings in the New Testament the words for *Holy Spirit* and *love* are used almost interchangeably, and in his famous letter to the Corinthians he says, "Without love I am nothing."

One of the earmarks of mature love is that it seeks more to give than to receive. Only as we have felt loved and accepted and healed of our pain and anger can we turn toward others and care about their hurts.

Another characteristic of mature love is faith, for it is practically impossible to believe in a caring God without the nourishment of warm human love. Courage, another byproduct of love, is gained only when we have confidence in the ultimate caring nature of reality. It is love which gives that reality meaning and expression.

Becoming as a Child

Yet another means of sharing concretely in spiritual reality is spending time with children, for in relating to them we contact our own inner child. It is often our hurt inner child, starving for affection and attention, who causes us trouble as adults until we take time to nourish and love it. A child has a fresh, vivid, unspoiled way of looking at the world that puts us in touch with our sense of wonder and imagination. Consider, for example, the following short poem authored by a seven-year-old:

> Lightning
> Who made you?
> Did some great giant
> Write you with a flashing pen?
> Did he?

The originality and sensory quality of her words put us in touch with our own childlike awe of God's creation, and with the poet and artist in each of us.

Spending time with children also gives us a renewed sense of the importance of play and recreation. In his *Homo Ludens* (man the player) Johan Huizinga contends that human beings experience the essence of their natures while they are at play. Likewise in *The Joy of Running,* Thaddeus Kostrubala cites instances of joggers and runners at his California therapy center who experience a sense of childlike abandon and delight as they forget their cerebral cares for a time and engage in hard physical exercise.

Art

The sixth way of experiencing the presence of the supernatural in our lives is through art. Each of us can become an artist when we allow our encounter with the divine nature to be expressed creatively through painting, weaving, writing, sculpting, dancing, or some other such medium. Art and religion are akin in that they are both concerned with the powerful experiences that occur when the divine and the human intersect. The reality of such an intersection demands expression and all real art speaks of the fire sparked in such an encounter; otherwise, art becomes mere entertainment.

The reason so many people today experience futility is that they have no sense of the transcendence which comes with the divine encounter. Art which reflects only this sense of futility cannot properly be called art, for it is empty and absurd. The great artists of the world—like Shakespeare, Goethe, Da Vinci, Bach, Handel—have all expressed the reality of the spiritual world through the triumph and grandeur implicit in their works.

Neurosis and Psychosis

Certainly God has provided many ways for us to encounter him. One highly unpleasant but extremely effective way is through neurosis or psychosis. Sometimes when nothing else can convince us that we are starving for God, a neurotic complex can do the job nicely. We come to the end of our rope so to speak; we must find the divine or die.

A complex can be a very healthy sign in disguise, for it may show us that we can no longer stand being stultified by a purely physical environment. Instead of being a meaningless curse, an anxiety neurosis may be the pains of spiritual rebirth, for in admitting that we cannot find our own way, that we are in despair and cannot function, we realize that we must give up our highly-cherished ego adaptation and cry out to God in anguish. Psychosis may result from living only in the psychic realm and having inadequate contact with material reality.

It may be that God can only reach some of us through the neurotic crack in our personalities, for we seldom unmask and seek help until our agony becomes unendurable. Giving up our ego adaptation is a form of death, and we fight it tooth and nail. Yet Jesus said that if we want to find our life, we must lose it. Thus neurosis may well be termed the "sacred illness" that forces us to seek meaning, for we do not voluntarily give up our ego adaptation while we are comfortable and painless. As Elizabeth O'Connor says in *Search for Silence,* "Our chance to be healed comes when the waters of our own life are disturbed."

Spontaneous Religious Experiences

The eighth way we can experience the divine is through spontaneous religious experience. Today the charismatic movement in both the Roman Catholic church and in Protestant denominations is gaining ever greater numbers as more and more people experience the spiritual world through such phenomena as tongue-speaking and healing.

Although many people believe that glossolalia only occurs in an atmosphere of uncorked emotionalism, the evidence proves otherwise. This phenomenon has taken place frequently in quiet meditational settings—and has happened to unsuspecting church members who previously would have been appalled at the thought of anything so blatantly charismatic.

Tongue-speaking is defined as a spontaneous utterance of uncomprehended and seemingly random speech sounds. It rarely occurs outside certain religious groups and is not controlled or directly understood by the speaker. After the tongue-speech has been completely uttered, it is usually spontaneously interpreted—either by the speaker or a group member. Those experiencing glossolalia report a sense of great joy and deep religious emotion.

Although glossolalia is the subject of great controversy within the church, there is biblical evidence to support the phenomenon. Some psychologists also believe that tongue-speaking can be expressive of deep contents in the psyche of an individual which connects to the transpersonal or collective unconscious of humankind.

Certainly tongue-speaking accompanied the gift of the Holy Spirit to the apostles in the New Testament. In the Acts account of Pentecost we read, "And they were all filled with the Holy Spirit and began to talk in other tongues as the Spirit gave them utterance." Later Acts records the story of the Gentiles receiving the gift of tongues after Peter has preached to them. Although references to tongue-speaking are not as frequent as references to dreams, visions and healings, they are an important part of the New Testament.

Another form of spontaneous religious experience, healing is being experienced once again in the modern church after many centuries of deviation from the practices of the early church and the New Testament. Primarily because the institutional church made no room for the healing experience, sects outside the mainstream of the church sprang up to practice the laying on of hands and prayers for spiritual and physical healing. The Camps Farthest Out, begun in the 1930s by Glenn Clark, have made spiritual healing a reality in many lives, and the Order of St. Luke, started by Dr. John Gayner Banks, has become active in several countries.

Such persons as Alfred Price, Louise Eggleston, Tommy Tyson, Olga Worrall, Kathryn Kuhlman, and Oral Roberts have all had an active healing ministry. Along with her husband, the Rev. Edgar L. Sanford, Agnes Sanford, author of *The Healing Light,* founded the schools of Pastoral Care to introduce both clergy and laity to a healing ministry. Both the Anglican and the Roman Catholic churches have recently taken stands on the importance of healing in the church.

Several new books have been written to shed more light on the subject of healing. Don H. Gross's *The Case for Spiritual Healing,* Bernard Martin's *The Healing Ministry in the Church,* Francis McNutt's *Healing* and my own *Healing and Christianity* all attempt to offer a framework for belief in the reality of healing.

The Death Experience

The ninth way we may contact spiritual reality is through the death experience. Because technology has made it possible for us to prolong life and even to reclaim the lives of persons who have "died" for a short time, we have access to descriptions of the reality encountered by those whose spirits have left their bodies when vital bodily functions ceased.

In his *Life After Life,* Raymond Moody details characteristics reported consistently by these persons. Nearly everyone who had had such a "death" experience reported that language could not possibly capture the quality of the experience. Almost all persons reported a sense of timelessness and an ability to see more lucidly than in earthly life. Many encountered a being they described as beautiful, loving and luminous. Others reported the ability to see a rapid review of the events of their lives.

Frequently participants in this "death" experience said they had experienced no desire to return to earthly life. Many persons reported that they were no longer afraid of death, although they said they could never believe in suicide. Moody found all the "dead" persons he questioned to be emotionally stable. He also noted that the similarity among the characteristics of these experiences tended to reinforce belief in their validity. I have described other experiences of contact with the deceased in *Afterlife: The Other Side of Dying*.

The Trance or "Slaying in the Spirit"

The tenth way one may experience spiritual reality is through a trance or what is commonly called "slaying in the Spirit." Perhaps the most dramatic of all the *charismata* being experienced once again in the modern church, this phenomenon frequently occurs among what may be called "enthusiastic" religious groups.

My first contact with "slaying in the spirit" occurred during a healing conference when I laid my hands upon a minister during a dedication service. As I performed the ritual act, he lost consciousness and slumped to the floor. This man later described his experience as a spiritual dying and rising and he maintained that it was the start of a new era in his Christian ministry. Later on I became acquainted with the ministry of Kathryn Kuhlman and attended one of her services in Los Angeles. Almost everyone in the long line of persons who came forward for the laying on of hands fell over backwards, unconscious, to the floor. No one was hurt, and it was obvious to me that these experiences were usual occurrences at Miss Kuhlman's meetings.

Although many people feel that such ministry is often fraudulent, my impression was that the experiences I witnessed were genuine and not overly emotional. Certainly these kinds of experiences are not sought out by everyone, nor should they be. Persons who do experience "slaying in the Spirit," however, report that they feel a great sense of calm, peace, and abandonment to God. Often they describe the experience as a loss of conscious ego control and a submitting to the Holy Spirit. Sometimes a floating sensation accompanies the experience.

Frequently persons report permanent changes in their lives as a result of being slain in the Spirit—either physical healing or emotional healing that brings a lightening of some psychic burden. It appears that in these slaying experiences the ministering person is the mediator through which one may experience the power of the spiritual world.

Hypnosis

Another means of contacting the spiritual world is through hypnosis. By responding to the hypnotist's softly spoken instructions, the subject enters a state resembling a trance during which he or she becomes susceptible to the hypnotist's suggestions. Because hypnosis opens up one's unconscious mind to another human being, it is a powerful process and must be executed with great care. In fact, it is so powerful that surgery can be painlessly performed through its use.

Many attempts to test the validity of hypnosis have recently been performed. Dr. Burton Glick, chief of psychiatric research at Mount Sinai Hospital in New York, tested a young nurse on his staff to discover whether or not clairvoyance is possible through hypnosis. The young woman's ability to accurately describe a picture inside a sealed envelope convinced the doctor of the validity of ESP through hypnosis.

Occasionally hypnotic experiments must be discontinued when it becomes increasingly more difficult to bring subjects out of their trances back into normal outer reality. Although hypnosis may be used effectively by competent, trained individuals, one needs to exercise caution in dealing with this type of access to the non-physical realm, for some practitioners use it to gain power over other individuals. In addition, not all the psychic contents unearthed through hypnosis can always be dealt with adequately by a subject, particularly if he or she is emotionally unstable or undergoing stress. Hypnosis, used with care, is a valuable tool.

Mediumship

Mediumship is a twelfth way of experiencing the supernatural. A medium goes into a trance in order to contact the dead or to attain ESP information through such contact. Frequently this practice becomes an end in itself, a brand of religion, rather than a means to an end. Although many mediums are fraudulent and do damage, particularly to recently bereaved persons, some genuine, sensitive psychics can use mediumship advantageously.

Edgar Cayce, for example, whose phenomenal gift is well documented, was able to help many sick persons as a result of tapping his unconscious contents during a trance. He had the ability to psychically contact a person in poor health, diagnose the malady, and accurately prescribe remedies. A dedicated Christian and authentic medium, Cayce never accepted payment for his gifts.

Both the Ouija board and automatic writing are also ways of contacting psychic forces but they can spell potential danger for participants because they unlock unconscious forces that easily overwhelm some individuals.

Oracles or Divination

Oracles or the practice of divination is yet another means of experiencing ESP. A common example of this practice is opening the Bible at random and letting a pointer pick out a verse to serve as a guideline in some particular problem or situation. In the East throwing coins or sticks to consult the *I Ching* serves the same purpose.

The practice of divination rests on the belief that a spiritual meaning pervades the universe so that random clues may mirror that meaning. Oracles can give us insights, but if we regulate our lives merely according to them, we may give up our independence. Astrology is the most common form of present-day divination.

Drugs

The last way we experience the other realm is through drug use. Although for many people drugs are a retreat from reality, increasing numbers of individuals, particularly young people, are using them as an experiment with altered states of consciousness. According to Andrew Weil, author of *The Natural Mind,* most people who use hallucinogenic drugs do so because they have found no other way to relate to the spiritual world and they are hungry for an experience outside the space/time world.

Weil contends that our innate desire for spiritual experience is so great and if society provides no means for its attainment, then people will invent or find their own means. If we deny the reality that drugs lead to, then we certainly cannot deal adequately with the problem of their use. If the church is to help this problem, it will need to provide ways for individuals to experience the mystical and the imaginative, for these are the spiritual elements that drug users are seeking when they smoke marijuana, pop pills, or take LSD trips.

4

Von Hügel, Mysticism and Mature Religion

That the English language has only one word—mysticism—to denote a direct experience of God shows the religious poverty of our culture. The Greeks had 12 words to describe the breakthrough of the spiritual world into human experience, and the Hindus have 34 or 35 such words. Because Western society is primarily extraverted in its adaptation to life, it has neglected the introverted aspect of Christian practice, and both attitudes must be developed if we are to be mature in our religious life.

One of the greatest Christian theologians was Baron Friedrich von Hügel, author of *The Mystical Element of Religion.* Von Hügel's life and philosophy were changed as a result of studying the life of St. Catherine of Genoa, an Italian noblewoman of the 1400s. She had one day gone to church and seen a spontaneous vision of the blood of Christ filling the church and washing her clean. As a result of this vision, Catherine started attending mass daily, fasting, and ministering to the sick, some of whom were healed by her touch.

The intensity of Catherine's love and devotion and the beauty of her mystical life, which reached out in service to others, touched von Hügel so deeply that he became convinced of the direct experience of God in human life. He altered his philosophy of idealism (that the spiritual is the *only* reality) and as a result of Catherine's concrete living example, came to believe in the reality of both the spiritual and the material worlds.

Because of this integrated belief system, von Hügel set out to show that a mature, effective religious life must incorporate several elements—the institution, mystical experience, and critical thought.

The Institution

First, there can be no development of real spirituality without being rooted in the traditional practices, beliefs, and morality of the church. People who try to "go it alone" without belonging to the institutional church are deprived, for they lack the nurture and guidance the body of Christ can provide. One cannot fulfill his or her religious potential without support, encouragement and teaching. The church can provide guidelines to the experience of the inner world while keeping its members rooted in the stability of rituals and extraverted practices.

The idea that each person's religious opinion is of the same value is nonsense, for there *is* a body of knowledge which is tested by time that can be transmitted by the church to believers.

The danger in limiting one's religion *only* to the institution is very real, however. Religious belief can degenerate to mere superstition if a ready-made dogma with a set of hand-me-down beliefs is accepted without question or study. An obsession with detail, organization, and blind obedience to the church's authority can cause sterility, which drives people away from the church and causes the institution itself to lose its vitality. The symbols and rituals of the church lose their richness and mythic qualities, and the church becomes a set of rules and regulations.

Mystical Experience

The second element essential to mature religion is mystical experience, or the direct apprehension of God by human beings. Many Christians believe that mysticism is merely a flight from reality and responsibility and would thus subscribe to the remark of Joseph Fletcher, author of *Situation Ethics,* that mysticism begins in mist and ends in schism.

But religion that consists entirely of institutional practices and intellectual knowledge is dead indeed. A direct, vital encounter with God *can* be experienced, and it can occur in three main ways—through sacraments, through contemplation, and through an inner perception of the divine in images.

Sacramental Mystical Experience

Sacramental mystical experience brings us into contact with the divine through contact with a material object. The inward and the outward work together. The bread and wine of communion, for example, mediate the atonement experience to us. The more collective the culture or group that participates in the sacramental, the less differentiation is made between the object and inner reality. Confession, absolution, saying the rosary, and performing the stations of the cross are all rituals that help us experience God. Certainly the Bible can be used sacramentally too.

Contemplative Mystical Experience

The second form of mystical experience is the contemplative, which is not generally advocated here. This type of union with God involves no material objects or symbols, merely the individual and his or her perception of the divine presence. Contemplative practice seems to have originated with the philosopher Plotinus in the third century and is not based on the New Testament or the practices of the early Church Fathers.

This particular type of union with God has as its goal the loss of ego and absorption into cosmic consciousness. Detachment from emotion, images, and material reality and an ultimate loss of ego result from this form of mysticism.

It is easy to understand why certain Eastern religions would practice this form of mysticism, for in large countries such as India, where starvation and every form of human misery are so apparent, it is little wonder people would want to disengage themselves from physical reality.

The contemplative saints of the Middle Ages also need to be understood in context. Theirs was a world full of disease, barbaric invasions, and poverty. Escape into otherworldliness through merger with the divine is understandable.

Von Hügel helps us to distinguish between the positive and the negative forms of mystical practice by pointing out that healthy mysticism promotes growth, harmony and action, while unhealthy mysticism brings passivity, fixedness, and indifference.

Such great Christian mystics as St. John of the Cross and St. Teresa of Avila were careful to incorporate contemplative practice with sacramental mysticism and a life of active service to others.

Mystical Experience Through Meditation Upon Inner Images

The third form of mysticism, meditation on images, is experienced when we turn inward and make use of our imagination. As we do this, we find an inner realm of reality gives birth to all kinds of images—dark and threatening ones, vital life-giving ones, and universal archetypal ones.

Mystical experience that makes use of the imaginative emphasizes the journey or process itself more than it emphasizes any particular end result. The growth which the mystical journey provides as we experience God's energizing love never comes to an end although we may find times of rest along the way.

We should note here that we can only be in earnest about mystical experience if we truly believe in the existence of spiritual reality. Because Western society, including most theologians and many clergy, is caught in a materialistic worldview, we need to make sure that allegiance is to a worldview that includes both physical *and* psychic reality.

Certainly the incarnation embodies this viewpoint, for God, who is spirit, revealed himself to human beings in a specific flesh-and-blood man, Jesus of Nazareth.

Meditative mystical experience gives us access to this same Jesus through the use of images. In his *Spiritual Exercises* Ignatius of Loyola shows how New Testament images can be used in this way.

Meditative prayer has always been the basis of the religious practices of The Society of Friends or Quakers, who would listen to the inner voice of God in silence and would then follow the guidance of the spirit in going out into the world and offering their lives in service to others. But they could only go out and act after they had listened to the inner voice.

As one engages in this type of mystical experience via inner images, one may imagine oneself in relationship with images from Jesus' parables, such as the tale of the prodigal son. Or one may imagine taking part in an event from the life of Jesus, such as being present at the feeding of the five thousand. Early Christianity believed that by relating to these images one could contact the reality they represented and were a part of.

Ironically it was not the church that showed me how to engage in this sort of mystical experience. Rather, it was psychologist Carl Jung who showed me that such meditative work can open us to the riches of spiritual reality.

In her book *Dark Wood to White Rose,* Helen Luke of the Apple Farm Community in Three Rivers, Michigan, shows how to use Dante's images from *The Divine Comedy* meditatively. And in his *Psychosynthesis: A Manual of Principles and Techniques,* Italian psychiatrist Roberto Assagioli discusses his encounters with the Christ within. He calls his meditative practice psychosynthesis and verifies that changes occur continuously in the lives of his patients who use this religious practice.

Just as we run into spiritual danger if we try to base our lives only on the religious institution, so we will court disaster if we concentrate solely on mystical experience to the exclusion of the other elements of mature Christian life. We run the risk of becoming disengaged from outer reality, of being passive and inert. We also short-circuit God's love, for Christianity must be practiced in community, in the hard realities of honest encounter, if it is to be as God intended. We are, after all, called to "make connections between the human story and the divine story," as Henri J. M. Nouwen says in *The Living Reminder*.

Critical Thought

The third element of mature religion, says von Hügel, is critical thought. Certainly one reason the early church proved to be so powerful as it stood against the pagan world was that it not only outlived and outdied that world; it also outthought it. Christians need to be well versed in theology and religion, but they also need to keep abreast of modern scientific and psychological discoveries and to read such books as T. S. Kuhn's *The Structure of Scientific Revolutions* and John Macquarrie's *Twentieth Century Religious Thought: The Frontiers of Philosophy and Theology 1900-1960*.

Some Christians are fearful that if they exercise their critical thinking capacity, they will lose or weaken their faith. On the contrary, honest searching and openness to secular disciplines can lead us back to our faith. After all, it is such modern-day scientists and psychologists as Teilhard de Chardin and Carl Jung who have pointed out truths about spiritual reality that most theologians and clergy have never thought about.

One reason that many young people today have taken up Zen and yoga is that they are attempting to throw away their heads as a result of their disillusionment with the intellect. Certainly the intellect alone cannot provide life with meaning, but our minds, too, are God-given and we must not discard them; rather, we must integrate critical thinking into the other elements of mature Christian practice.

Relationship with Other Human Beings

The fourth element of mature religion, which I have added to the three proposed by von Hügel, is a familiarity with the nature of human beings—as they react to themselves and to one another, on a one-to-one-basis, and in groups. If love is the center of the universe, then one cannot stay in relationship to it unless one reaches out to others. Effective reaching out means that we need some knowledge of the structure of the human psyche and an awareness of the communication process. Perhaps most essential of all is developing the ability to really listen to others—not merely to hear the words they say.

Listening is being silent with another person in an active way; it is participating in another life in a creative, powerful way. It is the essence of what the Bible says when it instructs us to "bear one another's burdens." Listening to another means forfeiting the wall of words by which we usually insulate ourselves from others. It also means being silent inside ourselves—not judging or censoring the one who talks. Listening is love in action.

Certainly familiarity with the human psyche and reaching out to others do not by themselves constitute mature religion. The logical extension of too much outward relationship with too little critical thinking, institutionalism or inner experience is the free-love commune where everyone lets it all "hang out" and ends up by hating everyone else. The mature Christian life needs all four elements we have discussed.

Proposal for a School of Spiritual Direction

Few Christians are aware of the importance of balancing the four elements of religion we have mentioned—the institution, mystical experience, critical thought and human relationship. Fewer still know how to set about actually living a healthy, balanced religious life. Using the insights of Baron Friedrich von Hügel and Dr. Carl Jung, I have constructed a proposal for a School of Spiritual Direction which would train individuals first to develop their own spiritual lives, and secondly to train others to become religiously mature and vital.

Jung acknowledged the importance of the elements of mature religion which von Hügel outlined; in addition he felt that a knowledge of the complex structure of the human psyche was essential to one's spiritual and psychological growth. We cannot neglect our own inner journeys if we are to be of service to others as they try to become more whole. The blind cannot lead the blind.

There is an acute need today for instruction in living an integrated, wholistic Christian life, for the essential elements of mature religion seem so varied and separate that a Christian struggling toward integration and individuation is left to make lonely sense out of seemingly disparate elements.

For example, currently individuals desiring to use Jung's psychological insights to develop their spiritual lives usually find themselves working with analysts who have little training or background in theology or historical Christianity. Frequently these analysts express animosity toward the church's attempts at counseling and working with searching, struggling human beings. Many religious leaders, priests, pastors, counselors, etc., on the other hand, express hostility toward psychiatrists, psychologists, analysts, and other secular persons who use depth psychology in dealing with human problems.

Thus one is often forced to choose *between* the offerings of religion and those of psychology when actually the insights and discoveries of both are needed to grow spiritually. Most individuals are not equipped to make the necessary integration between the two fields, for skill and training are needed to form a satisfactory synthesis.

During the last 25 years as I have preached, taught, counseled and written, I have become aware of the desperate need for a school which would help individuals integrate psychological insight and religious experience. The model which follows is specifically based upon insights received through seven years of graduate teaching and counseling with ministers and religious at the University of Notre Dame.

The program of spiritual direction which I have outlined would be based upon the following contentions:

1. There exists a deep inner religious and psychic life into which individuals may be introduced. In addition, the church possesses a vast collective wisdom which needs to be made available to individuals, for by oneself one cannot come to this same body of knowledge. Thus, if one is to be a Christian spiritual director, he or she must have a thorough knowledge of the Bible and of the church.
2. A spiritual director must have a sufficiently inclusive and sophisticated worldview that he or she can deal with the spiritual doubt and distrust bred by our materialistic worldview. The director must also be aware of the recent developments in Western philosophy which enable one to enlarge one's view of reality, thus allowing individuals to believe that it is possible to relate to God here and now, and that religion is not an opiate, but a living reality.
3. A director must be versed in the phenomena of religious experience so that he or she understands and is comfortable with mystical experience, psychic phenomena, and altered states of consciousness, and is able to see these approaches to spiritual reality in a meaningful context. The director also needs to be familiar with the personal experiences and writings of mystics and others who have traversed the inner pathway.
4. The director must be familiar enough with the field of human dynamics that he or she can understand the complexity of the human personality. He or she must understand the workings of the unconscious part of an individual's being and how it affects both outer behavior and inner relatedness to the divine. A person who believes that human

beings are merely rational and cognitive cannot be a competent spiritual director.

a. A spiritual director must realize that individuals will not reveal their inner depths until a trusting relationship is ensured between two persons or in a group. Thus a director must be nonjudgmental and accepting, attitudes which preclude the director's knowledge and acceptance of his or her own psychic shadow or darkness.

b. The spiritual director must be expert in using both one-to-one encounters and group dynamics as ways for an individual to come to a better self-knowledge.

c. A director needs to be familiar with dream interpretation, for as the language of the unconscious, the dream expresses the aspects of one's inner life not being dealt with. Thus paying attention to one's dreams is essential to growth and wholeness, and a spiritual director is deficient in competence without some training in dealing with dreams.

The tenets upon which the program would be built would ensure that priests, ministers, psychologists, social workers, medical doctors, and lay persons with the proper qualifications would be well trained cognitively, affectively, and religiously. (By this use of the word religious, I mean that complex of institutional and personal experience of the Divine.)

For those professionals who wish to train others, a three-year individualized program would be constructed so that ministers could concentrate in the psychological area and in the area of religious experience, while the medical doctor or psychologist could concentrate in the area of religious experience and institutional religion.

For those persons who do not wish to later train others, a one-year program could be instituted. Those professionals near the end of their three-year programs could be utilized in the one-year training programs. This shorter program could take place during three or four successive summers.

An outreach program of two-to-five-week seminars could be used to augment the skills and training of persons already working in the service professions. These mini-programs might also arouse interest in the longer programs.

Professional individuals trained in the three-year program could bring their expertise to seminaries and theological schools.

With regard to structure and mechanics of the training programs, I would envision a fully developed center staffed by five full-time teachers and leaders, equipped to train about fifty students. After the first year, some individuals in the advanced program could assist the five teachers. The program would consist of the following activities:

1. Classes based on the seminar model, composed of not more than fifteen students in which the following subjects would be covered:
   a. A survey course of Eastern and Western philosophical and religious thought providing a base for the value and need of spiritual direction. The study would extend from Shamanism and Plato to Gödel, Heisenberg and Skinner.
   b. The Biblical tradition and its significance within the philosophical/religious framework studied.
   c. The history and meaning of myth, symbol, dream and ritual.
   d. The various psychological traditions which have emerged in the last 100 years, their intrinsic value, and their value for the spiritual director.
   e. The devotional masters, East and West, their teachings and practice.
   f. The phenomenology of religious experience, a study of the various ways in which the Divine breaks into human life.
   g. Exposure to some of the varieties of the religious experience in a practicum.
2. Each student would have a counselor or spiritual guide to meet with at least one hour a week to help him or her in the inner spiritual journey, for the undirected cannot direct.
3. Group process in communication and education (rather than therapy) would be stressed, for a potential spiritual director needs to be cognizant of his or her relationships with others in a group context.
4. One-to-one encounters, as well as group dynamics, need to be made available and used toward individual spiritual growth.
5. Applicants for entrance to the program would be screened by psychological testing and interviews to ensure that an individual has a sufficiently strong ego structure to undertake the program.
6. The program leaders would meet weekly to ensure the development of their individual spiritual growth and the continuance of healthy relationships.

Because an academic degree in spiritual direction might seem somewhat incongruous, a certificate verifying completion of either the three-year or the one-year program could be issued.

It is sadly true that because the clergy are often not equipped to be competent guides on the spiritual/psychological journey, psychologists, medical doctors, and other members of the helping professions are called upon to bridge the gap. These persons, although competent in their own areas of expertise, are unskilled in certain areas of the inner journey too. Thus the need is critical for individuals in all the helping professions to become cognizant of the areas outside their specialities and to learn to integrate these disciplines so that human beings searching for wholeness may be provided with highly trained, sensitive Christian leadership and guidance.

There are three attempts to put some of these ideas into practice in a concrete program. At the San Francisco Theological Seminary at San Anselmo, California, plans are being laid for such a program with many features of this proposal. A program for spiritual guides has been started at Wainwright House in Rye, New York. In Pecos, New Mexico, the abbot at the Benedictine abbey has instituted a program in spiritual direction.

FOR FURTHER READING

Kelsey, Morton T., *The Other Side of Silence: A Guide to Christian Meditation,* Ramsey, N.J.: Paulist Press, 1976.
Nouwen, Henri J. M., *The Living Reminder: Service and Prayer in Memory of Jesus Christ,* New York: Seabury Press, 1977.
Von Hügel, Friedrich, *The Mystical Element of Religion as Studied in Saint Catherine of Genoa and Her Friends,* Vol. I and II, London: J. M. Dent and Sons, Ltd., 1927.

5

The Dream as Religious Experience

In Western Christian society today there is practically no encouragement for a person to attempt to understand dreams as a source of religious insight into life. Most twentieth century Christians simply assume that the idea of finding religious meaning or reality in dreams is a fallacy.

This attitude is strange for several reasons. In the first place, the early Christian church viewed the dream as one of the most significant and most important ways in which God revealed his will to human beings. Dreams were understood to give people access to a reality that was difficult to contact in any other way.

Not only do we find this view in the Old Testament, in the New Testament, and in the Church Fathers up to the time of Aquinas, but it is the attitude of nearly every other major religion of the world. Some of the most astute observations about dreams were made by the early Christian thinkers, and this evidence has not been systematically presented to the Christian public in our time.

The Fascination with Dreams

The dream has also been given serious attention by psychiatry and clinical psychology. These two branches of the healing profession view the dream as revealing the autonomous psychic depth of human beings called the unconscious. They see the dream as a means of treating forms of nervous and mental illness.

Some medical persons also view the dream as revealing the collective unconscious, a vast realm of experience beyond the individual's ken, touching realities of a religious and spiritual nature. The work of Dr. C. G. Jung and his followers in particular has revealed the religious implications of the dream.

In addition, current research on sleep and dreaming has shown that dream experience is universal, and that it occurs in a regular pattern night after night in spite of most people's total amnesia the next morning. The person who is convinced he or she never dreams is simply not aware of what is going on below the level of consciousness.

Studies have demonstrated conclusively that something is going on practically all the time we sleep, and about every ninety minutes a vivid dream occurs, completely absorbing almost every reaction of the dreamer. This research suggests how limited most Christians have been in their attitude toward dreams and dreaming.

Certainly human beings are fascinated by dreams. Ever since there were words to talk about them, these strange happenings in the night have been the subject of wonder and discussion wherever people gathered to talk about their hopes and fears. Literature is full of dreams.

Even in this day of sophisticated rejection, after a few cocktails people begin to talk about the funny dream they had the night before. Whenever I lecture and mention my interest in the serious study of dreams, the questions about them begin to come out, and people invariably show their hunger to talk and to hear more about the meaning of their dreams.

I once visited the pastor of a large, smoothly organized urban parish, a man who admitted that he had probably not been bothered by an illogical thought since the first grade. When I mentioned that I was doing some writing on dreams, he could not wait to tell me of the dream that had awakened him a few nights before with the picture of an accident so real that it terrified him.

The next day he had learned to his horror of an accident that had claimed the life of a close friend that night. He was still shaken by the experience when I talked with him, and he expressed the hope that someone would write of dreams in religious tradition, for he could find no material relevant to his experience in modern religious writing.

Yet it is easy to forget how many people are still concerned with dreams. The average person in the street is concerned enough to keep a big business going in dream books, which can be found in the paperback racks of almost any newsstand or corner drugstore. There are dozens of these books in print, and they are turned to by millions of people even though the basic ideas in them are highly questionable.

Most popular dream books try to separate out specific dream images and assign meanings to them in order to foretell the future or to explain certain life situations. All this is quite contrary to the legitimate study of dreams. These books, however, are interesting because they do show how great is the popular interest in the subject, and how persistent and pervasive the "commonsense" attitude toward dreams continues to be.

Dreams as Nonsense

The most common attitude in western culture is that dreaming is an essentially meaningless experience. It is viewed as "nothing but" the rehash of yesterday's half-forgotten experiences, thrown up mechanically, without any kind of order, before the sleeping consciousness. It is the feedback that occurs as consciousness rewinds itself for another day's activity.

Vivid dreams, according to this point of view, result from some immediate stimulus, like dining late on too much chutney or overdoing the mince pie; or they can be caused by something that happens during sleep, like the siren of a passing fire truck, the creaking of a door, or by letting in too much night air. To be concerned about dreams then is silly; it simply indicates a superstitious mind.

This attitude was very nearly universal among the intelligentsia of the eighteenth and nineteenth centuries, and it is still held among those influenced by the positivistic science of this period—in other words, by most of us. It was first suggested 2200 years ago by Aristotle in three little papers on dreaming and was supported by Cicero a few centuries later.

After centuries of unpopularity, this view was revived to become the accepted point of view—without ever being subjected to scientific inquiry. It was considered so obvious and certain that there has been no need to spend time and effort verifying it, or even to spell it out very clearly. In fact, it is hard to find this view fully expressed in written form, although it is assumed in much of the writing in every field of our society. Yet there is nothing in the present careful research on dreaming that particularly supports this point of view. Instead, the actual studies frequently seem to give both analytical and empirical support to the opposite point of view.

Dreams and Dr. Freud

This quite different point of view, which finds dreams highly significant and meaningful, has been held in practically all other cultures. Indeed, wherever peoples have not been touched and influenced by our Western worldview with its belief that we are limited to sense experience and reason, the dream has been viewed as the chief medium through which nonphysical (or spiritual) powers and realities spoke to people.

Although some dreams were seen as meaningless or unintelligible, it was important for people to consider their dreams, for through them they might obtain intimations of things to come or guidance and confrontation from greater than human powers. All of the major religions of humankind have held this view, and as we have shown, it has never been entirely displaced by the skeptical view of the scientific community.

Instead, the modern support for this view has come from a strange source. Beginning in 1900, with the publication of Freud's carefully documented *Interpretation of Dreams,* the subject has come in for serious consideration by the medical profession. Their research makes it rather hard to avoid the significance of dreams.

Freud first saw dreams as the royal road to understanding our submerged personality, that hidden nine-tenths of the human being which we now know as the unconscious. Jung, if his record can be believed, followed then by witnessing dreams that gave hints of the future and offered suggestions to people superior to their conscious knowledge and attitudes. Recently, the studies of Dement and others carrying on similar research have demonstrated that dreams are so important to mental health that simply being deprived of them may lead to mental breakdown and even psychosis.

These findings, particularly those of Jung, certainly suggest that the dream—which has been valued and interpreted by all religious groups, Christianity included—is worthy of serious religious consideration and may be one very important access to knowledge. It is true that in the past this understanding has sometimes led to an uncritical and superstitious concern with dreams. Still, Christian dream-interpretation is an ancient, long-held, and carefully considered religious practice. It deserves to be reviewed and evaluated.

The British writer J. B. Priestley has added a modern voice to this ancient understanding. Commenting on the importance of one early experiment with dreams, Priestley concluded:

"We are not—even though we might prefer to be—the slave of chronological time. We are, in this respect, more elaborate, more powerful, perhaps nobler creatures than we lately have taken ourselves to be. . . .

"Our lives are not contained with passing time, a single track along which we hurry to oblivion. We may not be immortal beings, but we are something better than creatures carried on that single time track to the slaughter house. We have a larger portion of Time—and more and stranger adventures with it—than conventional or positivist thought allows."

When we are perfectly honest we find the two opposing attitudes toward dreams struggle with each other within us. Much of the time we are dominated by the attitude of the Enlightenment, which devalued dreams as meaningless, and we ignore them.

Then there are times when we awake from a vivid dream strangely moved and troubled, hardly able to shake off its influence throughout the day. Or we read of Lincoln's premonitory dream of his assassination and wonder what it means that dreams sometimes have reality and significance like that. What meaning do dreams actually have? And what is a dream?

Physiology and Dreaming

It may seem hardly necessary to define anything so familiar as a dream, but in defining the familiar we discover how little we know. Most commonly the dream is understood to be a succession of images present in the mind during sleep. And here, as Nathaniel Kleitman has shown in his *Sleep and Wakefulness,* we are getting into one of the least-understood of human activities. We cannot even say precisely what is meant by sleep except in terms of a certain kind of consciousness.

According to Dr. Kleitman, sleep is best described as that period in which there is a temporary cessation of the waking state. From time to time in this period anything from a single picture or figure to an elaborate story may be vividly perceived, which is in no sense a direct perception of the outer physical world. Normally this happens four or five times every night, and it can also be "watched" or predicted by keeping track of the sleeper's brain waves, eye movements, and certain other reactions. Indeed, vivid dreams seem to come spontaneously and to be almost as free from our ego control as our perception of the outside physical world.

This process is not the only one that happens in sleep, however. There is a second process closely related to dreaming which can be recalled best between the periods of vivid dreaming. This conceptual activity, simply "thinking," is apparently continuous in the parts of the brain which do not go to sleep. Apparently most of the brain goes right on working whether we are awake or asleep.

Whether we are conscious of it or not, vivid dreaming takes over alternately with conceptual activity, which is constantly at work changing perceptions into thoughts and ideas. The psychologists call these processes "primary-process activity" and "secondary-process mentation," and together they produce the underlying psychic life that seems to be basic to conscious thinking and activity. It is no wonder that psychiatrists like Lawrence Kubie have pictured the mind as a magnificent computer, as if designed expressly to the scientists' specifications.

It is from this level of psychic life that the sharp and discrete religious intuition probably comes. These intuitions, which are so valued and prized by religious people for direction and guidance, are in most cases the end product of this kind of secondary-process mentation turned upon religious contents. The religious intuition is therefore of the same nature as the dream (and also the vision), and shares in the same reality.

A third form of dream activity is the spontaneous image or vision that appears to a person in the borderland of wakefulness when one is not sure whether one is awake or asleep. These dreams and visions—they are termed hypnagogic or hypnopompic, depending on whether the dreamer is falling asleep or waking up—are usually flash pictures focused on a single impression, but in some cases whole scenes, even fairly long stories may appear.

At times these images coming on the edge of sleep can seem so tangible that the dreamer really does not know whether he is awake or asleep, whether the images belong to the outside world or the figures of the dream. And this leads us to the last and closely related form of dreaming.

This final form is the waking dream or vision, in which the dream images are intruded into the waking consciousness. The images themselves are apparently no different from those which can be experienced during sleep, except that they reach the field of consciousness during periods of wakefulness. They rise as spontaneously and with as little ego control as the dream, and in most cases the visions are involuntary.

However, there are persons who are able to cultivate the ability to look inward and observe this spontaneous rise of dream images because they wish to experience them. This experience, which we shall simply call fantasy, seems to be very similar to dreaming; in it the same kind of images and stories arise within one as in dreams. In other cultures and other times the experience of visions has been far more common than it is among most people today. In fact, as we shall show, the people of other cultures have not distinguished as clearly between the dream and the vision as we do today.

There is an activity, however, which is common in our culture today that is not always so carefully distinguished. This is the daydream, which is different from fantasy. In daydreams the flow of images is not spontaneous, but is directed by the conscious center of personality, the ego. The daydream can be created and also changed at will, fantasy, like the true dream or vision, cannot—it must be met with and observed. At times the line between fantasy and daydreams may be a fine one, but unless it is maintained, fantasy loses the spontaneous quality that is characteristic of both dreams and visions.

Dreams and Visions —

One other distinction must be kept quite clear because of the popular modern attitude toward visions. Most people are quite suspicious of visions. They probably would not go so far as to find the dream dangerous or pathological. But even the dream is so closely related to the vision that at times the two cannot be distinguished; visions are feared as a sign of mental disintegration.

Most of us automatically assume that any person who experiences a vision must be mentally ill, that any vision must be hallucination. On the contrary, the real visionary experience is quite different from the hallucination in mental illness.

The true visionary experience is seldom mistaken for giving immediate knowledge of the physical world, but only of the "dream" world, or quite indirectly of the physical one. The vision is superimposed on the physical world, or the two may in some way be synchronized, but they can be distinguished just as easily as the dream is usually distinguished from the experience of waking.

Hallucination in mental illness, on the other hand, is a definite sign of pathology. Here the same kind of content one finds in a dream arises spontaneously and is attributed directly to the world outside where it does not belong; the "dream" world is mistaken for the physical world of sense experience.

Persons subject to this kind of hallucination have lost the ability to distinguish between these two kinds of experience and so project their inner images directly upon the outer world. Because they cannot distinguish between the two they are not able to deal adequately with either the outer world or the inner one. Their actions become inappropriate and they are seen as sick. Such hallucination is a common occurrence in several kinds of mental illness where the ego under stress cannot distinguish between experiences that come to consciousness from psychic reality and those that come from the outer world.

It is not possible to discuss dreams without considering the thought process that goes on in sleep, the true vision, and fantasy as well. The four experiences are basically the same in nature. They are intrusions into consciousness of activities over which we have little if any conscious control.

In the past these spontaneous images and thoughts, distinct from outer physical reality, have been valued as a sign of contact with religious reality. Whether the image was presented in sleep or in wakefulness, whether breaking in unexpectedly or sought and cultivated, it was understood to come from a different world, and nearly all religious groups everywhere have considered that the ability to observe and interpret these images was a religious gift.

This was essentially the common Christian tradition from biblical times, through the Church Fathers, and up into the seventeenth century; in isolated instances it has continued to the present time. In this tradition dreams were significant because they revealed something beyond humankind which gave purpose and meaning, warning where spiritual disaster impended. In Jung's terminology dreams can express the reality of the collective unconscious, the objective psyche. In religious terms, they kept the people in touch with the purpose and direction of spiritual reality.

Dreams and the Church

At the beginning of the twentieth century there was almost no educated person in our culture who seriously considered this way of looking at human experience. After Freud had broken the ice with *The Interpretation of Dreams,* the reaction to his work showed how deeply people were concerned about this area of their lives. But even when the thaw set in, and people of all kinds began to show an interest in the study of dreams, there was still one major group in our society with nothing to say about the subject.

The Christian clergy, the theologians, are still silent, and this is surprising in itself in a group not noted for silence. It is more surprising when we realize how much there is about dreams in the Christian tradition from the Old Testament on. It is also surprising when we consider the attention given to other aspects of the inner life.

There are groups of Christians interested in spiritual healing, in speaking in tongues, or preparing for the imminent end of the world, and even in the ritual handling of snakes. But there is no significant group that suggests that Christians should listen to their own dreams or make any particular study of the many dreams in the Bible and in subsequent church history.

In fact, I cannot help recalling the consternation I caused in speaking to one group devoted to glossolalia when I spoke about dreams. It seemed to them that the idea of taking dreams seriously was much farther out than the practice of tongue-speaking. What does this mean? Is it just dreams that we have neglected, or is it something more?

The trouble is that the dream comes to us neither from the acceptable material world nor from our well-ordered and controllable reason. To value the spontaneously given content of the dream one must postulate the reality of something in addition to the material world and reason. Depth psychology calls this reality the unconscious; the early Christian community called it the spiritual world; and these two different terms may well refer to the same reality, as the Catholic theologian Victor White has suggested in *God and the Unconscious*. Unless we believe that there is such a realm of reality which can be experienced, we will probably not look very hard for meaning beyond the material world.

Indeed, if there is no meaning beyond the physical world, then what place is there for dreams to come from except the meaningless tag ends of yesterday's sensation? Dreams are then simply the commonest example of the human mind or psyche out of commission. They show how irrational its action can be when logical thinking is switched off.

Of course, sense experience is also nonrational in the sense that it is not guided or directed by reason; it is just given. But since it is believed that there is a real physical world that is revealed in sense experience, this essential irrationality hardly bothers anyone except a few philosophers.

The irrationality of dreams is something else again. So long as we "know" that there is no other world for them to reveal, no world beyond the material one, there is nothing else for dreams to show us but irrationality—our minds at their most irrational, illogical, in fact.

There is no controversy on dreams as there is with glossolalia; the subject simply does not come up for consideration except very rarely. It is very difficult for modern persons to imagine meaningful psychic reality beyond the grasp of his or her reason or his or her physical senses.

Indeed, the greatest thrust of mid-twentieth-century theology is to maintain unequivocally that human beings have no direct or immediate contact with any nonphysical or "supernatural" realm, and so there is no natural religion. This brand of theology also denies the value of depth psychology in human transformation, for once it is admitted that lives are changed in the psychologist's office, then the church is faced with a realm of reality that is neither physical nor rational, and which is sometimes revealed in dreams.

Once the dream is taken seriously and regarded as having religious significance, then it is inevitable that there is some direct and "natural" contact with reality other than material or rational. Then the door is open and anything can happen, even transformation. Dreams may well be a doorway to religious significance and a new theology, as well as to the unconscious.

FOR FURTHER READING

Kelsey, Morton T., *God, Dreams and Revelation,* Minneapolis: Augsburg Publishing House, 1974.
————, *Dreams, A Way to Listen to God,* Ramsey, N.J.: Paulist Press, 1979.
Sanford, John A., *Dreams and Healing,* Ramsey, N.J.: Paulist Press, 1979.
————, *Dreams: God's Forgotten Language,* Philadelphia: J. B. Lippincott, 1951.

6

The Dream and Christian Tradition

In the last four centuries the Western world has emphasized the development of conceptual thought to the point that symbolic thought has virtually been ignored. As a result of this development, the church has lost contact with many aspects of its rich symbolic tradition—particularly the dream.

If, however, we examine our Christian heritage, we will discover that the early church did indeed listen to the dream and receive, as a result, insight and wisdom from God.

The Apostolic Fathers

The first Christian authors, who probably knew the apostles, wrote apocryphal gospels and epistles, although these were eventually excluded from the canon of holy books because they appeared more fanciful than factual.

One of the most noteworthy of these early works was the *Shepherd of Hermas,* based on the author's dream-vision. A portion of the book is very similar in subject matter to *Pilgrim's Progress.* The power of this piece and the fact that it was widely read for three centuries shows how deeply symbolic truth was at work in this inspirational book.

Another significant example of the role of the dream or vision in the lives of the early Church Fathers is described in the *Martyrdom of Polycarp,* which shows Polycarp seeing a vision forewarning his capture and death.

The New Testament Apocrypha

The apocryphal writings display the same sort of emphasis on dreams seen in the New Testament. For example, the *Acts of the Holy Apostle Thomas* record that God gave Thomas missionary instructions through a dream, while *The Testament of Abraham* relates Isaac's dream of Abraham's coming death. *The Clementine Homilies,* written in the second century, show Peter and Simon discussing dreams.

Post Apostolic Times

The post-apostolic era, which began in 150 A.D., saw Christians being persecuted severely by the Roman Empire. As the church attempted to write down the meaning of Christian experience, the Church Fathers became interested in philosophy and writing intelligently about the place of Christian belief in the world.

The worldview of these Church Fathers was based on Plato, and this view, coupled with the experience of Christ they had had, produced a powerful theology. These early Christians believed that God spoke directly to human beings through dreams. How far church theology today has strayed from these original beliefs!

The Apologists

Justin Martyr, the first Christian to write down an interpretation of Christianity for the Roman world, was martyred in 165 A.D. He believed dreams allowed human beings to experience spiritual reality and that they were sent by both good and evil spirits.

Irenaeus, bishop of Lyons in the second century, who wrote *Against Heresies,* emphasized the importance of dreams in such New Testament accounts as the Acts 10 story of Peter's dream and the Matthew report of Joseph's dreams.

Tatian, a follower of Justin, who believed that demons speak through dreams, discussed his philosophy in *Address to the Greeks.*

Two of the most intellectual Church Fathers, Clement and Origen of Alexandria, emphasized the important role of dreams in Christian life. Clement stated that sleep provided human beings a special contact with spiritual reality and was a means for human beings to receive revelations about their destiny.

In his *Against Celsus,* Clement's pupil Origen wrote that the dream was a means of relating to the divine and to future events. It was also Origen who believed the dream spoke symbolically and revealed the nature of spiritual reality. He further maintained that God used the dream as a means of conversion.

Tertullian

Originally from North Africa, this controversial third-century Latin apologist was a prolific writer whose theory of dreams is expressed in his most important work, *On The Soul.* Tertullian believed that all human beings dream and that in sleep we are overwhelmed by a form of reality different from what we experience in our waking hours as sense experience. Tertullian cited a phenomenal number of references to support his beliefs about dreams—among them Homer, Herodotus and Cicero.

Tertullian believed that dreams may come directly from God, from demons, or as a result of the natural workings of the depth of the soul. Tertullian emphasized that it was not he alone who believed in dreams, but Christians in general who experienced God in their lives in this way.

St. Perpetua, only one of many saints who received visions and dreams from God which sustained them in the face of persecution and martyrdom, saw a golden ladder reaching toward heaven, forewarning her own death and that of friends.

Theologians Who Documented Their Dreams

Emphasis on the importance of dreams did not stop with the Apologists or Tertullian. Such leaders as Cyprian of North Africa and Hippolytus in Rome believed that wisdom was directly imparted through dreams and visions. Cyprian, bishop of Carthage, believed that God guided the church through visions and he was even prepared for his own martyrdom by a vision.

Two disciples of Origen, Gregory Thaumaturus and Dionysius, found great comfort and sanctioning of their faith through dreams, and Julius Africanus, also of Alexandria and reputedly bishop of Emmaus, wrote that the King of Persia had foreseen the birth of Christ in a dream.

In Rome, Hippolytus wrote many works dealing with the importance of dreams. In addition to showing that the biblical prophets had been given instructions through visions and dreams, Hippolytus also analyzed at length the dreams of the prophet Daniel.

Arnobius in the Latin church was said to have been converted to Christianity by means of a dream, while Lactantius, his disciple, maintained that knowledge of the future came through dreams.

Dreams of the Victorious Christian Church

The issuance of the Edict of Milan in 313 as a result of the victory of Constantine brought a virtual end to the persecution of Christians. All of the monumental church leaders who emerged in this period of new freedom believed that God reveals himself to humankind through dreams and visions.

In fact, it was apparently as a result of a dream-vision that Constantine became Emperor of Rome. The writer Lactantius tells in his account concerning the battle between Constantine and Maxentius that prior to the engagement, Christ appeared to Constantine in his sleep with the sign of a cross of light, commanding him to use this sign as a safeguard.

The Church Historians

Generally speaking, the church historians of this period were little concerned with dreams. However, one writer, Socrates, did refer to the story of the Empress Dominica who received warnings through a dream about the forthcoming death of her child. Another writer, Theodoret, made mention of the fact that the Emperor Theodosius dreamed of receiving the imperial crown. Still another historian, Sozomen, recounted Constantine's directions from God via a dream to give up rebuilding Troy and was then led to erect the marvelous city of Byzantium. Sozomen also detailed his friend Aquilinus' healing one night as a result of a divine vision.

As the church ceased to be persecuted from outside, problems arose within its own gates—especially problems of heresy. One of the giants in church history of this period, Athanasius, bishop of Alexandria, believed the dream to be of paramount importance as a means of revelation from God. It was this great churchman who wrote the marvelous *Life of St. Antony,* and the effect of the saint's life and extrasensory spiritual gifts upon the author cannot be overstated.

Greek Orthodox Leaders

Three of the most important theologians in the history of the Greek Orthodox Church—Basil the Great, Gregory of Nazianzen and Gregory of Nyssa—all believed that God communicated with human beings by means of dreams and visions. In his *On the Making of Man,* Gregory of Nyssa maintained that while we sleep, our reason and sensory functions lie dormant. Then our nonrational side may emerge, and it is through this nonrational side that God speaks to us.

Basil the Great maintained that dreams were intended to be obscure so that our wisdom and mental perception could be prodded into growth. In several of his works he discusses God's direct contact via dreams with the Old Testament patriarchs. Basil did have trouble, however, accepting the fact that dreams constitute a method of compensating for our unbalanced conscious attitudes.

It was as a result of the appearance in a dream of two maidens—Temperance and Virginity—that Gregory of Nazianzen decided to lead an ascetic life. Another great figure in the Greek church, St. John Chrysostom, believed that dreams not only reveal spiritual reality to us, but also show us the state of our souls and can affect our actions. He further stressed that we are not held accountable for the subject matter of our dreams. Chrysostom also wrote detailed commentaries on the importance of dreams and visions in the Bible.

Early in the fifth century Synesius of Cyrene, who became bishop of Ptolemais, wrote a sophisticated book on the subject of dreams which made a great impact upon the Eastern world. A complex work which synthesized most of the important Christian thought on the subject, Synesius' study maintained that the meaning of the universe was given its best expression in the dream and that through the dream human beings may know the future, correct bodily malfunctions, gain hope for the future, and come to love the Divine. Synesius also suggested that one ought to keep a record of dreams and that there is a vital connection between dreams and mythology.

Doctors in the West

In the Western church, four influential men emerged who believed in God's revelation through dreams and visions—Ambrose, Augustine, Jerome and Gregory the Great. Ambrose refused to celebrate the eucharist before the Emperor Theodosius because of a dream, and he also discovered the bodies of two martyred saints as a result of directions from a dream. Ambrose's works stated that the Holy Spirit speaks through dreams and that in the Old Testament the great wisdom of Solomon, Joseph and Daniel was seen in their ability to interpret dreams.

Augustine

The man who was to lay the foundation for Western Christian theology for a thousand years, Augustine, believed that there were two basic realities—the material and the spiritual. He maintained that through dreams we may gain entrance to the nonphysical world where spontaneous contents await us. Augustine recounted a dream his mother, Monica, had of the conversion of her son which gave her fortitude to keep praying for him during all his wayward years. In both *The Confessions* and *The City of God* are stories of fascinating, unusual parapsychological dreams.

Jerome the Scholar

Jerome of Aquileia on the Adriatic is noted for translating the Bible into the Latin Vulgate. Converted to Christianity by a dramatic dream in which he saw himself surrounded by a bright light before the judgment seat, Jerome became the head of a monastic community in Bethlehem. Jerome believed that dreams must not be sought for their own sake but for the revelations that God is sending.

Another scholar of the Western world, Macrobius, author of *Commentary on the Dream of Scipio,* had a great influence on medieval thought. He spent a portion of his work explaining his classification of dreams into five types—the enigmatic dream, the dream foretelling the future, the oracular dream, the nightmare, and the apparition. It was from the works of Macrobius that the Middle Ages learned what it knew of Platonism, for this author attempted to summarize the wisdom of Greece and Rome and pass it on in a rather oversimplified form.

Another important personage of the fourth century, St. Martin of Tours, a missionary to Gaul, was the subject of a biography by Sulpicius Severus which detailed Martin's beautiful vision of Christ clothed in the half-cloak he had given to a naked beggar.

Gregory the Great

The next major figure to write about dreams, Gregory the Great, is more closely connected to the Middle Ages than to the classical period, for between his lifetime and that of Augustine and Jerome the Western Empire had fallen, plunging Europe into the Dark Ages. Although his *Morals and Dialogues* discussed the sources of dreams and supported their importance as revelations of the divine, Gregory became increasingly fearful of dreams and later advocated belief in God through faith rather than as a result of visions or dreams.

Gregory's attitude was a precursor to the philosophy of Aquinas, which viewed dreams in an Aristotelian context and thus completely negated their significance. It was the belief that human beings can only experience reality through sensory perception and reason that caused Christians to cease interpreting dreams and thus lose contact with a rich source of spiritual experience.

Dreams in the Modern Church

Although modern Christianity has placed little credence in dreams, the early Church Fathers have not been the only persons to find enrichment and guidance through dreams. The following stories illustrate the importance of the dream to modern-day Christians as well.

The first dream, that of a Baptist minister named A. J. Gordon, occurred at the end of the nineteenth century. In the dream, Gordon was standing before his congregation about to begin preaching when a stranger of compelling presence entered the church and sat down. Although Gordon wished to greet the man at the end of the service, Gordon could not get to him before he left. When Gordon asked one of his parishioners who the man was, the parishioner replied, "Did you not recognize him? It was Jesus."

The impact of this dream—with the sorrowful expression on the stranger's face—radically changed Gordon's life and ministry. He later wrote, "It was a vision of the deepest reality. Apparently we are most awake to God when we are asleep to the world."

The second dream, that of Anglican minister John Newton, author of "Amazing Grace," was, by his own testimony, the most important event of his life. Captain of a slave-trading ship at the time of the dream, Newton saw himself on a sailboat in Venice. Suddenly a strange man presented him with a ring, telling him that happiness was his as long as he possessed the ring.

Later in the dream, accosted by a man who ridiculed the worth of the ring, Newton dropped it into the sea. Just then he looked up, observing a huge fire in the Alps. Fearfully he stood gazing at the raging fire and reflecting on his stupidity for parting with the ring. Suddenly the stranger appeared who rescued the ring from the water and promised to hold it in trust for Newton so that he could always feel its power. Later on, Newton was confronted with an experience which this dream helped him to deal with.

The third dream, that of St. Therese of Lisieux, who died in 1897 at the age of 24, took place during the course of a long illness and subsequent depression. In the dream, three Carmelite nuns and the Mother Superior of the convent appeared to her. She asked to remove the veil from the face of one of them. Granted permission, she recognized the nun as Mother Ana of Jesus, a saint who had introduced the reform orders into France. As an incredible light shone from the nun's face, Therese felt a great love and warmth surround her. As a result of this experience, Therese was able to write, ". . . I knew beyond doubt that heaven was a reality. . . . My heart melted in her love and I became inflamed in love, joy, and thankfulness, not only to her but to the whole of heaven."

Interpreting a Modern Dream Series

Just as dreams have been sources of guidance and revelation to the early Church Fathers, to ministers and saints, so too they can provide encouragement and direction for men and women today.

The following series of dreams was experienced by a young man reared in the Catholic faith who had rejected his religious heritage. Alienated from his family, he had left home and was living in a commune in Indiana. His life was practically devoid of meaning and he felt directionless.

The first dream of the series showed the young man returning home, encountering his weeping father. His brothers and sisters, by contrast, were joyful at his arrival.

This dream was pointing out the young man's basic problem—his confrontation with his father, the outer symbol of the youth's inner father, or the old traditional way of doing things. Because the young man realized he needed to separate himself from his distorted father image, he turned to his inner child, who responded.

The insights from this dream enabled the young man, who was attending college out of a sense of duty, to drop out of school and deal with his personal life.

The second dream pictured the youth in the desert, encountering a wise old Indian chief. The desert in this dream portrayed the young man's directionless state, but the Indian chief was a hopeful symbol—an important figure representing an alive spiritual reality. Subsequent dreams showed the young man that he must give up the reality he knew and explore his identity and life pathway more thoroughly.

Shortly after these dreams the young man left Indiana and hitchhiked across the country, a trip which brought him insights and altered his personality.

While staying at a monastery in New Mexico, the youth had a dream that he was dying of a heart attack, but that after the "death" experience his spent heart was replaced by a larger, stronger one. This dream is symbolic of the death of the old ego adaptation, making way for a new life.

The next dream found the youth in the mountains contemplating some nearby cliffs. Even the Indians who had inhabited these mountains showed fear in their legends when they spoke of these cliffs. But the young man decided to climb the cliff alone. Proud that he had conquered the heights alone, he eventually looked down on the people below and began sneering at them for never daring the climb. A few minutes later, however, the cliff gave way beneath him, and he fell into an abyss.

Paradoxically, if the young man had not had the courage to climb the mountain, he never would have fallen nor experienced the transformation which it brought about. It almost seems that the sin of pride brings about redemption here. The experience is reminiscent of Paul's question in Romans 6: "Should we sin that grace should abound?" Paul was almost grateful for his own failures for they permitted grace to work in his life.

As the dream continued, the cliff cracked and the young man changed into a weed, symbolic of the valueless, the unusable. The young man was incapable of recognizing his own limits and mortality. In order to come to a new view of himself, he had first to try to achieve so much that he fell into an abyss as a weed. Then the youth saw the weed burn up and the ashes spread over the bottom of the abyss. This image is reminiscent of the Phoenix, which rises from its ashes and is often used in Christian symbolism. And now, from the depth of the dream, a great but gentle voice came forth pleading, "Jesus, Jesus," and with the sound of this voice, the young man was resurrected.

The next dream showed the father figure again, but under a new guise—that of a strong, tall, black-clad cleric. This image was representative of the traditional, severe, religious attitude in which the young man had grown up. This black-clad figure came toward him, poked a finger at him, and derided the resurrection experience of the previous dream.

The young man, deciding to confront this negative figure, turned to him and said, "No, you are wrong." As a result of facing his own inner doubt in this manner, the youth's life started to change. He was able to actualize the potential pointed out to him by his unconscious.

The young man returned to South Bend and began to take his church life seriously in spite of its negative side. He returned to the university to finish his education and began a genuine Christian journey. The full text of these dreams is found in my book *The Other Side of Silence* and is also discussed at length in John Sanford's *Healing and Wholeness*.

The dream continues to speak to human beings just as it did to the members of the early church, making us conscious of the workings of the Spirit within us and helping us attain God's potential for our lives.

FOR FURTHER READING

Kelsey, Morton T., *Encounter with God,* Minneapolis: Bethany Fellowship, Inc., 1972.
———, *God, Dreams and Revelation,* Minneapolis: Augsburg Publishing House, 1974.

7

How to Interpret the Dream

In order to understand the fundamental principles of dream interpretation, we must familiarize ourselves with the different kinds of dreams that we see played out before us nightly. We also need to bear in mind that if we oversimplify dream interpretation or try to reduce our dreams to pat meanings their value and vitality will elude us.

Types of Dreams

One type of dream we encounter frequently is that which deals with recent occurrences from our outer lives—often with the events of the preceding day. The emphasis the dream may place on merely one or two happenings can alter our viewpoint of the whole day and put it into a new perspective for us.

An especially important type of dream is that which deals with elements of ourselves we have repressed. Frequently a dream will resurrect forgotten actions or buried attitudes that can help correct our unconscious and one-sided views of ourselves. If we faithfully and honestly deal with our dream contents, they will enable us to face up to qualities in ourselves to which we would have preferred to remain blind. The new honesty resulting from our dream insights can help our personalities grow toward wholeness.

Sometimes our dreams center primarily upon other people who are present in our everyday lives. Upon working with these dreams, we will discover that these people often represent parts of ourselves which are similar to them in some way. These outer representatives of our corresponding inner figures help us to discover how much of ourselves we are projecting onto other people and whether or not we are relating to them authentically as individuals or merely as extentions of ourselves.

Another type of dream deals with archetypal contents. These dreams usually image for us some great mythical symbol, like the child, the wise old man, or the maiden. Although these images may arise from the deep structure of our own psyche, they most frequently come from the spiritual or psychoid world of which our individual psyches are a part, just as our bodies are a part of outer physical reality.

Extrasensory perceptions can also arise from our dreams. A personal incident may serve as the best explanation of this type of dream. On a weekend vacation with my family in San Diego, I had the embarrassing dream that I was putting a pair of stockings on one of my parishioners—a little old lady who had been a missionary to India. Although I found the dream nonsensical at first, I later found out that the old lady had suddenly become ill and died. The dream showed me that she had died, but in a symbolic way.

The dream of a friend of mine is a particularly good illustration of an extrasensory perception type. Although my friend was aware that I was looking for a publisher, he had never heard of a Mr. Allan Williams of Little, Brown and Company, about whom he dreamed one night.

As a result of my friend's dream, I wrote to Mr. Williams and subsequently had several books published over the years. Amazingly enough, the dream had even revealed some details of Mr. Williams's personal life which were later verified when I became acquainted with him. This particular type of extrasensory dream is called telepathic or clairvoyant.

In another dream, a close friend cried out to me for help. Later I discovered that my friend's son had almost died in an accident in the mountains.

One final illustration of the extrasensory perception dream also arises out of my parish ministry. The father of one of my parishioners had deserted his family, demanding a divorce. Although he was hiding from the family members, the dreams of his daughter revealed the names of the hotels where the man was staying, enabling the family to contact him.

The spiritual world may confront us directly via the numinous dream. A close friend, Ted Sanford, the 75-year-old retired pastor of an Anglican church, had an important dream while he was painfully sick.

In the dream Mr. Sanford saw first his boyhood home, then the boarding school he had attended. Then he saw his missionary parish in China and his church in New Jersey. Finally he saw himself in his room, lying on his couch. Looking up, he saw that the clock on the mantel had stopped at 11:00. As the mantel changed into a doorway, a path of pure light shone through, and Mr. Sanford got up and went along the path of light through the opened door.

Mr. Sanford's pain and anxiety disappeared after this dream and about a week later he fell asleep in his chair and never woke up. It seemed that he had walked down the path of light through the door in the dream.

Two types of dreams that occur less frequently are the clear dream and the numinous dream. In the former, the dream is completely self-explanatory and acts as its own interpreter. The numinous dream, which touches us to the depths of our beings, conveys a direct and immediate sense of the presence of God.

Guidelines for Dream Interpretation

If our dreams are to help us on our spiritual journey, we must subscribe to some basic rules or guidelines that provide us with the discipline essential to the inner pathway.

First, if we are to understand our dreams, we must write them down. Keeping a written record, a journal, indicates that we mean business about our spiritual life. The daily recording of both dreams and reflections is essential to our inner development.

As the dream laboratory of the United States Navy in San Diego has found, 95% of all dreams not recorded within five minutes after awakening are forgotten. The reason for the military's interest in dreams is that it wanted to find out how much sleep personnel could be deprived of without being nonfunctional or unable to follow orders.

Secondly, if we do not take our dreams seriously, we cannot profit from them. Our attitude toward dreams, which are as delicate, complex and alive as human beings, is of paramount importance. When we do take our dreams seriously, we discover that they have some powerful and transforming messages for us.

For example, one of my dreams, which pictured a group of young men in a military school, showed me how undisciplined my life was. Another dream showed heavy road construction going on. This image was alerting me to powerful changes about to occur in my spiritual life.

Thirdly, our dreams are filled with all sorts of inner images which we need to get to know. By paying attention to these images, we can come into contact with forces within ourselves that need to be dealt with. For example, during one period of my life I often dreamed about my brother, who differed from me in many ways. One of the major differences was that he was agnostic and I was Christian so that the fights occurring between us in the dreams showed me my need to deal with the agnostic brother inside me.

War is a frequent subject of dreams, and they are often interpreted as indicating fear of war or as remembrances of traumatic experiences during wartime. Usually, however, this type of dream is signifying an inner battle being waged within the dreamer.

Because dreams show us particular problems that need to be worked on, they often portray graphically some characteristic we usually do not credit ourselves with.

I once dreamed that I owned a cabin in the mountains in a national park. Since the cabin was on United States property, the park ranger had the right to tell me what color to paint the cabin and how to take care of it. Furious at his intrusion into my private business I verbally attacked the park ranger in my dream.

Later, in discussing the dream with a friend, I discovered that the unreasonable and autocratic park ranger was actually a part of my own personality. Much to my surprise, this truth was later substantiated by my wife, who claimed to be well acquainted with this part of me!

The fourth guideline in dream interpretation is to make associations with the dream symbols that occur. The image that started me on the road to spiritual growth was a pink peach pit I saw in a dream. From associations I made with the peach pit I was able to uncover some sore spots in my life and deal with some problems long repressed because I was afraid of unpleasant confrontations.

Fifthly, we need to be sensitive to dream repetitions. If a dream occurs more than once, it is usually important and may even be viewed as a friendly warning that we better take it seriously.

For example, I used to dream repeatedly that my boyhood home was on fire. In many of the dream sequences I tried to put the fire out. When I confided the dream to a friend, he suggested I allow the house to burn to the ground.

Through using active imagination, I reconstructed the dream and watched the house disappear into flames and then kicked the ashes to be sure the house was really destroyed. This imaginative action allowed the fire of the Spirit to burn much that was childish within me and allow room for new maturity and growth. The dream was never repeated.

Sixthly, it is extremely important to find a trustworthy friend or spiritual companion with whom to talk over our dreams. Because our dreams are the expression of our unconscious, it is difficult for us to understand our dreams by ourselves. The traits and characteristics in ourselves of which we are unaware are often perfectly obvious to others.

An expert is not necessary to shed light on our dreams. An intuitive person whom we trust and who is open to the Spirit can be of great help. Certainly a friend who can shed light on these nightly dramas enacted on the stages of our souls can help us recognize the forces working within us so that we may become more conscious in our choices and in our life directions.

A friend of mine once wrote:

> Although it takes years of familiarity to interpret dreams well, since it is truly a specialist's work, a craft as well as an art, it still takes no great cleverness or special knowledge.
>
> We can always let this friend, the dream, ramble on in a reverie, spinning along; and then the observer can ramble on associating and amplifying, remembering incidents, plays on words, parallels from the Bible, mythology, and film.
>
> I let it speak and I speak to it rather than analyze or interpret it. By speaking to the dream, one addresses the mood and images and encourages the dream to go on telling its tale.
>
> Here it is necessary to take care throughout that the atmosphere of the dream is respected and the images given validity and dignity, which may be given best by courageous reactions to the dream as one must react courageously in a friendship.
>
> By encouraging the dream to tell its tale, I give it a chance to tell its message, its mythical theme, and thus get closer to the myths which are operating in me, my real story which is operating within, rather than my case history which is observed from outside. I become my own mythologist, which originally meant "teller of a tale."

Another rule for those who would heed their dreams is to learn to understand archetypal symbols. Symbols of this type are universal in nature and therefore have a meaning that transcends the purely personal.

One of the most common archetypal symbols is the shadow, which is the unknown entity in us, often the undeveloped, primitive, threatening element in us. It is the part of ourselves which we may constantly attempt to ignore or repress because we view it as uncivilized and think it will cause us problems.

This dark shadow will cause trouble, however, if it is ignored and will often be projected outward onto such scapegoats as blacks or other ethnic minorities who in our society are often made to bear the brunt of our repressed natures.

In our dreams the shadow often takes the form of a criminal or a pursuer with a knife. How common is the dream of being chased by some sinister figure and then awakening with a sense of fear. This attacking figure must be confronted, not escaped from, however, if we are to integrate its potential richness into our personalities.

Another archetypal figure, the anima, is the unconscious feminine part of a man's psyche. It is the anima which usually controls a man's moods, gives him belief in a divine nature, and provides him with the ability to love.

Likewise, the archetypal animus is the unconscious, undeveloped masculine side of a woman. This inner man is responsible for a woman's argumentative side and also enables her to deal with facts and relate them to a larger truth of which they are a part.

Certain images which occur repeatedly in the dreams of many people are significant archetypal symbols. For example, in our culture the automobile frequently represents the ego—a means of dealing with the world and moving around in it.

If I dream that my little red sports car is zooming down a road at 80 miles per hour and crashes into a guard railing by a river, I had better stop and take this warning dream seriously. It is indicating that I am moving too fast and am about to lose control. If I apply the brakes in time and regain control of my vehicle, I can avert the impending disaster.

Animals often serve as archetypal symbols. Dr. Carl Jung was once counseling a woman who dreamed that a horse leaped through a window, killing itself instantly Because Jung knew the horse was a symbol of physicality, or the body, he interpreted the dream to mean that the woman's body was destroying itself. At Jung's advice the woman went to a medical doctor, who discovered she had cancer. Because of the dream, the woman was able to have surgery and avert almost certain death.

Other animals often appear in dreams as symbols too. Dogs may represent an animal type of masculinity, while cats often symbolize one aspect of femininity. Some women, for example, are referred to as being "catty."

Some time ago I dreamed about a bear. Being unable to discover any implications this dream might have for me, I discussed it with a friend who asked me how I would interpret a bear symbol if it appeared in a cartoon. I responded that it would probably be a totem of Russia, just as the eagle represents the United States. From this association of images, I made an important discovery about myself.

Frequently dreams of going to school and school classrooms represent a new growth or reorientation about to occur in us. The house in which we find a room we did not know was there shows us that our capabilities and possibilities as a person exceed what we imagined.

Other common archetypal symbols include the sea, representative of the unconscious from which humankind's conscious life emerged; trains, hotels or motels, and airports, which may symbolize collective or group values and mores; and earthquakes or other natural disasters, which often point to a significant change impending in one's outlook or life.

A Word of Caution ... and of Encouragement

Contrary to the claims of many of the dream books on the market today, there is no shortcut to dream interpretation. One cannot reduce dream images to ready-made meanings and expect instant insight.

Learning to understand our dreams is as slow and difficult a task as persevering on our religious pathway. We need to approach the unconscious in an unbiased way, open to receive whatever meaning the dream has for us.

Dream images and symbols are understood only in relationship to one's entire life—so it is important, whether we are listening to our own dreams, or those of others, to see them in the perspective of one's whole life. Living widely and well is one of the best preparations for understanding one's dreams.

Certainly dreams can alter our outer lives directly as well as change our inner lives and attitudes. One concrete example of this can be seen in the following story.

I had been working with one young man approximately one year when he dreamed that his father and brother were black. As we started to discuss the dream, the young man expressed to me how wonderful he felt his father and brother were. I pointed out that the dream showed that his unconscious attitude toward them was negative (often signified in white persons' dreams by blackness).

At this point the young man began to look more deeply into his feelings about his family. He discovered that although his material wants had been well supplied, he felt that his family had never provided adequate love and emotional sustenance.

The counselee could not begin to have an authentic relationship with the members of his family until he was consciously aware of his feelings toward them. Neither could the young man deal with his other interpersonal problems until his family relationships were mended. Change could come only with awareness, and it was this awareness that the dream provided.

Although our dreams often provide us with unimaginable insights, they never show us more than we can stand to know. It is on this point that dreams and hypnosis differ. In my own experience I have never seen anyone psychologically injured by dealing with the contents of the dream. Importantly, the dream almost always encourages interpersonal relationships and points out unloving or selfish attitudes.

The power of the dream to bring us to a greater consciousness and thus set us on a new pathway is seen in one final example—that of a young woman faced with a major life decision—whether or not to get a divorce from her husband of seven years. Although the marriage was in a shambles, the woman's whole religious background caused her to view divorce as a catastrophe. In addition, because so much of her energy had been put into her marriage, she felt useless, purposeless and meaningless at the prospect of a breakup of her home.

The first dream a counselee brings to the counselor is usually highly significant and often points the direction that the analysis will take. The first dream the young woman brought to me pictured her best friend, securely married and a new mother, as a drug addict. The woman felt sorry for the friend's child and attempted to interrogate the family to find out more about the friend's addiction.

As we discussed the dream, it became apparent that for this young woman, her marriage and its place in the collective value system were preventing her from going on her own separate, individuated journey. In her attempt to conform to all the expectations of society's mores, she had abandoned her consciousness; i.e., she had become a drug addict.

This dream and subsequent dreams gave the woman the inner strength and sense of purpose necessary to go through the following painful months and to start making a new life for herself.

As this young woman discovered, there is a vast difference between knowledge through deduction and reason, and knowledge through experience and confrontation. Deduction and reason can teach us a great deal, but they alone cannot give our lives meaning. Only a direct experience of the spiritual can do that, and it is the spiritual world which is mediated to us nightly as we dream.

FOR FURTHER READING

Jung, C. G., *Memories, Dreams, Reflections,* recorded & edited by A. Jaffe, New York: Pantheon Books, 1963.

Kelsey, Morton T., *Dreams: A Way to Listen to God,* New York: Paulist Press, 1977.

———, *Adventure Inward: Christian Growth through Personal Journal Keeping,* Minneapolis: Augsburg, 1980.

Sanford, John, *Dreams: God's Forgotten Language,* Philadelphia: J. B. Lippincott, 1951.

8

Rediscovering the Power of Christian Myth

M any Christian leaders today are suggesting that the symbols, myths and rituals of our faith are outmoded and ought to be discarded in our scientific secular era. These leaders feel that perhaps we have outgrown the traditional practices of the church and that we can learn to rely on reason alone.

Certainly dogmas and practices essential to Christianity in the past have recently crumbled. Vatican II heralded the winds of religious change in our times. But rather than view the change as a precursor to a new vitality in our faith, many see the turbulence of these changes as merely a crisis and a signal that perhaps modern secular thought and traditional Christian faith are at odds with each other.

Actually, there is no need for this confusion. The belief that the secular and the spiritual are at war is naive and springs out of our Western contention that all knowledge comes to human beings consciously as a result of sense experience and reason. This view leaves no room for belief in a spiritual reality which can be known through intuition and imagination, through unconscious perceptions. Our view of the nature of human beings is too small and we limit ourselves to seeing only one-half of our capacities—the conscious half.

The church, too, in professing a primarily materialistic belief system, has promulgated the idea that engaging in the language of the unconscious—through images and symbols, stories and legends, sagas and myths—is primitive and nonsensical in a modern world.

All we need to do if we want some clues to the existence of a psychic or spiritual reality is to watch the nightly drama of dreams that unfolds from our conscious mind night after night. Dreams, religious experiences, intuitions, and extrasensory perceptions all indicate the existence of this other realm of reality about which myth and symbol have been speaking for centuries.

Myth is essentially the way human beings talk about their religious encounter with God and the spiritual world. If we demythologize our Christianity, it will become meaningless and poverty stricken.

Myth . . . a Definition

People commonly believe that myths are fabricated stories, embroidered products of imagination that have little or no relationship to real life. This view is terribly limited, however, for myths are really pictures of a reality that cannot be captured in ordinary language. They are a series of images reflecting the truths of the spiritual world. Thus myths and truth are not at odds with each other. Factual truth describes outer physical reality; myth describes inner spiritual reality.

Myths rise from our unconscious and speak of the significance of spiritual reality and its relationship to the material world. The early Christians believed in a spiritual world and they used myths and stories to describe human interaction with that world.

If we dismiss myth as irrelevant to our modern age, we lose a valuable means of encountering spiritual reality. The real stature and depth of human beings has been overlooked by much of modern thought, but it is through myth, which points toward meaning, that we can rediscover our great human capacity for relationship to the spiritual.

As a result of one-sided, rationalistic thought, which claims that the spiritual world is non-existent, men and women have been forced to contrive their own meanings for life. Even the church has discarded rich myths and religious traditions and has begun to suggest that mature people must learn to live in a world where only skill, science and reason matters.

However, people have found that without any religious roots to anchor them and give them meaning, their own fabrications of reality have been meager indeed. Depression, the common cold of modern psychiatry; neurosis and psychosis; drug addiction and alcoholism are but a few of the results of loss of meaning. Only by coming into contact with the creative reality or the center of meaning about which all great myths speak can we rediscover a sense of purpose in life.

The Importance of Myth in History

One of the myths that is powerfully replayed throughout history is the myth of the dying god. That myth is alive and affects us in the modern world is demonstrated by the assassinations of two American presidents—Abraham Lincoln and John Kennedy. The mythic proportions of the deaths of these two men bear examination. These two tragedies, so uncannily similar in many details, stirred the emotions and imaginations of Americans and people around the world, altered lives, and changed the course of history.

The death of Lincoln seemed to be felt psychically before the actual occurrence. Of course, Lincoln himself had a dream showing his body lying in state, surrounded by mourners. In three separate towns the news that the President had been killed was issued before he had actually been assassinated. The death itself and the funeral cortege attracted multitudes of people who eulogized him and compared him to Christ. The details of his life were enlarged and a variety of religious sects tried to claim Lincoln as one of them, although he was not affiliated with any religious institution.

Likewise, several psychics attempted to warn John Kennedy not to go to Dallas. I personally know of two dreams that seemed to forewarn his death. A handsome war hero and member of a colorful family that captured the imagination of the public, Kennedy was the sort of figure ripe to be mythologized. The rituals of the funeral processions, the riderless horse, the march down Pennsylvania Avenue, kept millions glued to their TV screens as they took part in this event of mythic proportions. In each case the assassin was a man caught up in the turmoil of an inner world where destructive powers ruled supreme.

Many primitive cultures practiced the ritual murder of their kings, often using human sacrifice. The Greek story of the Phoenix which rises from its own ashes is a myth which pictures death, but it is a death which precedes resurrection, offering hope and meaning.

Certainly the Christ myth (which was lived out in actual history) depicts a destructive power at work—a force which succeeds in killing the Son of God. But Christ's resurrection shows that this destructive power cannot win. Rather, Christ has conquered evil through his sacrificial death on the cross. Through ritual imagination we too can participate in the power of myth and deal triumphantly with the noncreative elements of the universe.

Mythology and Evil

It is practically impossible for us to ignore the effects of evil in our world today. The media are full of descriptions of murder, rape, arson, and political assassinations. Although we see clearly the effects of evil all around us, many of us are loathe to identify these happenings as a result of a destructive spiritual reality that makes its presence felt in material reality. We consider ourselves too sophisticated to take evil that seriously. Yet movies like *Bonnie and Clyde, The Exorcist,* and *In Cold Blood* as well as books like *Frankenstein, Dracula,* and *Faust* all clearly show the reality of evil.

The Christian myth offers a solution to the problem of evil, but it is not the only myth existing in our world. There are a number of other myths, or ways of approaching reality. Let us examine how each one deals with evil.

Materialism and Evil

First, the belief that matter and energy are the only realities in the universe is a faith of sorts that promotes the idea that we ought to construct a materialistic utopia achieved through operant conditioning. In this framework evil is merely whatever prevents human beings from achieving this goal.

Nowhere in this scheme of things is there a belief that a spiritual reality, composed of both creative and destructive elements, is at work. Instead, we find only the thought that evil is an accidental lack of perfection. This mythology is hardly powerful enough to deal with the horrors of such evils as the concentration camps at Dachau or the multiple slayings of a Charlie Manson.

Eastern Religions and Evil

The mythology of the East—both Hinduism and Buddhism—maintains that the physical world is illusionary and that the only reality is the spiritual world. It believes that God, who is at the center of the universe, encompasses both good and evil and that one finds truth by merging his or her own ego into the will of God.

This belief system emphasizes the absorption of the individual into cosmic consciousness to the exclusion of extraverted efforts. Thus social outreach or a ministry to the sick or dying is neglected in favor of each person's working out his or her own karma.

The Mother Goddesses

The third mythology, that of many primitive cultures, centers around the great mother goddesses of nature. Certainly this viewpoint offers proof that a destructive reality exists, for natural forces are often annihilative and devouring. The ravages of hurricanes, tornadoes, stormy seas and preying beasts show that beauty alone does not characterize amoral nature.

One of the early goddesses in Aztec mythology wore a belt or girdle of skulls, connoting the devouring mother. Another goddess was depicted with a snake in her lap, while the Greek siren Circe was shown circled by fanged beasts. In their attempt to deal with nature's destructive element, primitive peoples often made sacrifices to these goddesses to appease the evil side of their nature.

The Wotan Myth

The fourth mythology is that of Wotan, god of the forest, who ruled the world through sheer naked power without thought for justice. A concrete example of this god in action was seen in the infectious form Naziism took in Germany in the 1930s. This warrior god who embodied the principle that evil is weakness and goodness is strength wreaked havoc upon the Western world, and his presence is still felt wherever might is viewed as right.

The Yahweh Myth

The Hebrew God, or Yahweh, of the Old Testament constitutes yet another mythology. This God, who loved justice and whose actions were governed by law, is a contrast against the amoral nature of the primitive mother goddesses or numerous pagan gods of darkness and light. Because in this myth Yahweh was considered to be the only God of the universe; he therefore had to incorporate both good and evil.

As a result of the anguished cries of men and women suffering at the hands of the dark side of God, this mythology maintains that God sent his son to redeem human beings from the dark into the light. The Book of Job presents this problem of evil clearly.

Gnosticism

The gnostic construct of reality views matter as the source of evil and spirit as the source of good. The earth, according to this viewpoint, was formed when the world of the spirit underwent an explosion which sent some of its contents into the chaos outside the spiritual world, creating the earth. Spiritual fragments then settled upon the earth and developed into human beings.

But the spirits longed to escape their material, bodily entrapments and return to the only good—the world of spiritual reality. As a result of this attitude, sexuality became the chief sin for it propagated more human beings entrapping more spirit in flesh, imprisoning it on earth.

Zoroastrianism

In the sixth century B.C. lived a man named Zoroaster (also called Zarathustra) who made some important contributions to our understanding of evil. Zoroaster believed in one God, Ahura Mazda, who had two sons, one of whom chose good and one evil.

Eventually this myth was altered to indicate that the evil son had really coexisted with Ahura Mazda from the beginning of time as a god named Ahriman. According to the myth, Ahriman had fallen into an abyss as a result of a struggle with Ahura Mazda, who gave the beings he subsequently made a choice—to remain as static spirits or to be born as flesh and blood into a world where they would encounter evil and struggle with it. In time, a savior would come to give the mortals on earth a means to become immortal.

This Zoroastrian myth gradually merged with the myth of the dying and rising god which was prevalent in the land of the Hebrew religion and which was the precursor of the Christian myth.

The Dying and Rising God

The New Testament presents Jesus as the incarnation of God who defeated evil by dying and then rising again, making his victory over the destructive forces of the universe available to his followers. The myth was essential to Christianity, but after the Middle Ages, when modern rational thinkers began to discard belief in a spiritual reality, intellectuals perceived the universe as a mechanism run by physical laws which certainly wouldn't permit a phenomenon like resurrection from the dead.

In addition, mythological study showed the existence of other myths that resembled the Christian viewpoint. This discovery led many to believe that the New Testament record was merely the attempt of primitive people to find meaning in the universe. If, however, we look more closely at these myths, we will see that the rational attitudes toward them is simplistic and erroneous.

The Pagan Myths

The most common myth of the dying and rising god is that of Adonis and Aphrodite, which tells of Aphrodite's love for the youth who is gored to death by a boar. The goddess mixes her beloved Adonis' blood with a sweet mixture that drops to the earth, causing flowers to bloom every spring. The stories of Tammuz and Ishtar, of Osiris and of Isis, from whose blood violets sprang up, are similar.

Each of these myths deals with death and life, winter and spring, sacrifice and resurrection, and was the basis of ritual celebrations that took place at approximately the same time that we celebrate Easter. These myths also mediated the divine to the peoples who celebrated them and gave them a ritual participation in the cycles that sustained rhythm, order, and meaning in the universe.

Myths of dying and rising showed humankind grappling with the destructive powers of the universe, with unconsciousness and evil. In each case, only through a positive spiritual power could victory over death be ensured. The ritual celebrations of these stories allowed human beings to actually experience or act out the archetypal struggle between good and evil, to symbolically partake of the victory over death and to express the story of the individual toward consciousness and light, away from the dark instinctual forces pulling them into inertia. The problem in each of these myths, however, was that no real human being had ever enacted this death and resurrection in time and history, thus freeing it from its unfinished cycle of mythological timelessness.

Judaic and Christian Myths

It was as an outgrowth of the Jewish myth of Yahweh that time and place were to eventually change the unfinished cycle of the pagan mythologies. In the Judaic myth Jehovah symbolized consciousness, light and the masculine principle of discrimination, the antithesis of the all-encompassing, dark, devouring earth principle of the mother goddess. The Old Testament prophets continually decried the feminine deities and celebration of the pagans. But in his justice and strength and majesty, Yahweh became unfeeling and legalistic.

Thus it was left to the Christian myth, a further development of the Judaic myth, to bring together the conscious masculine principle, represented by the Lord God, with a humanized compassionate form of the great mother, represented by Mary. This union of opposites created Christ, the symbol of wholeness and transformation.

Psychologically speaking, Mary's impregnation represents the myth of the soul of humankind (the inner feminine) being impregnated by the masculine and so bringing about the creative union of these sides of oneself and thus new life, the "new man in Christ."

And so, the myth of the conquering hero who is victorious over evil reaches its ultimate expression in Christianity. But Christianity also differs from all previous myths in that Christ was born in history, physically, as well as in myth, spiritually, so that the myth was anchored in outer reality and no longer required yearly reenactment. Christ died once and for all and human beings could participate in its ritual celebration in the mass. Christ's victory over evil becomes the participant's victory as well.

Attempts to Demythologize Christianity

Although some thinkers maintain that the pagan myths parallel the Christian one, making it implausible and reducing it to the level of fanciful tale, this argument is naive and fallacious. It does not see the nature of myth as representative of existing spiritual truths, as a pattern of the structure of reality, not merely a human contrivance that wildly attempts to inject meaning into a meaningless universe.

And although there are many rich parallels among the myths, Christianity is the only one that incarnated God in human form, setting myth free to act in an inner *and* outer way upon the lives of men and women.

Because myths do express existing spiritual realities, their patterns emerge in the dreams, fantasies, and imagination of human beings. We ignore myth and its expressions at our own peril, for without them, we confine God to the rational realm and deprive ourselves of a living and vital faith that transforms our whole person.

Despite the attempts by many churches, clergy and theologians to make religion rational and "intellectually respectable," Christianity still maintains its mythic, life-given quality. One of the best expressions of this mythic power is in the sacraments.

Myth and Sacrament

The divine realities of which myths speak are mediated through religious ritual, meditation and sacramental action. Whether we as individuals in a modern society realize it or not, we participate in myth in our secular lives merely by belonging to a collective group or culture.

One such myth is lived out through war, for the unconscious demonic aspect of our nature takes shape in the rituals of battle. Today we like to think that we are so highly civilized that we have erased the tendencies to violence and aggression which we associate with primitives. But the annihilative events of two world wars in this century alone prove us wrong.

The rituals of reconciliation, healing and transformation which require consciousness and commitment are available to us if we choose to participate in the victory of Christ over the demonic. But we must bring our whole selves to this commitment; intellectual allegiance is not enough. In a materialistic society that depends on Santa Claus and the Easter Bunny for celebration, the profound rituals and sacraments of Christianity are desperately needed to nourish our underfed souls.

If we elect to disregard the creative rituals of Christianity, then we run the risk of succumbing to those of a destructive or barbaric myth, for human beings are religious by nature and ultimately make a commitment to something.

Carl Jung once stated that the structure of Christianity offers us the best possible opportunity for psychological wholeness. Unfortunately most modern individuals are cut off from this structure and thus they try to content themselves with a relatively superficial existence, avoiding confrontation with the spiritual issues of life. Those who do not confront spiritual realities, however, run the risk of being devoured by this powerful world unless they are protected and accompanied by the rituals and sacraments of the Christian church.

There have been people who confronted this stark reality alone, as did Carl Jung, who survived, but he maintained that the only thing that saved him during this experience was his convction that he was obeying a higher will which would get him through. The confrontation was so powerful that he felt as if he were being deluged by high boulders attempting to crush him. Then there were others who attempted the confrontation alone and were annihilated, like Nietzsche.

Symbols of Transformation

The two major rituals of the church which mediate the power of Christian myth to us are the Eucharist and baptism.

As we partake of communion, we participate in the myth of the hero preparing for the sacrifice. The light from the candles symbolizes the light of the world shining into the darkness. The bread represents the earth element associated with the Great Mother, while the wine speaks of masculinity. The breaking of the bread signifies the death of Christ, and as one partakes of both elements, the union of the masculine and feminine gives birth to the Christ within, who secured victory over darkness through his resurrection.

Whether or not one understands all the symbolism is, to some degree, irrelevant for the power of myth is not so paltry that it can be maimed by our lack of conscious knowledge. By celebrating the ritual, we experience the myth and integrate it into our lives.

Those who claim that the rituals of the church are dead and without meaning do not have an acquaintance with their dreams and imaginative life, for these mythic patterns emerge time and again as I counsel people and listen to them reveal their inner realities.

Baptism speaks of dying with Christ and then rising to new life in him. The rituals of washing and making the sign of the cross also suggest transformation.

Other sacraments that mediate the power of Chirstian myth include laying on of hands for healing, anointing with oil, exorcism, marriage, and confirmation.

The desperate need of our time is to learn once again to enter into that world of myth and symbol, rite and sacrament, which can put us in touch with the center of creative reality without which life is sterile, arid and meaningless.

FOR FURTHER READING

Campbell, Joseph, *The Hero with a Thousand Faces,* Princeton: Princeton University Press, 1968.

Jung, C. G., *Collected Works* Vol. II (*Psychology and Religion: West and East*), New York: Pantheon Books, 1958, pp. 201–296.

Kelsey, Morton T., *Myth, History and Faith: The Remythologizing of Christianity,* New York: Paulist Press, 1974.

9

Using Imagination to Enter the Inner World

There are many ways to enter the strange, beautiful—and sometimes terrifying—territory of the inner world. The methods mentioned here are well-tried ways of using imagination for religious purposes. Persons who become familiar enough with ways like these can then branch out on their own, for these forms are meant to be stimuli to encourage each individual to work with his or her own images.

One way to start is to enter a biblical story in imagination. By stepping into an actual event or taking part in one of the stories told by Jesus, one can participate in images that are already formed and share in their deepest meaning. The opposite way is to wait for images to arise spontaneously from within and then follow them as they move. If they become too threatening or destructive, we can call upon the Risen Christ to support and save us.

A third method is quite similar. Instead of trying futilely to ignore a bad mood, or going right out to celebrate a good one, one can enter the mood and allow it to be expressed in images which can then be worked with, again turning to Jesus to bring renewed vitality and a sense of direction. Outer expressions, like imaginative writing, gardening, weaving and sand play can also be used to bring images into focus for this purpose.

Still another method is to listen to one's dreams, which are a natural expression of the inner world. They come without knocking or asking leave, and seem to vanish again into nowhere. But if their images are given quiet, meditative attention, they can be invited back and figures can even be persuaded to speak of meanings from all levels of being. By using this natural bridgehead to the inner world, one begins to discover that the ways of communicating with the Risen Christ are just as natural and actually not very different from making contact with an inner dream figure.

Some people find that the experience of tongue speaking provides just as natural a bridge to the inner world, opening up communication with the Holy Spirit and allowing images from many levels to arise. For others, quiet prayer does much the same thing. Simply the act of affirmation—affirming that one centers on Christ and the love that goes both ways—will open many people to reflections and insights which are a form of imagination in action. The effort to share that love through intercessory prayer often works equally well to open some persons to the same kind of insights, and also to the value of learning to use the imagination.

Imagination is the key that unlocks the door to the inner world, because images give us a way of thinking that brings us closer to actual experiences of the spiritual world than any concept or merely verbal idea can. The images that arise from the unconscious, much as dream images, for example, tell us about our inner being and how it is affected by forces from the spiritual world.

Ability to Think in Images

It is important to realize that the powers of the spiritual realm seldom deal with people just on a conscious rational level. God, of course, can reach an individual by a rational conversion experience, but such an experience is only the beginning of a journey into a deeper relationship with God. God seems to want the whole person and to be willing to work with our ego consciousness as though it were a slender life line that will grow stronger with deeper inner experiences. When prayer and meditation concentrate only on concepts, they do not touch the most profound part of our being except when it happens accidentally. Conceptual thought does not have the same power as the ability to think in images.

Although every one of us needs logical, purposeful thought to analyze problems, set up goals, and measure results, we must be aware that logical thinking follows different rules and is used for different purposes than imagination is.

Images come from the inner world where we have the most intimate contact with realities that are usually hidden from view in the outer world. They have the power to contact these realities and offer us ways of relating to them so that we can gain the insight and drive and energy which they hold potentially for our use.

Images also help us work with the emotions that are generated by these highly charged experiences of the spiritual world. When one is overwhelmed by a negative experience, it is almost impossible to get at the root of the problem without images that will show us what the negative force is, and then enable us to bring the Risen Christ into the picture by the use of the imagination.

Because Western civilization has stressed the importance of logical thought, people frequently consider imaginative thinking suitable only for primitives and artists. Many individuals fear that their imaginations may interfere with their rational conceptual thinking and, as a result, with their control over their lives.

It is true that imagination requires a very different capacity. With imagination one does not have conscious control of the images worked with. They cannot be called up or stopped at will like concepts can. Images are more like living beings with a life and purpose of their own. Often they take the individual into strange territory where he or she does not know the terrain well enough to take direction and has trouble enough simply trying to follow where the images lead.

Only a few of the most creative thinkers today seem to realize that our ability to understand and deal with the world around us depends upon using *both* imagination and conceptual thought. As scientists have studied the source of their knowledge and ideas, they have come to realize that even the most carefully developed concepts rest originally on images which first came up from someone's unconscious as a flash of insight does.

Far from stopping each other, logic and imagination go hand in hand. Imagination is needed by logical thinkers fully as much as logical reasoning is needed by intuitive people in order for both to know the world, and to realize and share the full value of the experiences that are available to us.

If we are to embark upon a spiritual journey, we must learn how to use images to open up the depths of the psyche that have been virtually closed to modern persons. We can then look to the more difficult job of trying to understand the experiences found there.

The name C. G. Jung gave to this venture was active imagination. Others may call it psychosynthesis or meditation. But whatever we call this process, we are still referring to seeking that part of the real world that can be explored by turning inward and using the images dwelling there.

How to Start the Inner Journey

We must subscribe to two rules to start this inner journey. First, we must believe in the importance of thinking and experiencing in images. Second, we must be willing to set aside enough quiet time to break away from immediate concern with the outer space/time realm. Aside from these two rules, each person needs to find an individual technique to awaken the imagination, guided largely by the demands of one's own personality type.

Active Imagination

A variety of suggestions for sparking the imagination will be offered in the hope that one or another of them strikes fire within the reader. To begin, a most helpful approach was suggested by Dr. Jung in response to a request to explain the technique of active imagination.

First, Jung made sure to distinguish between idle daydreaming, which consists of movie-like, half-conscious episodes, and active imagination, whose essence lies in the fact that "the images have a life of their own and that the symbolic events develop according to their own logic—that is, of course, if your conscious reason does not interfere."

Jung then went on to give a personal example to clarify his statement. As a child, he often visited an aunt whose house was full of interesting pictures. One of them showed his grandfather, who had been a bishop, standing on the steps of his house looking down a pathway leading to the door of the cathedral. Often, Jung said, he would kneel on a chair looking at the picture until his grandfather came down the steps onto the path.

His aunt always told him he was mistaken; his grandfather was still standing in the same place. But the child knew perfectly well what he had seen. "In the same way," Jung went on, "when you concentrate on a mental picture, it begins to stir, the image becomes enriched by details, it moves and develops. Each time, naturally, you mistrust it and have the idea that you have just made it up, that it is merely your own invention."

It is usually not too difficult to start the process of active imagination by concentrating on something graphic. The hard part is realizing that something can move inside us without our conscious direction. It is vital to realize that in developing imagination the ego is not the only force operating within us. As Jung pointed out, anyone who writes or lectures knows that the writer is not the creator of the ideas, for the ideas come popping out on their own.

If we pay attention to our imagination, we find a spontaneous creative process working within. We can observe the forces of work, relate to and influence them, but we cannot create what they do by use of ego power. Through acceptance of what our imagination offers to us, and through action upon it, we are given access to many levels of the world from which dreams come.

To explain active imagination concretely, Jung cited the story of a young artist attempting to deal with inner images.

> I was treating a young artist, and he had the greatest trouble in understanding what I meant by active imagination. He tried all sorts of things but he could not get at it. The difficulty with him was that he could not think. Musicians, painters, artists of all kinds, often can't think at all, because they never intentionally use their brain. This man's brain too was always working for itself; it had its artistic imaginations and he couldn't use it psychologically, so he couldn't understand. I gave him every chance to try, and he tried all sorts of stunts. I cannot tell you all the things he did, but I will tell you how he finally succeeded in using his imagination psychologically.
>
> I live outside the town, and he had to take the train to get to my place. It starts from a small station, and on the wall of that station was a poster. Each time he waited for his train he looked at that poster. The poster was an advertisement for Mürren in the Bernese Alps, a colorful picture of the waterfalls, of a green meadow and a hill in the center, and on that hill were several cows. So he sat there staring at that poster and thinking that he could not find out what I meant by active imagination. And then one day he thought: "Perhaps I could start by having a fantasy about that poster. I might for instance imagine that I am myself in the poster, that the scenery is real and that I could walk up the hill among the cows and then look down on the other side, and then I might see what there is behind that hill."
>
> So he went to the station for that purpose and imagined that he was in the poster. He saw the meadow and the road and walked up the hill among the cows, and then he came up to the top and looked down, and there was the meadow again, sloping down, and below was a hedge with a stile. So he walked down and over the stile, and there was a little footpath that ran round a ravine, and a rock, and when he came round that rock, there was a small chapel, with its door standing a little ajar. He thought he would like to enter, and so he pushed the door open and went in, and there upon an altar decorated with pretty flowers stood a wooden figure of the Mother of God. He looked up at her face, and in that exact moment something with pointed ears disappeared behind the altar. He thought, "Well, that's all nonsense," and instantly the whole fantasy was gone.
>
> He went away and said, "Now again I haven't understood what active imagination is." And then, suddenly, the thought struck him: "Well, perhaps that really *was* there, perhaps that thing behind the Mother of God, with the pointed ears, that disappeared like a flash, really happened." Therefore he said to himself: "I will just try it all over as a test."

So he imagined that he was back in the station looking at the poster, and again he fantasized that he was walking up the hill. And when he came to the top of the hill, he wondered what he would see on the other side. And there was the hedge and the stile and the hill sloping down. He said, "Well, so far so good. Things haven't moved since, apparently." And he went round the rock, and there was the chapel. He said, "There is the chapel, that at least is no illusion. It is all quite in order." The door stood ajar and he was quite pleased. He hesitated a moment and said, "Now, when I push that door open and I see the Madonna on the altar, then that thing with the pointed ears should jump down behind the Madonna, and if it doesn't, then the whole thing is bunk!" And so he pushed the door open and looked—and there it all was and the thing jumped down, as before and then he was convinced. From then on he had the key and knew he could rely on his imagination and so he learned to use it. (From *Analytical Psychology: Its Theory & Practice,* by C. G. Jung. © 1968 by heir of C. G. Jung. Reprinted by permission of Pantheon Books, a division of Random House.)

It is important to observe that the first step in the young man's journey inward was his *desire* to discover this other dimension of reality. He was willing to work at the process. His first venture, essentially sacramental in nature, was an effort to enter the poster from outside. The second time he started with an inner image.

Almost any representation of outer reality can be a starting point. A picture, a statue, a myth or story, a crucifix can be brought into the psyche and encountered within. Many people find that great art stimulates their imagination. Archetypal religious symbols can also start the imagination working.

Furthermore, it is equally possible to start from within the imagination. One can begin with a dream that has bubbled up out of the unconscious, or the memory of a story. Or, one can simply wait in the stillness until an image appears and then follow it as it moves. These are some of the vehicles that can carry one to the gateway of imagination.

The artist in Jung's illustration was surprised at what he found in his inner world. If, however, he had been taking a Rorschach or a Thematic Apperception test, he probably would not have been so surprised.

When a psychologist asks, "What do you see?" one feels foolish answering, "an ink blot," or "an unfinished sketch." One lets the vague forms stir the imagination so that it brings up images from the deep recesses of the mind, or tells a story with an outcome that suddenly seems to fit the neutral outline of a picture. Thus one is in a world of limitless possibilities no longer restricted by the material outline of an ink blot or a half-finished picture.

It is important to note that the artist did not start out with any religious venture in mind, but imagination led him right to religious images. If religion matters to a person, imagination will produce the religious images regardless of the original intent.

In this story the realities of the divine mother and then of the evil, furtive creature lurking behind the altar hold our interest; we wish Dr. Jung would go on with the story. But he would probably smile and remind us that we all have access to this world and to experiences of our own that are just as interesting and directed toward religious meaning.

Ways of Awakening Imagination

There are dozens of ways of helping people get back into the imaginative realm they knew as children. But most adults have to learn first of all that there is nothing wrong with imagining and becoming as little children again, for parents often feel that a child's experiences of the inner world are signs that he or she is not adjusting to the ordinary, outer world. It is upsetting to them to see the child actually at home in both worlds; they are afraid the child will not be able to tell inner reality from outer.

The problem in growing up, however, is not to reject the inner world, but to learn to distinguish between inner and outer realities. The child is not yet able to tell the difference between inner and outer realities. But, as Laurens van der Post has shown with such depth in his novel *The Face Beside the Fire,* it takes years of restoring to undo the damage that is caused by punishing a child for inability to distinguish between inner and outer realities. Since the Enlightenment, generations of people have grown up trying to avoid imagination and the inner world. When a faculty like this is repressed, its power usually turns negative.

Just as children have to begin learning to think logically and to know the world outside, adults need to find once more the magical reality within and know that it can be terrifying or comforting. When we come to know the reality of the spiritual world, our lives will become less restricted, and we will be able to differentiate between physical and spiritual reality and feel at home in both worlds.

Rix Weaver's book *The Wise Old Woman* offers a good explanation and many illustrations of finding the inner way, while Roberto Assagioli's *Psychosynthesis: A Manual of Principles and Techniques* is packed with suggestions for developing imagination. He starts with simple exercises like imagining a blank blackboard and seeing a series of numbers gradually appear on it, and goes on to increasingly sophisticated techniques. One may imagine being in a meadow, on a mountain, visiting a chapel, and then report what happens. Archetypal symbols will often stimulate deep levels of the psyche. It may help to share images with another person or participate in a prayer group. In my book *Adventure Inward* I give many concrete methods of using the imagination.

By inventing stories one also reveals the depth of oneself. This technique has been used in English classes to have students make up their own fairy tales, and it is surprising how pupils are stimulated. Great literature reveals not only the depth of the writer, but also what is happening in the collective psyche and sometimes even the nature of reality itself.

Robert Louis Stevenson, for instance, expanded the images of a dream into his best-selling novelette, *The Strange Case of Dr. Jekyll and Mr. Hyde,* thus revealing his own split and the split of Victorian England grown rich and cultured on imperialism and the slave trade. Herman Melville, Shakespeare, and Goethe, for example, all depicted levels of spiritual reality in their writings.

One's own efforts at insight can start with dream images like Stevenson's, or by looking at a picture as Jung did, or by walking into a new scene as Jung's artist friend did. One can begin with images of one's own meaninglessness, as Dante did in *The Divine Comedy,* or by visualizing a Bible story.

Or one may simply wait for the right image to appear and then concentrate on it until it moves. Some people are able to sit down at the typewriter once the action has begun and record it as if they were watching from a press box. My own imagination has led me through three long sequences—one of them 80,000 words long!

Many people find that drawing, painting, or sculpting will open up their imaginations better than storytelling can. Many of Dr. Jung's patients used painting to work with their dream images. "Sand-play" is used by some therapists for both children and adults. Jung himself built a model village of stone in his backyard as a means of dealing with his unconscious material.

The important thing is to find whatever activity will help one to develop imagination, whether it is sculpting, building, weaving, gardening, dancing or acting. The relationship among dance and drama, religious ritual, worship, creative play, imaginative writing, painting and meditation is very deep.

Johan Huizinga has suggested in his book *Homo Ludens* that it may be a misnomer to call ourselves *homo sapiens,* and that the term *homo ludens,* man the player, may be closer to the truth. It is the human's ability to play creatively that keeps us in touch with the roots of reality so that we are able to find meaning and purpose. Our sense of the sacred, which provides our direction in life, undoubtedly springs from the merger of the playful with the imaginative.

The Importance of Religious Symbols in Imagination

If ordinary meadows and mountains can awaken a response from the depth of people, there is likely to be far more power in the deep, sacred symbols that spring from Christian ritual. Christianity's tapestry of symbols reveals God's concern for human beings.

The Bible is a moving story of how God works with people to overcome the evil that affects their lives. The Bible does not try to show us how to put this message logically in neat propositions, but gives us a picture of how we can find triumph over evil.

Using the imagination, we can step into the New Testament stories and be present at Jesus' birth in Bethlehem, at the feeding of the five thousand, or the crucifixion and the resurrection. In this way, we can participate in the eternal reality that broke through in history in Jesus of Nazareth and continues to break through whenever someone becomes truly open to the Holy Spirit.

The tragedy is that so many modern churches have tried to become intellectual and eliminate the rich, meaningful symbolism from their Christianity. If people can only learn how to step into symbolism, the stained glass windows, statues and images of the church can do more to feed the soul than all the concepts that could be put into a sermon.

The practice of using images in meditation has been rediscovered by modern psychiatrists trying to bring sick people to health again. Because they had nearly the same passion for healing as the first Christians, they were willing to try something that looked silly to many people. They realized that the excessive rationalism of modern times had cut us off from the inner world, causing mental anguish, neurosis, and physical illness. A number of depth psychologists began to teach patients to use imagination through techniques similar to the early practices of Christian meditation.

The results were surprising. By learning about their own psychic depths, using dreams and symbols and imagination, patients recovered their health and found religious meaning as well. Jung's experience with his patients made him quite certain that a neurosis could never be totally resolved until the individual came into touch, usually through imagination, with the reality of which all the great religions speak.

Christians need to learn a great deal from the healing professions, for it is through working with images that the church can get back to meeting the real needs of people, especially their need for a contact with the center of meaning. It is through Christian symbols that we are able to uncover the religious depth of the spiritual world.

FOR FURTHER READING

Assagioli, Roberto, M.D., *Psychosynthesis: A Manual of Principles and Techniques*, New York: Viking Press, 1971.

Kelsey, Morton T., *The Other Side of Silence: A Guide to Christian Meditation*, New York: Paulist Press, 1976.

———, *Adventure Inward: Christian Growth through Personal Journal Keeping*, Minneapolis: Augsburg, 1980.

10

Using Imagination to Deal with Negativity

In over 30 years of parish life ministering to all kinds of people, I have found no one whose life was totally secure and without need. This was true in a comfortable parish in suburban Los Angeles, and I have found it true in the academic community as well as in cities and villages across the United States and Europe. Among young and old, wealthy and poor, in lives seemingly rich and powerful, as well as those empty and oppressed, deep needs exist which are often difficult to express.

Behind their masks of confidence and capability, people are suffering, mostly in silence, because they do not see any place to turn. My encounter with the pain and need that fill almost every crack in our social facade has shown me that the most urgent problem of individuals is to find some meaning that will help them bear the inner, as well as the outer, suffering they feel.

Too often all people hear is advice to stay busy and get their problems solved, or else forget them and keep up a brave show like other people. The trouble with well-intended advice like this is that it leaves the pain and agony locked up inside the soul where most often nothing can touch it.

In fact, the deepest dread and pain, which existential writers reveal so well, seldom comes to the surface until people are relieved of the struggle for existence which keeps them busy all of the time. So long as they are completely absorbed by the problems of getting enough food and fuel just to stay alive, they seldom have to face the despair of meaninglessness.

Working with people at all levels of our society has shown me how often the greatest misery and pain occur along with great wealth. These people have no outer problems important enough to keep their attention diverted from the emptiness of their own being. With no outer problems, they are exposed to the reality of the inner or spiritual world. They feel as though they are naked and alone and are usually guided only by fear of what might be found if they looked within for meaning.

Anyone who is stripped in this way and forced to look inward usually faces fear and agony. Like solitary confinement, this exposes us to the depth of our own darkness. We often find whatever meaning we have known disintegrating; there is fear of finding only a void, fear of death and dissolution.

These are elements of the confrontation that are described over and over by writers from Paul Tillich to Jean-Paul Sartre. Although Tillich in *The Courage To Be* writes of finding the God beyond god, other people see us caught forever in a blind nothingness that most people try to escape. They are afraid of finding only the pointlessness of Beckett's *Waiting for Godot* or Sartre's *Nausea.*

This terror of looking directly into the void and finding only experiences that seem meaningless and devouring is worse than any sickness. Yet the darkness is there; the need is not to escape it, but to go through it and find meaning on the other side. There is still no better description of the darkness than the words of St. John of the Cross in *Dark Night of the Soul.*

The idea sometimes heard today that darkness can be avoided and we should find God only in joy and celebration, in peace and comfort, is a grave delusion that perhaps reveals our present lack of experience. We are apt either to begin this way in some darkness and depression or else be caught up by it somewhere along the way. Celebration is fine and comes after deliverance. Beforehand, celebration is often hollow, false, and naive.

The depression and anxiety resulting from the inner darkness and meaninglessness often force comfortable men and women to unmask and seek help. It was my own inner agony that sent me to seek help from Dorothy Phillips, author of *The Choice Is Always Ours,* and Max Zeller, a Jewish follower of Carl Jung, who started me toward healing and taught me to read the gospels again.

Here in these pages I began to find the reality of the loving, saving God whom the early church knew so well. I awoke to the fact that it is people's alienation from their religious roots, their lack of transcendent meaning to give purpose to their pain, that breeds neurosis and illness. It is only when the church really believes in the victory of Jesus Christ over the powers of evil that it touches people on a deep level.

As I reread the New Testament I began to understand something of the nature of the evil forces Christ defeated on the cross. Most of us fail to comprehend that evil is an autonomous force with a power to affect human life.

I remember a conversation I once had with a brilliant and creative theologian who was denying the reality of evil. We reflected a little together and concluded that he knew little outside of his sheltered college community. He had never known real tragedy or violence or inner agony personally, and in dealing only with rational concepts, he had no need to postulate the reality of evil and look for a power that could save him from it.

But if we look honestly at the outer happenings of our world, we must agree with Jung that only someone with a warped sense of humor could honestly claim that the death ovens of Dachau represented only an "accidental lack of perfection" or an absence of good. In our own time we have seen a cruelty overtake otherwise normal and civilized persons which one might call bestial, except that this maligns the instincts of the animal world.

Evil affects us inwardly as well as outwardly, however. Jesus taught us first of all to pray "Deliver us from the evil one." Then he told us to look within to identify the evil force within ourselves so we can stand against it.

It is often easy to identify this force within oneself which attacks through depression, anxiety, fear and rage. No matter how much one struggles against it, this force is always ready to tear one apart or drag one into icy isolation. The novels of C. S. Lewis and Charles Williams portray the primal force of evil in all its ugliness.

The idea that we have outgrown our need to turn to God for help in dealing with evil, or the belief that there is no such thing as cosmic evil would be humerous if it did not show such a tragic lack of understanding. This force has to be faced and dealt with or it will keep on turning our homes and our world into a battlefield. We sometimes find it hard to understand why Jesus said that the poor in spirit, the meek and sorrowing, are blessed, but perhaps it was because they are the ones who know they can't manage their lives by themselves.

Once a person realizes that there is a spiritual world as well as a physical one, he or she learns that there are forces of evil more destructive than the simply human ones, and that these spiritual forces of evil are those that the individual cannot deal with on one's own. They are more powerful realities, like the force of gravity or some other force of the universe, than many of the more recent ways of thinking about Satan would suggest.

When we do awaken and realize our own helplessness, our spiritual poverty, we become open to the inward way. It is then that we may ask the

Christ figure to come into our imagination, restoring and renewing us. If, in our time of meditation, we can actively imagine Christ coming into the deep, dark places with us to do his atoning work, we will find that a threatening, destructive mood can be faced, transformed into images, and finally conquered.

The first active imagination included here resulted from a feeling of meaninglessness and hopelessness.

The Desert

A feeling of separation and dryness is upon me. There is no destructive voice attacking. I only feel separate and alone, with no one who can take the whole of me. From the outside things go quite well. I function well enough.

But inside all is dried out, desiccated. There seems to be no place to go; no meaning, no future, no horizon. I simply grind out what is required, sleep, get up and do it all over again.

Life has lost its zest and sparkle . . . nothing to enjoy and nothing to look forward to. There is no particular fear; death does not seem to be on my tracks. Life is simply dull and dry.

I realize that I have had this gnawing feeling at the back of my heart for a long time. As I stop and look inward, I can feel it become more and more oppressive. I have a momentary desire to get back to busy-ness, to activity, and avoid the confrontation.

But I know that this is no escape. I must deal with the mood, with what I feel, or it will keep at my heels. If I try to escape it, I may even flee so hard that I fall and break a bone or make myself sick. And then I will have both the mood of uselessness and dryness and the physical pain as well to deal with. It is better to deal with it now. . . .

I sit down at the typewriter and start writing what I feel, stepping into the depth of the mood . . . into its very heart so that the dryness swirls about me like an arid desert wind, burning my skin with the heat and sand. . . .

It is then that the image comes. I almost seem to open my eyes to find out what direction the wind is coming from . . . and I am sitting on a mound in a great deserted valley like the Arizona or Mojave deserts. I look around. It is perhaps fifty miles long, with jagged, tiger-tooth mountains on either side. In the distance I can see that each end is walled in. Here and there a little whirlwind plays with the dry sand. One of them has swept around me.

There is only one sign of habitation in the whole desolate expanse, and that is where I am sitting . . . beside a desert shack that has fallen in. It has been abandoned for a long time. . . .

The windows are empty sockets. They look out on the debris of some former owner. A piece of tar paper flaps in the wind. A door, still hanging on its frame, whines as it swings back and forth . . . no other habitation in all that valley . . . just sagebrush and sand and rock. . . .

I wonder if it goes on forever. Is there any other place? Is this all there is?

I have a view, because the mound is higher than most of the valley. Then I look down and find that I am sitting on the dump-heap . . . the accumulated residue of years of desert living, now abandoned.

All sorts of useless things have been thrown onto this spot . . . the broken china, the tin cans, the donkey dung, some warped two-by-fours, the crumpled door of a car, pieces of corregated metal roofing. . . . The desert winds have poured sand around them and built a little mountain. . . . And there I sit like Job, examining the ashes and decay of former lives.

And the sun . . . always streaming down, now high overhead, burning, always bright, glaring day after day, drying out the skin, deadening the eyes, endlessly burning, relentless and incessant. . . .

And when it drops, the night and cold come quickly. The shadows move and coyotes howl, and then I shudder and long for the sun, for day to come. . . .

This is what life seems like, what it feels like . . . absurd, burning, dry, meaningless and useless, alone, separate. I feel the full brunt of the vacancy, the vacuum, the searing vacuum, the dry and burning nothingness. And where does one look for help and where is there to go?

Is life meant to be like this, I wonder? There is a story that we were made for glory, for transformation, for God and joy. I laugh to myself. There is a story that once God came as a man to rescue humankind from their desert and gave them life, to bring a promised land, a kingdom flowing with milk and honey, into their reach. . . .

What harm to think about it? I have faced all that there is to face here. It may even be cowardice not to look for more than just this all-encompassing emptiness. . . . Could there be one who would seek me out and bring me back to myself and into touch with other human beings? I decide that it will not hurt to explore this possibility. . . .

I say, "Lord, come to me; if you are real, come to me in my desolate isolation and make me human once again. . . . "

Of course, nothing happens. I expect a thunder clap, some lightning, and out of the explosion some triumphant figure with a chariot of fire to carry me away. But nothing. . . .

All a fraud, I think. . . . No, let's hope. I keep scanning the valley for a sign. . . .

And then on the far side of the valley, miles away, I make out a moving spot, tinier than the tiniest leaf from where I sit. But before long I can see that it is moving as if alive. Are my eyes deceiving me? I watch as the sun, past its height, begins to drop into the West.

The figure keeps moving, comes closer. Could it be coming my way, coming from the East? I keep staring dumbly as the figure comes still nearer. It really is a person, tall, a strong man in his very prime, erect, powerful, and yet he walks with grace. His clothes are very plain, but sturdy.

And when he comes close enough so that I can see his face, I see one that makes me truly hope for the first time in years . . . kind, warm, compassionate, with a smile of humor as if this were some divine joke, this trip of his.

He comes right up to my dump heap. I have not moved or said a word. Nor has he spoken. He reaches out a hand to lift me down. Automatically I stretch out mine toward him in return.

As I step down he embraces me with a great hug . . . as if he were my mother, father, brother and sister, friend, beloved, all rolled into one, and I a small pouting child . . . as if I had tried to run away from home and had been found tired and frightened on the edge of a gloomy forest with night coming on. . . . He embraces me with all of my grime and sand and dried sweat and caked hair, just as I am. . . .

Then I lay my head upon his shoulder and murmur, "Thank you." After a moment I stand straight and ask him, "Lord, why did you wait so long in coming?" And he replies, "Because you didn't ask. You thought you could do it by yourself. It is difficult to give you something when you don't know you want it. As long as people are satisfied with dryness or deserts or have no hope, they are so difficult to touch." I say, "Give me everything you have to give." "Come with me," he says.

Behind the dump heap where I had sat, a mass of granite rises from the earth, thrust up in some primeval age. He leads me there, he strikes the rock, the water gushes out. It falls into a basin below the rock.

When the pool is filled, the water makes a stream down past the desert shack. He bids me bathe in the pool, and while I lie in the cool water, he takes my clothes and washes them and lays them on a rock to dry. Along the little stream vines spring up and grow, and soon cover the broken shell of a cabin.

I come out of the water clean and so refreshed. I feel as if my skin was drinking in the moisture as the caked sand and mud melted. I put my clothes on again. . . . I had forgotten that my coat had once been brightly colored. I dance with joy as I see myself reflected in the pool . . . clean, even dapper.

He has a meal for me. There is milk and bread and honey, fish and berries. I look at him and ask why he has come and why he is so kind. He tells me that it is because he loves us human beings and he wishes to fill us whenever our hands are opened to receive.

That night I sleep in peace. No more haunting dreams. And in the morning we leave the pool of water and the vine-covered house. We cross one ridge, and still there is desert . . . another, and we see some junipers, and then pinon pine, and then the forest, green and rich.

The land is rugged, but at last we come to the coast where people live. And there I have fellowship with others who have opened their hands to him, and are beginning to open them to one another. And there I settle down to live and become stronger, and start to learn. . . . Someday I shall set out as he does. But for now it is the time to stay put and learn and grow. . . .

The second meditation, or active imagination, uses the joy and triumph of the resurrection story to successfully deal with evil and negativity. It was written by a psychotherapist friend, Dr. Andy Canale.

Resurrection

Dear Father, I am upset and "touched" this morning. I feel the need to cast off my concerns and come into the numinous, into my frightening dream of resurrection, in imagination with humility.

I ran from this, forced myself awake (whatever that may mean) and found myself alone in my room and not alone. All negative power seemed gathered around me in potential about to burst upon me at any moment. I prayed but avoided the Resurrection which frightened me even more.

Oh, how I fear you! How I fear life which is so much larger than myself!

And yet I want to do your will—given the two choices. The third choice of avoiding it doesn't seem to be offered. So I will enter the Resurrection scene now, praying for your help and your son's help, more hoping than believing in the utter transformation beyond my imagination.

It is a dark, dark cave and cold, musty, threatening to such a coward as

I. I don't know how I have found myself here, or by what teleportation. But it is cold and I am afraid.

In the darkness I can sense death, the presence of utter, complete death and I am horrified that I have retained consciousness, that I should have to know this. Have I died? Do I wait as Lazarus trapped in my death, waiting, longing for a release, for an impossible rescue?

Certainly I do. I do. I do.

Please, please find me, bring me life, resurrect me.

Now my eyes have adjusted—oh why have they become so powerful, so penetrating—I see on the slab dressed in funeral gown my battered, torn, dead Savior. He is dead, Father! Dead! There is no hope of salvation now. There is only complete death and this trapped eternity with my dead Savior. How can I ever survive this death, Father? Why, why have you forsaken me?

I bend over my dead Savior. Dear brother, Jesus, what have they done to you? You are torn, ripped and sore. And what you have had to bear, I cannot begin to bear for you. Oh Jesus, forgive the Pharisee in me, the proud saint and righteous man. Forgive the Sadducee in me, who feels victorious now in your death and lack of resurrection. I am not he, I am not the Sadducee, but there is a part of me that is like him.

Oh God, it is unfair that you have promised a Savior and killed him. Not fair! I would spit at you for your miserable humor. But I am afraid, Father, too afraid, too alone to spit for the spit lands hollow and echoes in this dark prison.

Oh let me die, let my consciousness perish, let all knowledge of this perish with me for I cannot stand this injustice, this death, this horror, horror. Let all plans for me be forgotten, let me no longer exist. Count me an unfortunate mutation and accept your mistake. For I am not big enough to accept my Savior's death. Now the earth is hollow, now there is only terror, now the cosmic thought becomes a horrid joke.

Dear Jesus, dear brother, oh how I love you though I am afraid. How I long for you to live. How I feel that I should die in your place. Oh rise, rise, make the universe make sense. Oh Jesus! Forgive my taunts, my laughter at your magic, my disdain for orthodoxy.

I am here as I am and that is all. I am here where I don't want to be—in the tomb with my Savior. If it is my lack of understanding come to me in my fear, transform me so that I can see you live, undo me. I need you, I want you to live.

Come alive as you are claimed to live. Come into my dead soul. Give it life and make it breathe again. Show it the possibility of glory. And accept my humble, feeble promise that I will be as open as I can, trying not to be possessed by the negative forces which tell me that I am all my life and the center of my universe.

I am willing to give up myself, fearfully in this numinous spot. I feel the power growing greater. This time I will try not to flee the Hound of Heaven. Come alive through your Father's power. Help me to bear this. I can bear no resurrection into everlasting darkness. Arise through the power, arise.

It is very quiet. I sit on the floor of the cave staring at him. An eternity of death passes and suddenly I am confronted with the Power. Suddenly there is an all-encompassing point of light which is everywhere and nowhere. Suddenly Jesus moves and I am utterly, totally, unredeemably afraid.

I want to flee, but being awake this time, awakening cannot save me. I pray, Dear Father, your will be done. Make him arise. Save me. Let me die if it is your will but grant me one glimpse of him in his restored life so that I might die peacefully, so that eternity wherever I may spend it will have this experience and knowledge to sustain me.

The cave becomes the Holy of Holies. My fear will kill me; that mystery which saves me is too much for me, will kill me. Please, God, let me first see the Life then do with me what you will.

I feel that I will burst, will become a conflagration of matter, bespattering the Resurrection for I am not up to the Power which restores, which can restore life.

Suddenly there is a pulling upward, an incredible victory over gravity which pulls me out of myself and pulls Jesus, my Savior, off the slab. He is filled with radiance and surrounded by lights which are activities and visions unseen by my untrained eye.

And then a fear even worse than before. Will he cast me out, unworthy sinful devil that I am? Will he send me away?

Jesus, I say, I am here with you. I have witnessed that which I should not. Forgive me for my trespassing. I could not help it and seeing you dead drew from me the deepest prayers for your living.

He stares at me, eyes me knowingly. I would run if there were place to go. But such a resurrected Person could always find me. He stands and comes to me and speaks.

Jesus: Get up, Son. Accept what you have witnessed, the conquering of gravity.

I am so afraid, my legs won't hold me. I try to stand but I cannot. His torn right hand reaches down to me. He grabs my shoulders and lifts me, as easily as he would a baby. And then I am looking in his eyes. There is no judgment there, only love and the love touched me and it is the transformed Power channeled through a human though no less immense for that. He opens his arms to me.

Jesus: Come, let me hold you.

I: How unworthy I am. I can never let you hold me.

Jesus: You are so like Peter. So set in your ways but I love you both, you stubborn goats. He would not let me wash his feet. You know my answer. Come.

He puts his arms around me and strokes my head, my hair, my back. I feel all my fears dissolving away. And then I put my arms around him and the dam bursts and I weep into his chest.

I: Oh I am so glad you live again, so glad.

Jesus: And I am glad that you have faced my resurrection. It happens once and forever in the hearts of those in pain who seek love. You have found me. I am here, alive in your center, in your very being. I am with you always. There is no need for you to ever die again. You are born again from above.

This cave of my death is the cave of your second birth. This is the end of a long process, a getting ready in you for me. I am here. You now begin again the arduous journey but this time not alone. Let us go forth.

Together we push the enormous rock covering the entrance and beautiful sunshine rushes over us. It is now that glorious point magnified which brings life to the whole world.

And there, a crying woman looks at us and shrieks—there is no gentler word for it—when she sees him. She kneels before him and he pulls her to her feet and they embrace. Then the three of us go arm in arm in arm down the road to tell the world the good news. He is risen! We too are risen!

II

Using Imagination to Participate in Stories from the Gospels

The only way I know of to be thoroughly familiar with a religious point of view is to live with it imaginatively. For Christians this means knowing the Bible in a way that is impossible so long as we read it only with our heads, to understand the concepts in it. For a long time it was understood that the Bible is not just an intellectual exercise. As Father Jean LeClercq makes a point of showing, well into the Middle Ages the Bible was read in the monasteries so that one could step into it, find its meaning inwardly and be transformed.

If we want to find such meaning in the Bible, we must imagine ourselves in it and moving with it. For instance, one can start at the beginning of the life of Christ, imagining what it would be like to be Mary pregnant by the Holy Spirit. How did she face village gossip, the fear of being rejected by Joseph, and then the long, hard trip to Bethlehem?

One example of a great poet's meditation on the birth narrative is W. H. Auden's *For the Time Being*. The whole story obviously came alive in him, including the attitude of Herod in slaughtering the innocents, and the flight into Egypt. One need not wait for Christmas to meditate on these events. Our purpose is to reflect on how the Christ Child can be born in each of us, and this is not seasonal. Giving oneself plenty of time to live with the story only adds depth of meaning to Christmas when it does come.

The boyhood visit of Jesus to the temple, or the period before his ministry can be lived in this way. We can start home with Mary and Joseph after the Passover celebration in Jerusalem, turning back frightened when we find that the boy is missing. Or perhaps one stands in the temple with Jesus, as amazed as the learned men at his answers to their questions.

What was in the hearts of Mary and Joseph, and how did Jesus appear in giving his answers?

Or later on, what were Jesus' days like in the carpenter shop after Joseph died? Did Mary worry secretly when he decided to leave home, even though the younger children were able to take care of her now? One can follow Jesus to the Jordan and try to see the heavens open as John baptizes him, or hear what words of approval are spoken as the Spirit descends. This kind of imaginative walking with Christ fills in the story and helps one grow with its depth. It cannot be done in a hurry; its reality springs only out of silence.

As unpopular as the idea of fasting is to most people today, few Lenten experiences can be fully real unless one takes the trouble to watch and wait and fast with the Christ as he meets the awful reality of evil in the wilderness. The encounter with Satan is a real one. Jesus does not project the evil onto any group or individual, but meets it head-on in temptations which have not changed much from that day to this.

T. S. Eliot bridges the centuries in his stirring play *Murder in the Cathedral*, showing how similar and yet contemporary the meeting with the evil one was in the death of Thomas à Becket. Evil is always tempting us to use power or good works or spiritual clout rather than love as our motivating force. I find only one way to set out living my life as Jesus lived his, fulfiling my own unique destiny. And that is to stand beside Jesus in the desert as he searched his own soul and listened to the devil's words and rejected them.

We can stand with Matthew at the customs table and listen to find out if one of us is being called to follow Jesus along with Matthew, or beside the lake with Peter and James and John. What came to their minds as they answered the call, and what comes to mine if I hear the call given to me? How did their situation differ from that of the rich young ruler who decided that the price was too high for what could be gained, or else that he would be a lost shadow without all his customary attachments? What new step is required of me that asks, "Are you Matthew or the rich young ruler?"

In the gospels many of the healings of Jesus are described in great detail. One can pick out any of these stories and try to sense its fullest meaning. How much did the persons involved realize beyond the sense of being physically well again? What lay behind their illness, and how did life change for them after the encounter with Jesus?

In *The Bible in Human Transformation,* Walter Wink uses the story of the paralytic who was carried to Jesus by his four friends to illustrate an imaginative method of using the Bible to transform human beings. His purpose is to show that the Bible can and ought to be used in this way, and the method he proposes can be used either individually or in groups. I have used it with groups and know how effective it is.

One can even be present at one of the resurrection appearances recorded in the New Testament and know the restoration of life to Jesus, the giver of life. Or be part of the crowd at the feeding of the thousands, taking the food in imagination and perhaps questioning the boy who brings the loaves and fishes and realizing what claims it makes on us to share in it. We can follow one of the group home and see the change in that person's life, or if there was none, find out why.

Sometimes I seem to be alone with Jesus in the garden as his soul is sifted and he wonders if he can go on. It almost seems that I have to see the bloody sweat and feel with him the decision in order to know that I am not alone in my own struggle to make the hard choices, to do his will and not my own. Then I can listen with Mary and John to the words of love and also of desolation from the cross, to see the body being taken down and placed in the tomb. I can realize that there is one who shares our agony when all our hope is extinguished.

Thank God, then, for the resurrection which tells me that I still have reason to hope. Knowing that his pierced and broken body was brought back to life makes me see in my own agony that I can be reconstituted, that my dismembered soul can be brought back together. I may watch with Mary as she walks into the garden to find only an empty tomb, or with the apostles huddled together in such fear that Jesus has to show them who he is. Or I may start out for Emmaus, perhaps with ones who have given up and are going home, and meet a stranger. I cannot help finding my own heart touched when he reveals himself by breaking bread with them in the little inn that is no longer remembered for any other reason.

There is a strange and important truth to living with Christ not only in his defeat but also in his resurrection. Life usually forces us to live out our sorrow and agony. In this way we are brought to search for some help outside ourselves, some way of finding a new beginning. But just as this search seldom starts until one can picture the nature of the need, so we usually stop short of finding new life until we are able imaginatively to experience the resurrection as a reality, a real possibility within ourselves.

Those who have not imagined the events of the resurrection again and again in concrete images can hardly know the power of the Christian message, the ability of light to conquer darkness. Without some kind of experience of Christ's rising from the dead, we can scarcely know the meaning of the atonement, or accept the power of the Spirit to touch and heal the gaping wounds of the world.

If one imagines only the sufferings of Christ and humanity, one can get stuck there. The door to victory over death and the evil one is opened only as people are able to realize—actualize in images—the victory of Christ over these forces. His victory and resurrection can then enter into the individual life and work transformation.

In addition, when one lives with Christ in these various experiences, Jesus becomes as real as the people with whom one sits down to eat dinner at night—or even more real. He becomes a person to whom one can turn and speak in the hours of quiet late at night or early in the morning. He becomes the friend who waits with open arms on the other side of silence.

In this same way one can relive the stories of the book of Acts and those later in Christian history. We can step imaginatively into the healing at the Beautiful Gate of the raising of Dorcas or the encounter of Peter with Cornelius. Reading this book meditatively, it is possible to imagine Luke present in the room and to ask him about a puzzling passage. We can, in fact, read any religious work this way. The basic idea of the communion of saints and the reason for keeping this idea enshrined as a creed is that there is communication among those who are joined in Christ whether they are living or dead.

We can also step into the pages of the Old Testament with the help of imagination, particularly the Psalms which express the whole range of human emotion and every agony of dereliction. We can relive Elijah's journey into the desert or suffer with Job or stand beside the burning bush with Moses. In *The Man Who Wrestled with God* John Sanford has shown how deeply these stories of the Old Testament speak to people in the modern world when God's truth is not reduced to just an event in history. In a profound sense these stories are myth and history combined. They reveal the eternal patterns of spiritual reality, which is the particular function of myth.

Imagination is equally valuable in finding the meaning of the parables and stories told by Jesus. He used the story form as a vehicle to reveal realities to people not only because this was the best way for that time, but also because stories are timeless in the same way that the unconscious is free of the limits of time. Of course, these stories speak to an outer moral situation, but at the same time they also speak to an inner one. They can do both at once, and the only way to unlock the inner meaning is to let imagination play upon the story.

As I read the story of the prodigal, I see myself first as prodigal, then as older brother, and often as both. The story of the Good Samaritan shows me that I have been set upon by thieves, that there are thieves within me, as well as a priest and a Levite who turn away from my trouble, and that I can also find a despised Samaritan in me to bring healing. All these parts of me can be awakened, opening me to a new reality in myself.

The parables about the kingdom of heaven have ways of speaking to us which are just as amazing. John Sanford's study of them in *The Kingdom Within* shows how profoundly these sayings of Jesus can speak to us, and also suggests a method of finding such a deeper understanding of them. Most of us are so accustomed to these usually brief statements that we often overlook the incredible wisdom they contain and how wisely they direct us upon the way of spiritual maturity.

In approaching either a parable or an actual event, the secret is to become silent and concentrate on the picture or scene that is presented until it comes to life and begins to move. Then I find that there is a choice. I can stay on the outside and simply observe the action as it unfolds, or I can step onto the stage and become a part of the action. I can even become one of the characters, sometimes sharing in their joy, or often in their agony and pain and then in transformation and victory. It is amazing how the life of Jesus and the parables he told open up to reveal a living, growing meaning within us if we allow imagination to awaken them again and draw us into their reality. They speak at a deeper level than the intellect, touching the total person as intellect seldom can.

To give a concrete example of an active imagination based upon the gospels, let us picture the birth of the Christ Child.

The Image Becomes Man

Birth is never easy. I know it is difficult to let the Christ be born within me. I wonder if I have the courage and strength to stand against the world. I am not even sure how to handle the ordinary problems that have to be faced this morning. What will I do about . . . ? I let the question die and try to put away all the other thoughts and concerns that slip in, and just be still.

I concentrate on Mary and Joseph and the problems they had to face so that the child could be born. First in Nazareth and then on the long trip to Bethlehem. . . . When another concern of my own breaks through, I try not to get upset. I simply tell it to wait and focus again on the images I am trying to awaken.

The image of Mary in Nazareth, the perfect image of the human soul . . . Mary, young, alive, obedient, open . . . standing by the village well, dressed in the garb of that time, a long embroidered dress, a veil covering her head. . . . As the pictures begin to flow, I see her standing there thinking back to the garden and the strange appearance of the angel with the startling news that the power of the Highest is to overshadow her and that she is to bear a child. . . . She is remembering her own words in reply: "I am the handmaid of the Lord . . . let what you have said be done to me."

How can the Christ Child be born in me until I am as willing as Mary . . . as open and as ready to take whatever comes? Lord, how is it possible for me to be accepting in the way that Mary was? She knew that the people of Nazareth wouldn't understand.

Now that I have actually entered the scene I can see the village gossips standing near the corner of the synagogue. They glance toward Mary knowingly and cluck to themselves. I can tell that she hears their voices murmuring away: "She always thought that she was so holy, and look at her now. Pregnant . . . poor Joseph . . . and her parents. . . . "

Even Joseph had doubted. She is feeling the pain of being doubted by those closest to her. How hard it is to withstand this pain. So often the doubters and the gossips have their way. How often we open ourselves to the Spirit and find new life, and then we back away because we cannot bear the criticism, the misunderstanding and derision and condemnation.

Wondering how Mary can take all this, I follow her back to the little dwelling where she lives with Joseph. It is a simple place with a dirt floor and few furnishings but a straw pallet. Even the poorest today have more. She prepares a simple meal, placing small loaves to bake on the open hearth. . . .

I watch as Joseph swings open the door and comes over to embrace Mary. His face is troubled and Mary senses that something is wrong. . . . He tells her right away: "An edict from the Emperor. Everyone must go to their own birthplace for an Imperial census. You know what this means. . . . We have seventy-five miles to travel to get to Bethlehem, and with you about to bear your child. How can we do it?" . . . How can any of us face the trip we have to make to our spiritual home where we can allow the Christ to enter?

It was not easy to bear the Christ Child then, but Mary and Joseph make their plans. The donkey that usually carries the carpenter's heavy beams will carry her. They will gather enough food together and start out in two days so as to avoid the Sabbath restrictions. They plan to wear their heaviest clothes, in fact the only warm things they have, because the winters can be cold. . . .

Bright and early they start out, leaving the little home locked, expecting to return. The sky is overcast and a cold wind blows . . . they trudge the dusty road, hour after hour, hour after hour. They pause at noontime by a ravine with a spring and eat some cheese and dry bread and then go on . . . there is rain and the dust turns to mud.

Evening and darkness are coming when they find a mill and knock on the door . . . wet and tired, and Mary only a few days from childbirth. The millers let them in and they sleep on the bags of grain in a corner of the cold mill. Outside the wind howls and the rain beats against the roof. . . .

During the night the rain stops and the next day they go on another thirty miles under the broken clouds. It is cold, bitter cold. They meet others traveling from their homes, huddled in heavy cloaks, who barely nod. Hour by hour, they go on; they break at high noon for rest and then go on again. It is no easy thing to bear the Christ Child . . . the sheer drudgery must be tasted to the full if one would bear the Christ Child and bring him to birth. . . .

This night an old villager and his wife let them sleep in a corner of their hut. It is good, they say, to welcome strangers. One may entertain God in so doing, and once we were all strangers when we left Egypt and wandered through a new land. . . .

Another long day . . . cold winds and snow on the mountains, but ahead the lights of Bethlehem . . . their destination. They had enough money for the inn. They had taken all their savings just for this . . . with the time of birth so near. . . . In hope and expectation Joseph knocks on the great door of the inn. The inkeeper opens the door. He is a hulk of a man, larger than life-size, framed by the light of a fire blazing on the hearth. . . . "Sorry, no room. . . . No, not even a corner." And, "No, I don't know what you will do. The villagers have all locked their doors and gone to bed . . . too bad. . . ." The heavy door clangs shut and the dark is even more penetrating.

Joseph stumbles down a little hill. The time is very close. There is a cave in the hillside with a shelter built in front of it . . . some straw in the back, and standing in the shadows a donkey and some oxen. . . .

It is an oriental stable . . . the dung is thick on the dirt floor of the cave

... the manger in the center gleams with the saliva of the oxen that have eaten there. It is better than nothing. . . .

Not a likely place for the birth of God, but perhaps the less likely the better. Then no one can say that his life is a less probable place. A runaway child sleeps on a pile of straw at the very back, a frightened child who has run away from the beatings of a stepfather and is now recovering. . . . The stable turns no one away. . . .

The child is born.

The Christ is born. They have some cloths to wrap him in. Some straw laid in the manger makes a crib for him, and the oxen are lowing softly in the background.

And so the Christ Child is born. . . .

Being Raised from the Dead

Another concrete example of dealing imaginatively with the gospel stories is this reflection on the raising of a man from death.

. . . And so Lazarus rose from the dead. So what? It showed that Jesus had unique power. He could heal the sick and raise the dead. I think that this happened, and that this was undoubtedly the event which turned the religious leaders against him once and for all. A thing like that could not be kept quiet and it gave Jesus a following which they couldn't tolerate. But does this event really speak to us today? Jesus gave his message by actions as well as in teachings and parables. And one of the best ways to learn from these events is to let imagination play upon them as if we were listening to Jesus telling a story. Such an event or action of Jesus is myth as well as history. The things that he did express our relationship to God and the nature of heaven which broke into the world with him. They can often tell us as much about his significance to us as the things he expressed in words.

The story of Lazarus begins when Mary and Martha sent for Jesus because they knew that their brother was probably dying. They knew that Jesus got the message, but he did not come right away. When he finally came, he found the sisters grieving. Their brother had died. They did not try to pretend that everything was all right and that it was the will of God. They said reproachfully, "Lord, if you had come our brother would not have died." And Jesus felt their sorrow and his own loss of a friend, and he also wept.

Religion so often fails right here. We won't come out and say it . . .

"Lord, we asked for something and you failed us." This kind of honesty is absolutely necessary if we are to find the power of Jesus. When we are phony there is not much that God or the Holy Spirit can do for us. When we are afraid or resentful or lost and bitter, we cannot get much help until we admit that this is the way we feel.

So often when we ask God to take over—in whatever kind of situation—he seems to tarry. He waits, needlessly, it seems, until what is sick in us has died ... our hope, our courage, our capacity to love may be sick unto death. And when it dies we are bitter and angry, and we need to admit that we are bitter and angry, and that it looks to us as if the world doesn't care.

This is another point at which much of our religion today fails us. It tries to avoid the dead parts of our lives. If we avoid them, we need not weep. If we avoid the stinking mess, we need not face our helplessness, and we need not come into real relationship with God by demanding to be helped by him. If we avoid it, we can do without the courage it takes to face the stench of death. But then we also do without the transformation ... no stench, no resurrection. ...

With the tomb open, Jesus prayed a prayer of certainty and called out in a loud voice, "Lazarus, come forth!" And Lazarus came forth, still bound in his burial wrappings. Then Jesus spoke to the people again with his final command: "Unbind him."

To come alive we have to be sorry for the dead part of ourselves, sorry enough to say what needs to be done, and strong enough to face up to the evil which caused it to die. We have to act with firmness, to cry out with a loud voice. We have to be sorry enough, and to want life enough to pray for it with all of our being. Then, with faith and certainty, we can call out in a loud voice.

And the dead within us comes forth, still in the cyst that was forming, and we are ready for the final action of setting it free. New life seldom comes forth without decisive action and a loud cry. Sometimes we remain dead simply because it is less effort and less painful than being alive. Yet the pain goes with the quickening, much like the pain of walking on a leg that has gone to sleep.

In their amazement at seeing Lazarus come out of the tomb, those people might have let the risen man smother in his grave clothes. But Jesus awakened them to action. The same thing is true when something has been raised within us. It must be set free or it can die again and negate the resurrection. We have to face the fact that it is dangerous to let the dead parts of us be raised. We probably let them die for good reason . . . usually for the reason that it is less dangerous just to be dead. . . .

Nothing is completely dead within us . . . so dead that it cannot be raised. And this story puts the question: What is the dead Lazarus within me? What part of me did I allow to die so that I am living as only a partial human being, busy getting more and more set in my one-sided, half-existence? This event, this parable, written in the fabric of history, tells what is necessary for the dead parts of me to come to life again.

After this meaning had unfolded before my imagination, I then prepared two sermons on the miracle of Lazarus and gave them on two consecutive Sundays. Shortly after they were preached, a young man with whom I had been working for some time without much success came to me with a dream. In it one of his brothers had died, and he stood by the casket and raised the dead youth back to life. With only a little prompting he realized that it was a part of himself that had died, and he soon found that it was his capacity to reach out to another person with love and caring.

He then went at the job of making the dream a reality, of bringing that capacity within himself back to life, and he was successful. The biblical story unfolded in its deep meaning, and the parallel dream brought the young man to himself and was a turning point in his life. He learned to love, and his whole life changed. He came alive. The image was verified. Jesus still raises people from the dead.

FOR FURTHER READING

Kelsey, Morton T., *The Cross: A Meditation on the Seven Last Words of Christ*, Ramsey, N.J.: Paulist Press, 1980.

————, *The Age of Miracles*, Notre Dame, In.: Ave Maria Press, 1979.

Sanford, John A., *The Kingdom Within: A Study of the Inner Meaning of Jesus' Sayings*, Philadelphia: J. B. Lippincott Co., 1970.

Sanford, John A., *The Man Who Wrestled with God*, King of Prussia, Pa.: Religious Publishing Co., 1974.

Wink, Walter, *The Bible in Human Transformation: Toward a New Paradigm for Biblical Study*, Philadelphia: Fortress Press, 1975.

————, *Transforming Bible Study, A Leader's Guide*, Nashville: Abingdon Press, 1980.

12

The Phenomenon of Slaying in the Spirit

In recent years there has been a tremendous increase of interest evidenced in parapsychology, meditation, extrasensory perception, and related phenomena. The church has felt these winds of change too, and the Pentecostal movement, which had previously affected only Protestant churches, is now influencing the Roman Catholic church. Religious phenomena are making headlines, and religious publishing is flourishing.

Although Pentecostalism has caused controversy among the mainstream denominations, in many cases it has revitalized the ministry of many churches. Cardinal Suenens has been influential in helping integrate Pentecostal emphasis into the Catholic church. The Cardinal has authored *A New Pentecost,* which details how Vatican II helped pave the way for a new stress on personal experience in Christianity and the contributions of the charismatic movement toward this stress.

The charismatic movement has brought an emphasis on direct contact with God, and as a result of this sort of experiential religion, healings, prophecies, visions, tongue-speakings, and "slayings in the Spirit" have been reported in many churches. This last evidence of charismata has not been the subject of as much study as the other gifts and has been widely viewed as an emotional phenomenon that occurs when religious fervor runs rampant among large groups of people. From my experience, however, it appears that slaying in the Spirit merits more study than it has heretofore received.

The Nature of the Slaying Experience
Let's begin our discussion by looking at the nature of the experience itself. My first encounter with slaying in the Spirit, as I already indicated, occurred at a dedication service I was conducting at the end of a conference on healing. As I laid my hands upon a minister kneeling in front of me, he

lost consciousness and fell backwards to the floor. Although I had never seen this phenomenon before, I had read of it and realized how quickly consciousness can be lost during intense emotional experiences. Later on, this minister stated that he viewed this occurrence as a death-rebirth experience which ultimately revitalized his ministry.

I had not even hear of Kathryn Kuhlman at the time of my first experience with slaying in the Spirit, but I was able to attend one of her healing services a few years later. The Shrine Auditorium in Los Angeles was filled with 12,000 people who were anxiously waiting for the service to begin.

In addition to many healings reportedly occurring throughout the auditorium, many experiences of being slain in the Spirit took place. It was obvious to me that these occurrences were frequent at Miss Kuhlman's meetings, for attendants stood behind the lines of people receiving the laying-on of hands, catching them as they slumped backwards. Enthusiasm ran high and the service was very extraverted, yet the events of the evening proceeded in an orderly manner and seemed to evidence genuine religious feeling.

Some persons who have experienced slaying in the Spirit at Miss Kuhlman's services report that they feel a loss of self-consciousness before falling over, a sense of abandoning their will to God. As a result of this giving up of ego control, they experience a sense of peace, joy, and communion with the divine. Others feel the lessening of emotional burdens.

It would appear that the person who performs the laying-on of hands is a mediator of the spiritual dimension of reality and as such, transmits a powerful current of energy that often causes a faint or temporary loss of consciousness. Two mediators, a Pentecostal minister and a Catholic priest, describe their experiences with the phenomenon of slaying in the Spirit.

Descriptions of the Slaying Experience by Clergy

An Oklahoma evangelist-healer has described his experience with slaying in the Spirit as feeling that a powerful current was passing through him. All the persons he touched immediately fell to the floor and others spoke in tongues.

The Catholic priest first encountered slaying in the Spirit at a Kathryn Kuhlman service where he himself did not have the experience but saw many others who did. Later on, at a priests' retreat, he had an experience of "leaving the body," which brought him a sense of great peace. He was also anointed at this time to heal others.

After he returned to his usual ministry, the priest found that he had indeed been anointed with power. People were slain in the Spirit when he prayed for them and some individuals prophesied. His ministry multiplied and eventually was the source of much controversy among other priests. Finally the bishop of the diocese intervened and asked the priest to cease practicing this phenomenon among large groups because of the sensationalism it produced, although he did say that its occurrences could not be controlled privately.

Later the priest engaged Pentecostal leader David du Plessis in conversation on the subject. Du Plessis felt that this phenomenon did little to build up the church and frequently brought discredit and controversy to the body of Christ.

As a result of this conversation, the priest did some serious thinking about slaying in the Spirit. He made several conclusions.

First, he noticed that the psychological state of the minister directly affected transmittal of the experience.

Second, he realized that this phenomenon frequently drained his energy away. He also discovered that the attitude of the group could promote or inhibit the experience.

Finally, he noted that the slayings did not always bring positive reactions and results. Furthermore, he felt that some ministers capitalized on the phenomenon to the detriment of the participants. As this particular priest became aware of the psychic complexities surrounding slaying in the Spirit, the phenomenon no longer occurred in his ministry.

The Trance Experience in Other Cultures

Certainly the phenomenon of slaying in the Spirit is not new. Throughout religious history this type of experience has been called by various names—*trance, rapture,* or religious *ecstasy.* All three words derive from Latin or Greek terms that refer to a form of death, loss of conscious control or seizure. It appears that Gautama Buddha found enlightenment through a trance or deep meditative state and that the Koran was given to Mohammed in a similar way.

Mircea Eliade has shown that shamanism, a form of ecstasy, has been a means of access to altered consciousness among many primitive people in the world. Eliade says that to be a shaman one must be able to ascertain knowledge of spiritual reality through a trance-like state and then mediate this wisdom to others.

In some cultures epilepsy was called the "holy sickness" because it brought seizures of unconsciousness. Likewise, dancing was often regarded as a religious ritual among primitives, with participants engaging in ritual actions in a trance-like state.

Frequently healings among groups of primitive people have resulted from the ecstatic state of the healer. John G. Fuller's *Arigo: Surgeon of the Rusty Knife* and David St. Clair's *Drum and Candle* document trance-state healings.

Certainly the group spirit that pervaded these primitive religious rituals cannot perform the same function in modern society because twentieth century persons have so highly developed their ego consciousness that they cannot allow their individual autonomy to be taken over by the collective psyche.

Similar to primitive practices, Eastern religious beliefs have maintained that individual consciousness is subsidiary to cosmic consciousness. This emphasis on the primal psychic reality has produced a culture that values individual consciousness less highly than Western Christian cultures do.

The West, of course, in its quest for personal development, has overemphasized the intellect and the ego, neglecting the primal roots so important to the East. As this neglect has brought us entrapment by our egos, we have developed neuroses and then sought to escape them, often through negative means of over-identification with groups at the price of healthy individuation.

Although religious beliefs do provide means for the ego to develop healthy relationships to primal realities, even religious sects can be taken over by powerful group impulses that may be negative. Because religious experiences can help us let go of our highly controlled egos, they provide access to new dimensions of reality. Certainly slaying in the Spirit is one such outer manifestation of an inner letting go. Our rationalistic society will often give credence to outward signs that it will never give to inner states, so a trance or evidence of religious ecstasy may assume undue importance as "proof" of the existence of the divine.

The Slaying Experience in the Bible

Although it is difficult and sometimes misleading to draw parallels between biblical and modern experiences, the Old and New Testaments both make reference to being struck by God's Spirit and falling down before him. There seem to be several reasons for this biblical version of the experience.

First, an ecstasy perhaps similar to that of slaying in the Spirit occurred as a result of feeling overwhelmed by a divine presence. Second, people often consciously prostrated themselves before God as an act of adoration and worship. Third, sometimes a deep sleep fell upon people, bringing visions from God. The implication of scripture is that these people also fell to the ground under the power of the numinous.

The Old Testament recounts many instances of people falling to the ground before God—among them Abraham, Moses, Joshua, David, Ezekiel, and Daniel. These prostrations often accompanied visions, revelations, and instructions from the Lord. Many of these "falling" occurrences were completely involuntary and were honored as a customary important part of religious life.

Likewise, the New Testament details accounts of people falling down before Christ. The Wise Men, Peter, the one leper who returned after being healed, Jairus, Lazarus' sister Mary, the tormented epileptic boy, and many others—all fell to the ground before Jesus.

Later on, the three disciples present at Jesus' transfiguration fell down in fear, and the armed men who came to arrest Jesus in the garden of Gethsemane fell backward to the ground. Again, the guards at Jesus' empty tomb were struck to the ground.

Acts recounts Paul's experience of being struck down, seeing a powerful light, and hearing a voice. John wrote the book of Revelation after an experience of falling down before a vision of Christ. These fallings were not always positive as one can see from the story of Ananias and Sapphira, who fell down dead after lying about their property.

Awe and holy fear certainly caused most of the falling experiences recorded in the Bible. Surely this is a natural reaction to encountering the divine, whether the cause is an unconscious psycho-physical one or a conscious adoration. These two states are not always mutually exclusive and distinguishable.

Slaying Experiences in Church History

Gradually the church began to move away from demonstrative occurrences like these falling experiences. In the second century extraverted outer expressions were distinctly discouraged and they became more and more infrequent. About 175 ecstatic experiences began to be classified as heretical, and such expressions only occurred in certain monastic orders that were relatively secluded.

During the Middle Ages some sects did arise which engaged in trance experiences and had ecstatic visions. Ronald Knox's book *Enthusiasm* provides a detailed, if somewhat biased, history of this period.

A Theory of Personality

In order to understand the slaying in the Spirit phenomenon, it is necessary to have some sort of theory of personality which explains both conscious and unconscious states of mind. One theory that may serve as a working model for us is detailed further in my books *Encounter with God* and *The Other Side of Silence*.

This hypothesis states that the psyche is composed of both conscious and unconscious elements. It also maintains that human beings are in

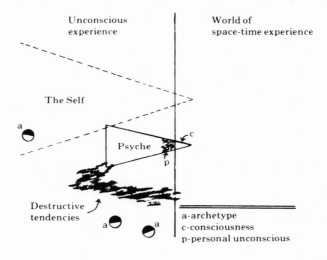

touch with two different realities—one via sense experience and the other via intuition and imagination. Just as the physical and sensate part of us is surrounded by a larger material reality, the psychic part of us is surrounded by a larger world of spiritual reality. The diagram below may help clarify this hypothesis.

Our control over our unconscious side is often negligible, and it is from this area that our neuroses often arise. Our repressed memories and the universal patterns of experience (archetypes) that determine our attitudes also reside here. Whether these unconscious forces are good or evil depends on who controls them—the creative or destructive elements of reality. Because we have so little control over these things of which we are unconscious, development of consciousness is vital to our growth and wholeness.

There are many ways of contacting unconscious elements; the trance experience is one of them. Sometimes unconscious material makes unsolicited appearances—as in dreams, visions, or various spontaneous extrasensory perception experiences. Slaying in the Spirit can be a spontaneous experience of this sort. Or it may be consciously sought out as a means of contacting psychic reality just as meditation, religious rituals, active imagination, drugs, autosuggestions, and hypnosis seek contact with the numinous.

Autosuggestion is a structured, programmed, positive-thinking approach to opening up the unconscious. Claude Bristol's *The Magic of Believing* discusses this particular method in detail.

Hypnosis/Suggestion

William Sargent's *Battle for the Mind* and Jerome Frank's *Healing and Persuasion* both show that there is some relationship between hypnosis/suggestion and religious experiences. It is important to note that just living as part of a collective culture is hypnotic in some degree and opens us to the values, opinions, and suggestions of others. The power of suggestion can be used for either positive or negative ends as we can easily see from the effects of such modern magnetic personalities as Adolf Hitler.

It is often hard to distinguish among the forms of suggestion in our society. Authority and mentor figures introduce us to the mores and norms of the culture through both subtle and blatant means. Likewise a group may be dominated openly or by surreptitious controls.

We must own up to the fact that genuine religious experience is difficult for most Westerners to come by because we have bought the suggestion that we live in a purely space-time universe. Yet we know from research that one's attitudes and expectations frequently determine the outcome of a given situation and that suggestion is therefore a very powerful factor. Hypnosis is really just an extreme form of suggestion.

Today a variety of suggestions are being offered to us concerning the nature of reality. Behaviorism and existentialism suggest that materialism is the only reality. Transcendental Meditation (TM) suggests that absorption into cosmic consciousness is the answer. Christianity suggests to us that we live in both a material and a spiritual reality and that we can meet and experience the center of all reality in Jesus Christ, for he was spirit made matter; he was the incarnation.

Causes of Slaying in the Spirit

Where do trance experiences come from? It appears that all the gifts of the Spirit, the charismata, are psycho-physical experiences; i.e., they are outer expressions of inner experiences. There seem to be seven main origins of this phenomenon.

1. We may suggest to our own unconscious minds that a trance-like state is to occur. The body may then comply with the suggestion (auto-suggestion).

2. A group with its increased intensity of expectation may suggest an ecstatic state.

3. A hypnotist may suggest a person into a trance-like state.

4. The trance may spontaneously occur either from the personal unconscious of an individual or from the larger collective unconscious just as dreams arise from these parts of spiritual reality.

5. A non-physical being or spirit may operate as a medium through which a person may be induced into a trance state.

6. A destructive or demonic part of spiritual reality can possess a person and cause a hypnotic trance.

7. The Holy Spirit or divine center of reality may cause this ecstatic state.

Because it is difficult to know from which source a trance or slaying in the Spirit emerges, discernment and discrimination are essential in dealing with these experiences. Neither complete repression nor total encouragement should be practiced. Those who have dealings with this area of religious expression also need to be well versed not only in their religious beliefs but also in an understanding of the human psyche and its pathological states.

Although many people find fault with slaying in the Spirit because of its emotionalism, it must be noted that great emotional stress is often necessary to any real change or conversion in one's life. Pavlov's studies of animal response patterns led him to conclude that living things have a certain point at which stress can alter behaviors and reactions which no other stimuli could change.

Slaying in the Spirit, then, could very well be the emotional stimulus to a real conversion experience. It could also, however, be an instrument of unhealthy group persuasion. In any case, we need to be careful to make neither a blanket condemnation nor a sweeping endorsement of this phenomenon.

Points to Consider in a Ministry Using Slaying in the Spirit

If a person is engaging in ministering through slaying in the Spirit, he or she needs to be aware of all the motivations involved. Some men and women use this ministry for their own personal power and profit. Others, whether intentionally or unintentionally, do psychological damage through this ministry. Occasionally individuals may be tempted to claim more power than they actually possess to enhance their success.

Still other ministers exert undue individual and/or group pressure on some persons in attendance, or they hold such lengthy meetings that tired individuals become overly susceptible to suggestion. Some leaders hold the foolhardy belief that they can control spiritual forces. Another danger is that the experience may be encouraged as an end in itself rather than as a means to a richer life.

Yet another temptation for some clergy and laity is to maintain their group authority by exploiting people through this experience. And finally, certain Christians tend to judge others as inferior if they have never had a trance experience.

Suggestions for Using the Trance Experience Creatively

First, the atmosphere and size of a religious group are extremely important, for if too many persons are present, group pressure and confusion can interfere with the workings of the Holy Spirit.

Second, because a trance experience can open a person up emotionally and make him or her vulnerable, an individual may later have negative reactions unless fellowship and support are made available. The trance experience needs to be synthesized into the rest of one's experience, and responsible spiritual direction can help a person put such a phenomenon into perspective. In addition, if the slaying experience has opened one to the unconscious world, then he or she will need a competent spiritual director to act as guide in this untraversed, sometimes frightening, territory.

Third, the emotional high from a trance experience should not be the motivation for engaging in the experience again. Slaying in the Spirit can be an initiation into spiritual reality, but it should not be used as a way of continuously recharging spiritual batteries that have begun to run low.

Fourth, a slaying experience can start one on the road to Christian growth, but it gives little content. God made human beings in his own image, and he came as a man to reveal himself. Imageless experiences fall short of the goal of that encounter. If these trance experiences start a person toward encountering Christ, they are useful. Otherwise, they may be detrimental.

Fifth, if love is manifested as a result of slaying in the Spirit, then it may be that the gift is being used properly. If there is a lack of love and a shallow relationship with both Christ and fellow human beings, then the motivation to this experience must be examined.

Certainly slaying in the Spirit has real value if it introduces one to new spiritual growth. When it is sought for itself alone, it can distract one from the true Christian journey and even cause harm to the body of Christ by diverting people from the love that is at the center of creative reality.

FOR FURTHER READING

Frank, Jerome D., *Persuasion and Healing,* New York: Schocken Books, 1969.
Kelsey, Morton T., *Discernment, A Study in Ecstasy and Evil,* Ramsey, N.J.: Paulist Press, 1978.
Kuhlman, Kathryn, *I Believe in Miracles,* Englewood Cliffs, N.J.: Prentice-Hall, 1962.

13

Personality Types and Meditation

Why do meditative practices vary so greatly and what makes the highly important religious practices of one person irrelevant to another individual? The answer lies amid the mysteries of our uniqueness; we know, for example, that each human being has a set of fingerprints different from that of any other human being. But we frequently have trouble understanding why an acquaintance can't seem to understand a point we try in vain to make. What seems crystal clear and logical to one person may be ambiguous and foggy to another.

The reason for our frustratingly different views is found in the fact that our acquaintances may perceive reality in quite a different way than we do. Our personality types filter incoming data and organize it according to contrasting viewpoints, often making communication difficult, if not impossible—until we realize that an understanding of our friends' personality types may provide us with some much-needed insight.

Theories of Personality Differences

Psychiatrist Carl G. Jung developed a theory of psychological types which can facilitate our understanding of how individuals perceive and relate to the world. Then Isabel Briggs Myers formulated an indicator for discovering personality types based on Jung's psychological typology. This instrument and others can provide us with a means to understand our own approach to life and also help us to be more understanding of other individuals' approaches which differ from our own. Thus insight can open doors to understanding and communication. We may not perceive reality the way our neighbor does, but we won't have to maintain that the motivation for his or her viewpoint is sheer cussedness.

Carl Jung was not the first person to develop a theory of personality types, however. Medieval thought saw people approaching reality in two completely different ways. The nominalists believed that reality could only be experienced through the senses and that abstractions or universals did not exist. The realists, on the other hand, maintained that universal truths alone constituted reality. The conflict between the two schools seemed to center around two possible ways of viewing reality—sensually and intuitively. Both realities existed, but individuals preferred to see the world through one particular viewpoint.

This ancient conflict continued to exist unresolved and was expressed in the Middle Ages through schism in the church. Some persons persecuted for heretical beliefs could well have been men and women who viewed reality from a different psychological stance than the average person.

In 1795 Friedrich Schiller devised a theory which separated people on the basis of emphasis on individual function as opposed to social function.

Later, in 1909, Nietzsche outlined two approaches to reality—the Appolonian and the Dionysian attitudes. The former emphasized reason and order, while the latter was based on spontaneity and abandon to instinct.

Shortly after Nietzsche developed his views, William James delineated two philosophical attitudes indicative of personality differences—the rationalist view, emphasizing abstract principles, and the empirical view, pointing out the importance of the factual.

All of the philosophers mentioned above can help us to understand why people view the world so differently, but Jung's highly refined and detailed analysis of personality types can provide us with further depths of insight into varied ways of viewing reality, and the implication of these variations for different meditative practices.

Jung's Theory of Psychological Types

Individuals approach the world in one of two different ways—in either an extraverted or an introverted fashion. The extravert is primarily interested and at home in the world of people, material things, and action. The extraverted individual finds it fairly easy to deal with social situations and to use a trial and error method of approaching reality.

The introvert, on the other hand, is more interested and at home in the inner world—the world of ideas and reflection. This type of individual will be comfortable spending time alone, while the extravert usually prefers more continuous social contacts. Although a mature individual will develop the flexibility to use characteristics of both personality attitudes, he or she will still maintain an extraverted or introverted *preference* in approaching the world. One realm will just be easier and more preferable than the other and this is as it should be.

According to Jung's personality theory, all people are either born with or develop early in life a preferred function and an auxiliary function. All individuals are able to use all four functions adequately to some degree but it is important for an individual to discover what his or her inborn or early preferences are and to develop these. If one tries to use or develop all functions equally he or she will find that they block each other and the individual will develop none of them well.

This is one of the big mistakes that many individuals make when they know only a little about type theory. They believe that development and maturity means developing all functions equally. This is not true. The great thing that personality theory can do for one is to help him or her discover what he or she was meant to be, independent of outside influences, and then develop these characteristics to the fullest.

Receiving and Organizing Data

In addition to believing that people approach reality in an extraverted or introverted way, Jung maintained that individuals also have a preference for one of two ways of registering the input of data from the world. One preference is called the sensing function, which takes in or perceives and registers data from the outer world according to the five senses. This type of person is practical, realistic, good at details and facts, is active rather than reflective, lives in the present as opposed to the past or future, and operates best in a familiar environment. He or she represents the "getter-doners" in the world.

The other preference, the intuiting function, is good at dealing with unconscious data, is innovative and enthusiastic, sees possibilities rather than facts, is imaginative, lives in the future rather than the past or present and works well with new ideas, problems, and projects but not with the details of working them out. This kind of person represents the "thinker-uppers" in the world.

The third set of variables (after extraversion-introversion and sensing-intuiting) is the pair of functions that organizes and arranges the data that was taken in or perceived through either sensation or intuition. Thus the thinking and feeling functions are performing a judgment or organizational operation, for they tell us what to do with the data we have taken in.

The person who employs the thinking function to organize his or her reality tends to emphasize logic and intellectual values. This individual will weigh facts and see time in an historical perspective, as proceeding in a straight line. He or she will regard analysis and logic as a more important tool for dealing with reality than human likes and dislikes. He or she is seldom aware of other people's feelings or likes and dislikes.

The feeling person, however, needs to evaluate data on the basis of human values, of how it effects people. The feeling function sees logic as less important than human lives and dislikes and regards time as circular, proceeding from present to past to present, thus enabling one to match current meaningful experiences from those from the past.

It is important to note that in this context the word "feeling" does not connote *emotion;* rather, it deals with *evaluation.* Thus a feeling person is not considered to be emotional and a thinker nonemotional. This theory does not in itself deal with emotions.

Finally, Jung believed that a person faces the stimuli of outer reality with one of two attitudes—either a judging or organizing attitude or a perceptive or open attitude. If a person is primarily judgmental, he or she will probably manage life in an orderly manner, controlling and planning his or her reality fairly carefully. In contrast, a perceptively-oriented person will probably have a more spontaneous lifestyle and will attempt to understand life, adapting in a flexible fashion to it rather than managing it in a more decided way as the judging person does.

Thus Jung outlined four pairs of personality variables which can be used to discover one's psychological type—extraversion-introversion, sensing-intuiting, thinking-feeling, and judging-perceiving. Only sensing-intuiting and thinking-feeling are considered functions, according to Jung's theory, however.

Jung's Sixteen Personality Types as Measured by the Myers Briggs Type Indicator

On the basis of these four pairs of personality variables, there are sixteen possible personality types, for each person will have a preference for outer or inner reality, will receive data through either a sensing or an intuiting mode, will organize this data according to either a thinking or feeling function, and will respond to life in either a judging or a perceptive way. The sixteen possibilities of combinations of these four pairs of functions will then look like this:

Table of Personality Types

	ST	SF	NF	NT
I—J	ISTJ	ISFJ	INFJ	INTJ
I—P	ISTP	ISFP	INFP	INTP
E—P	ESTP	ESFP	ENFP	ENTP
E—J	ESTJ	ESFJ	ENFJ	ENTJ

E = Extraverted	I = Introverted
S = Sensing	N = Intuitive
T = Thinking	F = Feeling
J = Judging	P = Perceptive

The first letter, of course, shows whether you are more interested in and at home in the outer world or the inner world. The two middle letters in each small box show first, the way one takes in data (a perceptive function), and second, the way one organizes this data (a judging function). The fourth letter shows whether one uses the perceptive mode (sensing/intuiting) or the judging mode (thinking/feeling) in relating to outer reality. For an extravert the process represented by the fourth letter (J/P) is one's primary function. An introvert, on the other hand, uses the primary process in dealing with the inner world because that reality is of prime importance to this individual.

Thus the introvert's secondary or auxiliary function characterizes his or her attitude toward the outer world. For example, the primary function of an INFJ (introverted-intuitive-feeling-judging type) will be intuitive (since intuition is a perceptive function and feeling is a judging function). But because this particular person is introverted, he or she will use intuition in dealing with the favored inner world, and the auxiliary function, feeling, to deal with the outer world.

The terms "judging" and "perceptive" always refer to one's outer behavior, describing the primary mode for extraverts; the auxiliary mode for introverts. Thus the saying "still waters run deep" is an accurate description of an introvert, for the best or deepest part of this type of individual only shows up after a relationship has developed beyond the introductory stages.

It is important to note that one's auxiliary function adds balance to the personality and is essential for growth and maturity. For an extravert to deal with the inner world, his or her secondary function needs development or else superficiality may shut off the ability to reflect and be alone. Likewise, an introvert needs to develop his or her auxiliary function adequately in order to have a stable relationship in the outer world of people and things.

The third and fourth functions, of course, are not so well developed in an individual, and undue attention ought not to be expended on these functions—at least until the first and second functions are highly developed and reliable. Otherwise, one may risk being underdeveloped in *all* areas of the personality. For example, an INFP ought not to concentrate heavily on developing his or her sensing or thinking functions until the intuitive and feeling functions are sufficiently developed to be very reliable.

Characteristics of Each Personality Type

Let us briefly characterize the sixteen personality types that the Myers Briggs indicator measures. The ESTJ (extraverted-sensing-thinking-judging) type makes for a practical, factual person concerned with getting things organized and done rather than dealing with people's feelings. The ENTJ (extraverted-intuitive-thinking-judging) person, however, is an individual of great curiosity, with a flair for ideas. He or she sees possibilities, likes solving complex problems, and develops interests of an intellectual nature.

The ISTP (introverted-sensing-thinking-perceptive) type, with a facility for facts, details, and mechanical things, tends to be painstaking, a lover of the out-of-doors, and good at making order out of chaotic details and data.

The INTP (introverted-intuitive-thinking-perceptive) individual finds facts valuable only as they relate to principles and is interested in pure science, mathematics, and research. Good at seeing possibilities, this person prefers to discover solutions to problems, letting others implement the solutions.

The ESFJ (extraverted-sensing-feeling-judging) type is interested in material things, routine details directly related to personal and other people's experience, and is well attuned to the facts and realities of a situation. In contrast, an ENFJ (extraverted-intuitive-feeling-judging) person will be insightful and aware of new ideas, theories, books and future possibilities. This individual may be adept at public speaking.

An ISFP (introverted-sensing-feeling-perceptive) individual is good at perceiving immediate needs and working out a solution to these needs. He or she performs best at work that calls for an attitude of devotion and loyalty as well as alertness. This person deals well with the outside world as well as the inner value-oriented world. An INFP (introverted-intuitive-feeling-perceptive) type, unlike ISFP, sees possibilities and likes to work hard on projects. The INFP has a facility for insight, ideas and language, especially writing. This person is loyal to his or her ideals.

The ESTP (extraverted-sensing-thinking-perceptive) person accepts facts and uses them. This person prefers to act rather than discuss and often tends toward math and science. The ESFP exercises great tact and diplomacy in dealing with people. Aesthetic appreciation and a facility for dealing well with the public mark this individual.

The ISTJ (introverted-sensing-thinking-judging) individual likes analysis and logic and is skilled at making decisions. This type is noted for being patient and willing to apply his or her energy to details. The ISTJ and the ISFJ are the most dependable people of all the types. The ISFJ (introverted-sensing-feeling-judging) person, unlike the ISTJ, is highly concerned with the feelings and welfare of people. Loyalty, tact and artistic interest characterize this individual. This person is also extremely stable.

The independent ENTP (extraverted-intuitive-thinking-perceptive) individual tends to be a planner of change in dealing with people, viewing them in relationship to the success or failure of his or her inventions, projects, promotions, or ideas. An ENFP (extraverted-intuitive-feeling-perceptive) person, on the other hand, has a facility for dealing with people, is interested in their development, and may implement this interest and enthusiasm as a teacher, salesperson or artist.

The highly individualistic, independent INTJ (introverted-intuitive-thinking-judging) man or woman is an organizer *par excellence* and needs to temper his or her executive abilities with a regard for people's feelings. This person tends to be an overachiever. The INFJ (introverted-intuitive-feeling-judging) individual is good at persuasive tactics, not coercive ones. Ingenious, he or she handles other people skillfully and may need to develop an appreciation for facts.

Practical Value and Application of the Myers Briggs Type Indicator

It is important to remember that the questions on the Myers Briggs Type Indicator have no right or wrong answers. The way one responds to the questions merely indicates one's own personality traits. We should also note that the Myers Briggs shows preference, not ability. We may be perfectly capable of dealing with hard facts but prefer to see possibilities. In this case we would do well to work more with the possibilities rather than the facts. Isabel Briggs Myers has written the finest and most useful book on types, *Gifts Differing.*

The Myers Briggs can serve several important functions. It can help us understand and deal with other people by showing us why it is that another person perceives the world in a different way than we do and thus operates on different assumptions. We can increase our tolerance and appreciation for those who differ from us.

Secondly, the Myers Briggs can help us pick priorities in a reasonable way. If we understand that values and things are important to us and why, we can use this understanding to make decisions and order our lives in a meaningful, fairly consistent fashion.

Thirdly, an indicator of this sort has great potential to provide guidelines for choosing a suitable vocation. In a day and age when many young people often have no idea what they want to do with their lives, this indicator may serve a valuable purpose as a guidance instrument.

Perhaps the most important thing that understanding our personality type can do for us is to clarify for us what type we really are. So often we function as we were trained to or as we feel we should, and not according to the way we were born to be.

Fourth, this indicator can help us see our areas of strength and weakness and perceive which functions are ours to rely on and develop into sturdy pillars for our personality. Functions are polar opposites—like right and left handedness; we will function best if we depend on our preferred functions to a high degree. We can later begin to develop our third function to give us balance and flexibility.

It is almost impossible for one to ever work adequately in the area of the most inferior function. One is usually unable to develop or work with this fourth or inferior function; thus it is often a waste of time and energy to try. However, sometimes through this fourth, inferior function we receive religious insight or experience. But when we do, it is usually something that is *given* to us, not something we work for or develop.

The psychological typology shown on the indicator also has tremendous implications culturally and socially. For example, it is helpful for an introvert in American society to realize that he or she is at a legitimate disadvantage and has every right to feel outnumbered by the ranks of extraverts this culture encourages. Such a piece of knowledge can make us feel better about who we are—particularly if our specific personality type is at painful odds with that of the general society.

The implications of personality theory for educational issues are also great, for Western school systems tend to be geared to the thinking intuitive person, so that a sensing-feeling type is not motivated in his or her area of excellence and therefore tends to do poorly and often drops out of high school. Intelligence quotient tests are also weighted in favor of the thinking-intuitive type, for these examinations are based on language and conceptualization. Thus, if we are to encourage the development of all persons in our schools, we will need to revamp our system to provide rewards for sensing-feeling types of persons too.

Finally, and most important with regard to our specific concerns, the knowledge of personality type can help us find the meditative way that best suits our psychological type and facilitates our personal relationship to God. Our differing attitudes toward prayer and religious ritual are outgrowths of our personality differences. God certainly does not require us all to worship him in the same way. We need to recognize that we each function differently and that these differences will reflect themselves when we relate to religious realities.

As individuals we must place primary importance on finding our own best way to relate to the divine out of our best functions. After that we are able to appreciate and share others' ways of meditating and perceiving spiritual reality.

Unfortunately, many pastors, priests, and lay leaders have assumed that their particular ways of relating to God are best for everyone. Our religious leaders need to acknowledge that there are many ways to relate to spiritual reality and they should encourage individuals to respond to their own unique ways.

It is interesting to note that almost all devotional booklets used by the church have been written by introverted-intuitives. An extraverted-sensing person is thus likely to be turned off completely by this particular aspect of the church's ministry. Another example of the religious problems caused by personality differences can be seen by looking at the procedures of Catholic orders, many of whom based their meditative practices on the methods of St. Teresa of Avila and St. John of the Cross, who believed in imageless meditation. Certainly this form suits some individuals, but other persons need to relate to religious reality more concretely—through images.

Preferences in Meditative Practice

Because the *extraverted person* is naturally outgoing, his or her religious life will often center around love of and service to others, certainly a valid way to implement meditation. The extravert's need, though, is to develop a time for quiet and reflection. The *introvert,* on the other hand, is already at home in the inner world, so meditation by reflection and/or contemplation will be easy. This individual's need, then, is to develop the ability to reach out in love and service to others. Otherwise, he or she may become overly detached from outer reality.

The *sensing person* is partial to the use of religious icons, pictures, Jesus beads, rosaries, etc. He or she often prefers the sacramental way with structured prayers and often uses the Liturgy as a means of meditation. This person needs to learn to understand and be open to the innovative, imaginative meditative practices of the intuitive, who may use active imagination and other means of practicing meditation. The *intuitive,* however, needs to appreciate the details of the sensate world that provide nourishment for the sensing individual. Often the intuitive person would neglect this aspect. Often renewal in the church is sparked by the interaction of these two polar opposites.

The *thinking type* finds that theology and ideas and logic are important in relating to God, for this individual's mind is of great value to him or her. This type needs to learn how to reach out for relationship to others to cultivate a balanced personality. And finally, the *feeling type* finds his or her best expression of meditation through intercessory prayer, prayer with others in prayer groups, and such rituals as the Eucharist, which emphasize intimate relationships in the presence of God. The feeling type may need to develop the thinking ability further by consciously paying attention to and thinking about, rather than reacting to, sermons, lessons, etc.

FOR FURTHER READING

Keirsey, David and Bates, Marilyn, *Please Understand Me, An Essay on Temperament Styles,* Del Mar, Ca.: Promethean Books, 1978.

Lawrence, Gordon, *People Types and Tiger Stripes,* Gainesville, Fl.: Center for Application of Psychological Types, 1979.

Myers, Isabel Briggs, *Gifts Differing,* Palo Alto, Ca.: Consulting Psychologists Press, 1980.

Silver, Harvey F. and Hanson, J. Robert, *The TLC Learning Preference Inventory,* Moorestown, N.J.: Hanson, Silver & Associates, 1980.

14

Time and Meditation

Carl Jung is said to have remarked, "Hurry is not *of* the Devil; it *is* the Devil." One of the best ways to avoid making progress on a spiritual journey is to fill our days with frenetic activity under the pretense that outer duties and cares are so pressing that we simply don't have time for God. If we don't take time to be silent and meditative, we certainly can't expect to develop a relationship with the divine.

Because a busy life efficiently filled with family, business and social commitments keeps our attention focused on external reality, it may often be more detrimental to inner growth than obvious escapes from confronting ourselves. After all, we are well aware of the effects of alcoholism and hard drugs on millions of Americans. We can't pretend that these avenues of escape are constructive; the emptiness and despair of the lives of addicts are too obvious.

Our society, however, sanctions good works, membership in civic organizations, participation in the Rotary Club and the church choir. Thus we can conveniently lose ourselves in meaningful activity and avoid, at least for a while, the Spirit that calls us to a time of quiet reflection alone with our own inner depths.

Sad to say, most of us have no idea how to be alone. Or if we have considered how we might go about it, the prospect of what we might find seems alarming. We fear we may find either a void or a disturbing, perhaps demonic, element which we have no idea how to relate to.

Sometimes it takes a disaster, a period of suffering, a deep depression, or a neurosis to finally force us to stop and confront ourselves. In times of such pain we don't have the energy to carry on life's usual functions, so we are forced to deal with these inner beings that have been crying out for attention but to which we have turned a deaf ear. Then we wish we had listened to the inner voice asking us to pause. Instead, we rushed blindly on, forcing life to strike us with a thunderbolt.

Stopping Time

Although most of us Westerners feel very caught up in clock time, in the immediacy of the moment, we need to remember that time has an eternal dimension. The people of the Eastern world seem to understand this dimension while often failing to pay enough attention to the temporal aspect of reality. We must learn that both the temporal and the eternal are important and worthy of our attention.

I find that the only way I can keep my life even nearly harmoniously balanced and in order is to schedule times when I can come to a complete halt. I am not interested in waiting for a calamity to catch up with me and force me into a painful corner. Unless I take time to be quiet and turn inward, I will lose touch with the center of creative reality and then I will fall victim to the meaninglessness that is so pervasive in our day and age. I find that St. Augustine was right—my heart *is* restless until it finds its rest in God.

The Importance of a Daily Time of Meditation

The first way to stop time is by setting aside a period of approximately 15 minutes to an hour each day. I began this practice while attending seminary; I went early to chapel services and sat in silence with a few other students before the service began. There in the quiet I learned to feel the presence of God seeking me out. Later on when I entered the ministry and felt the burdens and cares of parish life settle upon me, I frequently felt I could not take the time to sit in silent fellowship with my maker. It took me a long time to realize how much I was losing out by not centering down meditatively for at least a small portion of each day.

Certainly the church services and sacraments are nourishing, but they should augment, not replace, individual time set aside to commune with the Risen Christ. And the time we set aside should not be the remnant of the day when we are hazy and out of sorts. God deserves prime time, the best part of our day.

During the course of my ministry as I allowed myself to become too harried to take time alone with God, I began to be a victim of insomnia. I would sleep for a few hours and then be awake, stewing and fretting about my loss of much-needed sleep. One day after listening to my tale, a psychologist friend suggested to me that perhaps God was trying to reach me during the night since my days were clogged with rounds of activity. He also pointed out that in the Old Testament God communicated with Samuel in the night. I began to realize that perhaps my friend's suggestion was the key to revitalizing my ministry, for how could I provide nourishment to troubled parishioners when my own wellsprings were running dry?

This realization was the beginning of a practice that I have kept up for over 25 years now, five to seven times a week. I started getting up at night, first to write down my dreams and then to try to listen to God. This particular time for meditation proved to be my own prime time, for I was seldom disturbed by my parishioners or my children at this hour. I also discovered that after I had taken this time to put my spiritual house in order, I could get to sleep more easily. Another quieting device was for me to pray the Lord's Prayer breathing rhythmically according to St. Ignatius' suggestion.

I have discovered that this silent time in the night is my best source of inspiration and insight—and that my friend was indeed right in his suggestion that insomnia was the signal that God wanted me to spend some time with him.

Each person must find his or her own best time for silence and meditation. For some, morning brings a state of alertness and freshness conducive to listening to the inner depths. The house is quiet and the business of the day has not yet started to demand attention. One friend of mine schedules 9 to 10 A.M. as her private time with God and tells all callers that she is busy and will call back later.

For others who are at their best at night, a period of meditation near bedtime may be prime time. These people may find that the cares of their day have melted away, allowing them to concentrate fully on the spiritual concerns of their lives. Whatever time one chooses, the important thing is to have a particular time and place for communication with the divine.

The desperate need for the centering down quality that meditation brings to our lives is evidenced by the tremendous popularity of Transcendental Meditation (TM), which teaches thousands of Americans how to say a mantra for 20 minutes twice a day. Zen and other Eastern religious sects have also attracted scores of followers who have experienced positive mental and physical effects from their practice. Many find they are able to cope better with their everyday tensions and that their concentration improves as a result of the centering, steadying influence of a period of daily meditation.

One reason so many Westerners have turned to Zen, yoga, and other

Eastern practices and philosophies is that for the most part the church has been noticeably silent about instruction in meditation and turning inward. There seems to be a distinct lack of clergy trained to guide people on the inner journey. One reason for this state of affairs is that the church has been brainwashed by the rationalistic worldview of Western thought, which has faith in material reality, not spiritual reality.

Daily Prayer—Past and Present

The early church knew the importance of setting aside time each day for meditation. It was imperative that Christians living in post-New Testament times have daily communion with Christ, for they existed under the duress of belonging to an illegal religion, bringing the possibility of sudden apprehension and eventually death for treason. Only a daily encounter with God could provide the strength necessary to maintain a Christian witness in a pagan world. The daily celebration of the Eucharist, times of prayer and fellowship were essential to survival. Thus the early church needed no reminder of the importance of meditation, for circumstance reinforced its urgency.

As Christianity became the accepted religion of the empire of Constantine, the church no longer was forced to struggle for survival. The constant attention to meditation and the inner life that had been the source of the church's fervor began to wane as Christianity became legally and politically acceptable. Monastic communities developed for those who wished to maintain the discipline and rigors of constant attention to the spiritual realm. In these community groups the seven hours of divine office were practiced daily, and regular fellowship for prayer, meditation and celebration of the Eucharist were instituted.

While the outside world went on a downhill course toward the Dark Ages, the individuals within the walls of the monasteries pursued the development of a religious life little affected by the disintegration of outside society.

The body of Christ outside the walls of these cloistered communities, however, was experiencing the diluting effects of collective religion, for many pagan kings upon their conversion to Christianity, instituted mass baptism into the faith. Many individuals turned over personal responsibility for the development of their immortal souls to religious "professionals"—i.e., the priests, monks and nuns. Thus devotion to the inner journey and attention to meditation waned among Christians at large and the collectivism attending the Christianizing of nations spelled doom for rigorous individual attention to the devotional life.

The Protestant Reformation attempted to reinstitute among average Christians a sense of individual responsibility for the inner religious journey. But many persons saw religion as only an outer form to be followed according to the rules and regulations of the church. They excused themselves from taking their spiritual commitment too seriously.

Then, too, the scientific discoveries and secular advances subsequent to the Reformation discredited some of the church's dogmas and the church, in an attempt to save its intellectual hide, eventually joined secular society in a materialistic worldview. Thus most Protestants, discarding belief in the existence of a spiritual reality, had no reason to meditate or turn inward. For if physical reality is the *only* available reality, it doesn't make sense to give attention to a devotional life that rests on the premise that there is a spiritual reality that can be encountered.

Today many Protestant churches place little emphasis on the sacraments, on prayer and meditation, or other aspects of the interior life. Instead, many churches try to offer intellectual sermons, provide discussion groups, and engage in service projects in their communities. Certainly these activities are all worthwhile, but they become meaningless if they are not motivated by a rich inner life that provides sustenance for our individual souls. Christianity should consist of horizontal *and* vertical relationship; concern for others should be the natural outgrowth of our own individual relationship to the divine.

I remember how worried one of my seminary professors became when he saw several of us students consistently meditating in chapel before the rest of the students arrived. He indicated to us that he feared we were being too intense and might suffer a psychological imbalance from too much introversion. This unfortunate attitude, which has permeated the majority of churches and theological schools, has driven those sensitive seekers of the inner way to look for acceptance outside the church—in Transcendental Meditation or the beliefs of Hare Krishna or Zen. The human soul will not be thwarted; if it is not ministered to by the Christian church, it will go elsewhere.

Assuming Responsibility for Our Own Inner Journey

Even the practice of daily hours in Catholic communities has decreased, for the decisions of the historic Vatican II ushered in a new era of freedom within the orders. It is difficult today to find either Catholic or Protestant professionals who can offer instruction in a Christian way of meditation that makes sense to sophisticated modern-day persons.

Surely there are good reasons to deviate from the old enforced routines of prayer and silence in convents and monasteries. Our increasing individual consciousness demands that we follow our own separate ventures in the inner journey and not take the well-trod collective path which often exempts us from the pain and agony of individuation. Spiritual insight and wisdom usually comes only when it is in response to the urgent longing of the individual who searches out of his or her own particular needs.

Thus assuming responsibility for our own religious development and setting aside the time to cultivate it is the key that unlocks the door to meditative practice. But unfortunately many of the techniques people employ today to encounter the inner depths are imageless. Only through the use of images in our meditation can we actually open the door to the inner world and walk through it to experience the riches available in spiritual reality, for images and symbols constitute the language of the inner world. Unless we learn to think symbolically, not just conceptually as we do in rational reality, we do not encounter the full range of this numinous world.

Re-collecting Time

In its commandment to keep holy the Sabbath, the Old Testament is admonishing us to stop every active endeavor and turn to reflect with our spiritual brothers and sisters upon the Creator. The activity of worship, the cessation of the weekly routine, and the time for quiet listening to our inner voice allow us to do some spiritual housecleaning, straighten up our psychological closets, and take out the trash that has accumulated in our inner life.

Personally I have discovered that I need to set aside at least two hours each week to take stock of where I have been and where I am going. This time gives me some perspective on my life and is the culmination of my daily periods of quiet time. Sometimes I read the Bible or become completely still and receptive. At other times I examine the recent activities of my life against the backdrop of the priorities I have set for myself.

Then at least once a year I take a day or two for reflection all by myself, without family or friends. In her *Gifts from the Sea,* Ann Morrow Lindbergh has presented the value which many religious communities have recognized when they conducted retreats. In fact, it was as a result of an almost year-long retreat that St. Ignatius wrote down insights to be collected later as *The Spiritual Exercises.*

The reevaluation of one's life that can result from a time of retreat is invaluable for those who would progress on their spiritual quest. The retreat atmosphere allows us to go deep within ourselves to experience the reality of the spiritual world and to let it speak to the unconscious layers of our being. We can meditate upon the gospel stories and parables, relating to them imaginatively so that we participate in them, seeing ourselves as prodigal sons welcomed back by a forgiving Father. Or we may identify with the unclean lepers who were healed by Jesus, letting Christ touch that which is unclean within us. We may use this period of time to set new goals for ourselves or to record our dreams more completely than we usually can, and then work with their symbols.

After these wilderness times, we, like St. Ignatius, may come away refreshed, aware of the futility of unconscious collective life in the world. A spiritual checkup can put our stumbling feet upon the path once again so that in the midst of the ordinary preoccupations of life we can, like Brother Lawrence, practice the presence of God. For this humble, beautiful man, the mere picking up of a straw in the kitchen became transformed into an act done for the love of Christ.

I, too, find that my best work comes from a higher wisdom that releases creative ideas that I myself cannot take credit for. Often when I am speaking in front of a group I find that words and ideas are coming forth that had no place on my original outline. Yet these intuitive spontaneous statements are often the very ones that prove helpful to people. Because I have touched a deeper reality than the purely rational one, listeners are moved by the reflections of this spiritual dimension.

A short utterance like the Jesus Prayer—"Lord Jesus Christ, Son of God, have mercy on me, a sinner"—when repeated over and over, becomes part of the warp and woof of our being, altering our lives in ways we didn't think possible. *The Way of a Pilgrim* shows us how this form of meditation can change us and as a result, alter both our circumstances and those of others. The beautiful thing about this particular type of meditation is that it can be practiced while we are typing a letter, cooking a meal, or driving the car. It can be as integral to us as breathing. Time assumes a new depth and importance as we examine our lives in the light of such a prayer, for our priorities reorder themselves according to our commitment to a truly devotional life.

A very practical way to ensure that I use my time responsibly is to list

those things in life that hold importance for me. I include: My family—
my wife, children and their families; my students and counselees; my personal religious practice and my time for and at the Eucharist specifically;
my teaching and research; my writing and lecturing; my recreation; my
sleep. A review of this list from time to time shows me what percentage of
my time goes to each item and whether or not I am being frivolous in my
time expenditures.

Frequently I feel overcome by the mountain of tasks and activities that
confront me. Then I must consciously stop myself and see whether the tyr-
anny of time is driving me or if I am in adequate control of my life. Only
by assembling the multitude of demands before me in a quiet time can I
sort out the claims upon my life, for then I can ask for divine help in or-
dering my priorities.

The lives of some individuals can be compared to jewelry stores in
which the price tags have been capriciously changed so that diamonds sell
for a few cents and worthless baubles for thousands of dollars. Only by
closing the doors of the shop and taking inventory alone can we avoid
bankruptcy. Inevitably life seems to shuffle the price tags of our priorities
until we become baffled by the disorder. Only by stopping to reflect in silence can we redeem time and bring harmony into our fretful, busy lives.

The following meditation arose out of my own need to sink into silence
and put my inner house in order.

An Adventure Inward: The Soul-room and the Kingdom

Let us go on an imaginative journey from the marketplace to the sanctuary, from the crowded streets to the deep aloneness of the soul-room, to
see what we may find there.

First of all let us turn into the silence . . . not hurriedly or violently, but
quietly, like pulling off the leaves of an artichoke, one by one. Let us be
comfortable. . . . Then let us still the inner voices which scream and blast
away. Let us put away our longings, desires, and let us lie fallow, inert. . . .

What is this silence like? It is like coming into a quiet sanctuary set off
in a garden away from the marketplace, insulated from the busy-ness and
the confusion, the anger and desire outside. It is entering this sanctuary
which can be found within each of us.

As we leave the marketplace of bright lights and mechanical voices trying to sell and convince, with its struggling and contending, we hear a
voice booming out: "There is no place to go! You cannot escape the mar-

ketplace because there is nothing but sleep and nothingness beyond it. Just stay busy. Keep judging as best you can, fighting to gain what you want. Don't think too much about it. You can't move out of it."

Yet within us there is another voice which speaks without saying a word and tries to draw us out of the fleeing crowd, out of the heady, maddening confusion that is the totality of life for so many people. Wouldn't it be better to go into our own shabby, little soul-room where we can be still and think? Yet we fear to go there . . . we fear our shabbiness. . . .

We find the entry way to our little dwelling. It is dirty and ill lighted. Inside the room is gloomy . . . oatmeal wallpaper hangs in shreds from the walls . . . the curtains are dirty and tattered . . . except for a sagging sofa and a desk piled high with clutter, most of the furniture lies in broken pieces around the room. There is an odor coming from the corner where the sink is filled with dirty dishes and a heap of rubbish and garbage pours out onto the floor. Obviously we have not spent much time here. This is a room no one has cared for, a stopover when there is no other place to go.

Even here the television is turned on and a radio blares in the background. We dare not be alone. We carry the marketplace into the very soul-room via the TV so that we have no time to remember and see ourselves. We are afraid of the pain within us and of our own nothingness, of the old angry ego that never wants to give in.

I turn off the TV and the radio, letting stillness reign. I wonder if I can endure the silence. Then I hear a strange noise . . . I am petrified as my imagination goes wild.

Listening intently, I realize that even before the stillness began the noise was there, but mingled with the other sounds of life, it was indistinguishable from the rest. I can tell that the noise has been there as long as I can remember. . . . It is a soft, persistent, gentle noise . . . it almost calms my fears.

It is a knocking, determined but kindly, patient. It comes from the other side of the room. I had heard that there was a door there, but that it led nowhere. I was warned to stay away from it or I might go mad. . . . The sound draws me, I go toward the door and call out, "Come in." A voice replies softly, "I cannot. The door is bolted from within."

The bolt is rusty and so are the hinges. At first the door will not budge, but then it springs open . . . and there right before me he stands . . . lantern in hand, a crown of thorns upon his head, but worn with richer dignity than any jewels. He speaks:

"Behold I stand at the door and knock; if any man hear my voice, and open the door, I will come in to him, and will sup with him, and he with me."

I fall to my knees and cry out, "I am not worthy that you should come under my roof."

He speaks again: "Who are you to call him for whom I died unworthy?" He takes me by the hand and lifts me up and steps into my little soul-room, and the light of his presence transforms the dull shabbiness.

Swiftly his hand clears the confusion. In the twinkling of an eye what was torn, dirty, littered is cleared as if a river had run through it. I am fresh, clean, renewed, redeemed, transformed . . . the broken in me is mended.

For a long time we sit and talk. I pour out my anguish, my hopes, my joys, all of me. He listens comfortingly. I weep, and the tears are cleansing. Then he takes bread and breaks it and gives it to me.

FOR FURTHER READING

Kaestner, Erhart, *Mount Athos: The Call from Sleep*, London: Faber and Faber, 1961.

Kelsey, Morton T., *Adventure Inward: Christian Growth through Personal Journal Keeping*, Minneapolis: Augsberg, 1980.

Lawrence, Brother, *The Practice of the Presence of God*, Springfield, Ill.: Templegate, 1974.

15

Silence and Meditation

When many of us think of the word prayer, we associate with it a voicing aloud of our needs and concerns before God, alone or in a worship service. Frequently prayer follows traditional forms—words from the Bible, from the liturgy or the sacraments. Or prayer may indicate a spontaneous flowing forth of unrehearsed words and emotions issuing from the heart. In either case these types of prayer involve activity of some sort on our part.

Certainly the active prayers we initiate are important, but there is another type of prayer equally as important. Instead of actively presenting our cares, concerns and petitions to God, this prayer requires that we become silent and listen. The purpose of the silence is twofold: first, to listen to our own innermost needs; and second, to await the promptings of the spirit of God. This silent, receptive type of praying is the crux of meditation and is the beginning of one's inner spiritual journey.

Rather than being contradictory to each other, these two forms of prayer are complementary. Corporate prayer brings us together in the fellowship of common concerns and goals. But individual meditative prayer enables us to maintain our own inner contact with God and to be sure we are on the proper religious pathway. Formal corporate prayer can, because it is more structured, become arid and sterile if the participants are not nurtured by their own fresh and vital encounters with the risen Christ. Prayer that is merely an habitual act initiated by an institution can quickly degenerate into a meaningless activity. On the other hand, prayer that is *only* personal misses the dimensions which an historic church can provide.

Individual prayer begins alone and in complete silence. Anyone who has tried to still the tumult of mental and bodily activity ever present in human beings realizes that sitting in silence is no mean accomplishment. Both inner and outer activity must be stilled, otherwise the prayer process may resemble one's thinking about getting one's car tuned up while in the process of roaring down the freeway. The actual servicing cannot take place until one slows down, pulls into a service station, and turns off the motor.

Religious Traditions of Silence

Silence is heavily valued in the Eastern religions of the world. Yoga and some types of Buddhist meditation begin and end in silence. In Zen the lotus position facilitates stillness and the search for *satori* or ultimate peace. The Chinese also stress the importance of quiet as a way of learning to come into relationship with tao, or the center of reality. Some Islamic sects also emphasize the importance of inner stillness.

In his literary quartet dealing with the nature of spiritual reality, Carlos Castaneda describes the solitary process a shaman, or religious leader, goes through to encounter religious experience so that he can then make it accessible to others. Shamanism seems to be a world-wide phenomenon that was originally practiced among primitive peoples and has been known in Greece, India, Africa, Australia, and on the American continent, where it was practiced by the Indians as a means of initiation into adulthood.

Starting with the receptive silence that surrounded Abraham as God's covenant was given, the Hebrew-Christian tradition has emphasized the importance of silence, a fact that we have largely forgotten. The importance of silence in the life of Jesus cannot be overstated. A number of highly important events occurred while he was alone. For example, he spent 40 days and nights alone in the desert after his baptism. Repeatedly he went off to a solitary place for a retreat from the intensity of his life among people.

Despite the lack of attention to silence on the part of most Christians, segments of the church have emphasized the importance of silence as a way to approach God. Almost all the mystics from Origen to St. John of the Cross have practiced times of silence. Quakers emphasized times of quiet listening in their services. Certain Protestant sects and Catholic orders have maintained hours of stillness. The *Philokalia,* the writings of the Greek fathers, who emphasized turning inward, have been translated into English recently, and the Greek religious communities on Mt. Athos still practice Hesychasm, a form of quietism.

Søren Kierkegaard maintained that the deeper one's nature, the more time is necessary for solitude, and Bishop Fenelon suggested that silence ought to be practiced whenever possible. In his famous *Markings,* the former Secretary-General of the United Nations, Dag Hammarskjold, wrote that only his periods of reflection and inner quiet enabled him to withstand the embroilments of political conflict.

Because our extraverted society places so little emphasis on the inner life and silence, very few people attach enough importance to reflection to schedule time for it. If we are to become still, we need to unplug ourselves from the intense activity which fills most of our lives. We need to become detached, in some respects, from our modern lifestyle.

The Practice of Silence . . . Becoming Unhooked

As long as individuals cling to their collective habitual approach to reality, they cannot contact the deeper levels of life that the religious way speaks of. If we are captive to each outer incident and encounter in our lives, then we become like ping-pong balls, bounced back and forth between each extraverted stimulus we meet. To develop a deep and rooted center for our personality, we need to learn to detach from outer reality for a while and focus on our inner depths.

It is important, however, not to overemphasize detachment, for sometimes a pathological, distorted denial of life may emerge from such an attitude. God does not wish us to become one-sided persons who are not attuned to external reality. Rather, he intends us to be whole, balanced individuals who are on good terms with both outer *and* inner reality.

In his *Still Point,* William Johnston has shown how the practices of both Christianity and Zen work towards psychological maturity. Depth psychology maintains that when one is able to detach from habitual unthinking activity, one's individuation or maturing process has started to develop.

A person is usually not mature so long as he or she finds a specific person, activity or job *essential* to survival. A dependent existence is one which revolves around an outer order created by the presence of external factors *only*. A self-contained person, on the other hand, is usually able to create his or her own synthesis or reality that is not overly attached to a particular person or thing whose absence will cause chaos or disintegration. However, absence of this type will require reorganization and readjustment for the individual. If it comes too easily it may mean that the individual really is detached and unable to relate to the person he or she is close to or committed to. The inner-directed person, who is nourished by silence and relationship to the well-springs of being, is usually more able to relate to the whole world as a mature man or woman capable of giving and receiving love without attaching provisional clauses. Inner-directedness is easier for some personality types than for others.

Inner-directedness alone is no guarantee of wholeness or maturity, for one needs a balance between detachment and attachment. A totally detached person is usually far from mature. The inner-directedness needs to be implemented in the outer world. Otherwise, we fall into the same pitfalls as Eastern religion—becoming so detached from this world that we seek absorption into cosmic consciousness, thus ceasing to maintain our individualism and failing to relate to the world around us. Buddhism, Zen and yoga are all based on the principle of disentangling oneself from the world—physically, emotionally, and spiritually.

As we begin the process of withdrawal from our previously *unconscious* attachments and behavior patterns, we feel the emotional reaction to our loosening of the ties that we realize need to be unbound. The withdrawal of our projections and demands upon other persons and circumstances permits us to discover how the fragments of our responses and reactions can be synthesized into an integrated personality.

Learning the meaning of God's love for us, that we don't find him but are found by him, as one writer expressed it, enables us to feel the acceptance and value necessary to becoming whole persons. Then we, in turn, can give to others the love and acceptance we have found, without making them dependent on us because of our needs. This approach to integration and love is central to Jesus' life and teaching. His words, "He who would find his life must lose it," convey the essence of the process of detachment and reattachment—of giving up an old life and view of reality and finding a new life and view.

In the detachment process, however, one must beware of slipping into an attitude of otherworldliness that denies and rejects all that is natural, caring and human in this world. A dangerous brand of asceticism can result from this attitude. Whether it takes the guise of wearing hair shirts and spiked chains, eating only bread and water or just refusing to participate in life as it is in this world, any devaluation of the body or view of material reality as evil is a deviation from the teaching of Christ, whom the Jews referred to as a glutton and drunkard.

Unfortunately, many Christians, in their attempt to be "in the world but not of it," as the Bible admonishes, have become fearful of and intimidated by the world. Fear produces attachment just as surely as undeveloped love does, so the inordinate amount of contempt for the things of the world displayed by some religious sects and philosophies often masks a negative attachment that needs to be examined.

Discipline is certainly essential to practicing the proper spirit of detachment, for conscious detachment is not an overnight occurrence. The art of reflection, the putting aside of activity and business as usual, can be tortuous; for some it is a form of ego loss, a mini-experience of death. This death, however, can result in resurrection if we can but entrust ourselves to the being who is the center of creative reality. Silence can slow down the mechanism of our life so that it can be unwound and initiate an altered or different direction in life.

Although many persons today spend their time in an extraverted lifestyle and need to learn the value of introversion, some particularly introverted individuals need to be urged into a larger exploration of the outer world. If we do not develop stable relationships in the outer world, we can become unbalanced and susceptible to mental illness. A wise spiritual counselor trained in depth psychology can help us determine whether detachment is becoming an avoidance of and flight from life or is being used to bring perspective and enrichment to life.

Although silence has never been easy to practice, the pace of modern technological society makes it even more difficult. The church, forgetful of the rich wisdom from the past, has offered little or no guidance to the modern person interested in encountering spiritual reality in this way.

Finding a Quiet Place

The first essential to centering down is a place without noise and confusion where telephones and other outside intrusions can be avoided. Some people choose a quiet spot in a church, while others seek out a nature spot—a mountain, garden, or brook. Others simply take the phone off the hook and lock the door.

In the Old Testament as Jacob awoke from his dream of the ladder to heaven, he exclaimed, "Truly Yahweh is in this place and I never knew it!" He was aware of the numinous power of that particular spot much as Carlos Castaneda became aware of the power of a certain spot in front of an Indian shanty in the desert. Each of us needs to find our particular place where mana or power resides. Then our mere arrival at such a place can help still us and awaken our receptivity to God.

Ways of Approaching Silence

For some people, participation in a group seeking silence together can often help initiate one into its use and provide inspiration and some sense of community in the face of a difficult and lonely task.

Outer sensory stimuli also need to be eliminated so that our attention cannot easily be diverted to such tempting tasks as answering letters, reading the papers, or calling someone on the phone. Some people like to sit in a yoga position. Others are comfortable in an easy chair or on a bed, while some like to kneel.

In our attempt to become still we may notice that even though we are situated in a quiet place with no disturbances and are receptive to our inner depths, our bodies may give us signs that we are still tense. Certain muscles may twitch, and cramps may result from the position we are in. Although constant dealing with outer stimuli has trained our bodies to be ready to respond at a second's notice, our hypertense state may also indicate unfaced feelings deposited in our unconscious minds. One way to calm the body and prepare it for creative silence is to tell each part of the body, one after another, to relax and let go. Yoga has particular techniques to calm our bodies too.

Often gazing at a particular object, like a cross, either in our physical environment or in our mind's eye, can help us shut off the busy spinning of our minds and lull us into a cessation of activity. For others, concentration on a steady rhythmic sound can bring stillness and receptivity. The use of the Jesus Prayer (Jesus Christ, Son of God, have mercy on me), or the Rosary, or the mantra in Transcendental Meditation, or chanting according to the Hare Krishna custom, are all ways of stilling our whirling egos, which are full of plans and programs, ideas and goals. Knitting, crocheting, whittling, and drumming are all repetitive actions which can sometimes still our inner strivings.

Frequently, shortly after we have managed to turn off outer stimuli and quiet inner dialogue, we are disturbed by a noise or an inner idea that pleads for attention and will not be turned away. We may be tempted to become angry or frustrated, but we need to quietly put the stimulus aside into a "suspense file," as St. Theresa termed it, and return to an inner focus. Sometimes it is helpful to keep a journal on hand to record the interruptions that intrude. Thus we satisfy ourselves that we have given the intrusion recognition and can return to it later.

Then too, daydreams—our Walter Mitty "B" movies—may barge into our meditation time. Again, these stimuli need to be put aside while we return persistently to our central focus. We need to be mindful that silence cannot be hurried or forced. It is a slow process requiring patience.

After one is able to let go enough, the silence itself becomes active. Daydreams and personal experiences are surmounted by a relationship with a flow of images full of life, power and vitality. These images are akin to dream images, autonomous and of great psychological significance.

The Christian mystics, the masters of Zen and of yoga, all discuss meeting powerful images of this type that emerge out of silence. It is later on, in evaluating how to respond to these images, that we see the Christian approach as different from the Zen or yoga approaches.

It is no easy task to deal with the spiritual realities that we encounter as autonomous images. With just cause we fear the emotions that these images can arouse within us. But we also have reason to fear our failure to recognize these images, for they do not go away if we pretend they are not there. It is then that they may have the greatest power over us, for their repression can cause us to become possessed by them in a negative way. Individuals cause themselves overwhelming difficulties when they fail to respond in a healthy and conscious way to these universal spiritual forces which we encounter in the silence.

The Importance of Breathing

One of the most important factors in trying to still the body is breathing, the bodily function which is the most sensitive to our inner state. Worry, anger, alarm, amazement, tenderness, and trauma all call forth different breathing rhythms. The idea of controlling breathing in meditation, the way some Eastern religions do, seems foreign to us, but this is because our Western Christianity has involved our brain more than it has our body. Some Christian sects, unfortunately, have even viewed the body as an object to be scorned, rejected and almost totally concealed.

Yet the body is one of the essentials to a religious encounter, for both the body itself and the image we have of it have a tremendous effect on our personality. Controlled breathing can help us to be still and meet our inner images. The man who introduced us to deep breathing was a survivor of a Nazi concentration camp. He had used breathing techniques to hold onto his center in the face of inhuman atrocities. He also maintained that deep breathing increased his ability to use oxygen efficiently and thus decrease susceptibility to cold and disease.

Breathing, although an internal bodily function, can be consciously controlled fairly easily. Upon awakening, we can note the muscle actions that control our relaxed breathing during sleep and then learn to produce the same rhythm consciously. This type of breathing, which comes from the diaphragm, relies on the abdominal, not the chest, muscles. Although learning to breathe deeply and rhythmically takes discipline and concentration, it is a marvelous aid in dealing with sleeplessness.

Controlled breathing can reach into the unconscious areas of our being, permeating them with calm and turning them, with a centering action, toward quiet and receptivity. Interestingly enough, the word "spirit" in many languages is a derivative of the words "breath" or "wind." Some persons feel that lung diseases like tuberculosis and pneumonia are the result of problems of a *spirit*ual nature. Many runners and joggers have found their sense of well-being increased as they have had to learn to breathe more deeply and rhythmically to sustain their continuous movement.

Just as rhythmical breathing may lead us to a stillness and an ability to turn inward, so authentic religious practice may spontaneously change our breathing. One friend of mine just happened to notice, as she was engaged in the type of prayer the charismatic movement calls prayer in the Spirit, that she was breathing differently than usual. Brainwave research shows that this type of breathing is characterized by alpha waves, indicative of a meditative state.

William Johnston, author of *Christian Zen,* suggests several methods we may use to control our breathing. One is to count slowly in the following way: "one," inhale; "two," exhale; "three," inhale; "four," exhale, etc. Another method is to follow the rhythm of ocean waves. A third is to listen to one's own heartbeat, adjusting our breathing to its pace. Any of these suggestions can help us cease our mental activity and center down into the silence.

St. Ignatius certainly believed in the importance of rhythmical breathing, suggesting the use of the Lord's Prayer and the Hail Mary in conjunction with the inhalations and exhalations. He also believed that the rosary could be used in such a way that it could connect the tempo of life with religious symbolism. The Jesus Prayer is used in a similar fashion in the Eastern Orthodox religion. The *Philokalia*, a thirteenth/fourteenth-century devotional book, also details the importance of breathing.

Also in the fourteenth century two monks authored the *Directions to Hesychasts* which include the following instructions on breathing:

> 19. The natural method of entering the heart by attention through breathing, together with saying the prayer: Lord Jesus Christ, Son of God, have mercy upon me. This method contributes greatly to the concentration of thought.
>
> You know, brother, how we breathe; we breathe the air in and out. On this is based the life of the body and on this depends its warmth. So, sitting down in your cell, collect your mind, lead it into the path of the breath along which the air enters in, constrain it to enter the heart together with the inhaled air, and keep it there. Keep

it there, but do not leave it silent and idle; instead give it the following prayer: "Lord, Jesus Christ, Son of God, have mercy upon me." Let this be the constant occupation, never to be abandoned. For this work, by keeping the mind free from dreaming, renders it unassailable to suggestions of the enemy and leads it to Divine desire and love. . . . Another father filled with Divine wisdom, and experienced in this sacred doing, says the following in explanation of what has been said:

20. More about the natural method of calling on Lord Jesus Christ in conjunction with breathing.

A man who wishes to learn this doing should know that, when we have accustomed our mind to enter within while inhaling, we shall have learnt in practice that at the moment when the mind is about to descend within, it forthwith rejects every thought and becomes single and naked, freed from all memory but that of calling on our Lord Jesus Christ. Conversely, when it comes out and turns towards the external, it immediately becomes distracted by varied memories.

Using the Jesus Prayer as a Means
of Practicing the Presence of God

The Hesychasts, to whom the preceding instructions were addressed, combined the Jesus Prayer with controlled breathing as a way of coming to stillness and practicing the continual presence of God. The use of the long form of the prayer, "Lord Jesus Christ, Son of God, have mercy on me, a sinner," is repeated continually until it becomes a constant presence and underlies all one's waking and sleeping activity.

Eastern groups of Christians have always used this prayer, but the Western church was fairly oblivious to its practice until *The Way of a Pilgrim* was translated from the Russian in 1930. This small book tells how the life of an itinerant was changed because he was taught to use the Jesus Prayer. The persons practicing this prayer believe that the reality of Jesus is directly related to his name and that its repeated use will soak into one's being, transforming one's attitudes and actions.

So long as the Jesus Prayer is used as a means of becoming inwardly still so that one is able to find a relationship with God and be reshaped by it, it is a positive devotional practice. It is using the prayer as an end in itself that causes the negative reactions of some Westerners. But such Western men as Brother Lawrence, Thomas Merton, Jacques Maritain, Frank Laubach, and Thomas Kelly have all stressed the inward devotional life, not as a means of withdrawal from life in favor of complete introspection, but as a rich source of contact with God which then expresses itself outwardly in human relationship and loving action. It is to the deep center of quiet within, nurtured by attention to the Divine, that we can return again and again for renewal and regeneration.

FOR FURTHER READING

Johnston, William, *Christian Zen,* New York: Harper & Row, 1971.
Kadloubovsky, E. and Palmer, G. E. H., Translators, *Writings from the Philokalia on Prayer of the Heart,* London: Faber & Faber, Ltd., 1954.

16

Mystical Experiences and the Lives of the Saints

Westerners are used to being bombarded by external stimuli. Americans in particular find themselves continually assaulted by media and other forms of the collective culture that provide us with attitudes that eventually own us without our even realizing it.

The practice of silence can give us a new perspective and take us out of the world of constant sensory bombardment. It can help us still the whirring of our conscious minds and put us in touch with the wellsprings of a different reality.

Turning away from the outer world and awaiting the offerings of the inner one is comparable in some ways to the expectancy felt in the darkness of the theatre just before the curtain rises. In silence we are not turning from a vital outer life to an empty void. We are, instead, readying ourselves for the inner drama which awaits us whenever we are willing to let go of our outer busyness and turn to our rich interior life.

Sleep can be the gateway for us to enter this inner world too, for in our dream life we find that we participate in a world not bounded by space or time. The laws and rules that govern our outer existence do not apply in this world of images, a world which St. Gregory of Nyssa maintained was closely related to the experiences of Christian meditation.

Just as it is possible for us to slip unobtrusively and naturally from the rational wide-awake world into the spiritual world via our unconscious dream life, so too it is possible for us to move from the outer world to an inner one via a conscious meditative state. Images will arise in either case and even the physiological changes that occur in both dreaming and meditation are similar. Mystics have always noted the images that spontaneously appear when one meditates.

We have a choice—to pay attention to the images that appear, or to ignore them. It is my contention that paying attention to our inner images is essential to vital Christian experience. For the most part the church—both Eastern and Western—has forgotten how to turn inward with images.

Understanding Mysticism

Mysticism has a variety of connotations—many of them unpleasant. Very often the term is associated with being detached, in an unhealthy way, from normal reality, or with being pious and otherworldly. The religious poverty of the English language becomes apparent when we realize that the Greeks had twelve words to denote experiences not mediated by reason or the five senses; we have only one much misunderstood word connoting such an experience. Most Protestant theologians have shared this view, condemning mysticism as a flight from reality and responsibility.

One of the reasons, of course, why mysticism is generally rejected out of hand is that our worldview, which believes only in a material reality, precludes the existence of an inner spiritual realm. Thus anyone who claims to have experienced this supposedly non-existent realm is seen as suffering from delusions.

The shallowness of this rationalistic viewpoint has been superbly exposed by Baron Friedrich von Hügel in his *The Mystical Element of Religion,* which provides a philosophical basis for believing in mystical experience. Today we can no longer afford to ignore or belittle experiences outside the space/time box, labeling them as occurrences that happen only to the mentally unbalanced or the emotionally unstable. Andrew Greeley, for example, has shown in his sociological study of psychic experiences, *The Sociology of the Paranormal: A Reconnaissance,* that experiences of the supernatural have a high correlation with a well-integrated, mature personality.

The subject of mysticism raises disagreements among people, not only because many individuals consider religious encounters to be invalid, but also because spiritual experience varies so greatly among individuals that it is frequently difficult to find a common ground for communication.

Mystical experience is of three basic types—the sacramental, the contemplative, and the meditational use of images. Because human beings differ in their personality make-up, what constitutes a supernatural phenomenon in one person's life makes no sense to another.

Difficulties Involved in Mystical Experience

Thus mysticism is a slippery subject. There are no easy guidelines for those who wish to partake of spiritual experience. Rather, each individual must turn inward and seek for his or her own best way to encounter the divine. This is a confusing business, and the inner trek often brings with it a period of aridity or a sense of being lost. St. John's term "dark night of the soul" adequately describes such an experience—one which few people care to encounter. Yet for those who are compelled to go on the spiritual journey, there is no way *around* this experience; one must go *through* it.

Unfortunately, some partakers of mystical experience have deemed it necessary to order varieties of experience according to their supposed level of sophistication. For example, some persons have felt that the use of one's imagination in inner experience was a lesser form of mysticism than absorption into the cosmic consciousness. The use of images was regarded as inferior and thus mysticism became the province of the small number of people who experienced a sense of imageless union with God. The common person was not encouraged to become mystical, for the pursuit of union with God became a full-time business considered best developed in a monastery or some other place of religious seclusion.

There were other religious communities, however, in which a rather rigid form of meditative use of images developed. Because of the structured environment in which such prayer took place, this type of mysticism began to be interpreted as somewhat contrived, forced, and lifeless. Eventually individuals assumed that because of the rigidity of the practice, any use of images was also constricting and meaningless.

It is usually more difficult to offset the dangers done by mispractice than it is to institute a particular practice where there was none originally. Thus it took modern psychologists, who came to the use and value of images in therapy with a fresh viewpoint, to show us that our conclusions about the value of that type of meditative practice were wrong.

One of these psychologists, Carl G. Jung, has clearly demonstrated that the use of images can have a transforming, healing effect upon one's psyche. Although the church has long been alienated from belief in the value of images, it needs to realize what a powerful tool for wholeness it has been passing over.

Three Types of Mystical Experience

Let us briefly review the three types of religious experience—the sacramental, the contemplative, and the use of images. The sacramental variety of religious experience is mediated to us through an external from the physical world. The bread and wine of Communion, the Black Stone of Mecca, or a sacred statue are examples. Sacramental experience is usually most powerful where religion is heavily collective and the group subscribes to ritualistic experiences. Some Christians look down on sacramental experience as being naive and unconscious, but this view is somewhat narrow, for material objects and outer processes can indeed be the carriers of divine reality.

Union with the Imageless State

The second type of spiritual experience is that of union with reality in an imageless state. No external realities are involved in this type of experience, and the only elements are God and the individual who perceives him. The philosopher Plotinus was the Western originator of this type of meditation, and he greatly influenced later Christians like the author of *The Cloud of Unknowing*, St. John of the Cross, and St. Teresa.

The problem with this type of meditation, however, is that it favors a dissolving of one's ego *into* God rather than forming and maintaining an active relationship *with* God. The joy of becoming absorbed into the center of reality is viewed as the goal of one's religious journey and the result is passivity and withdrawal from external reality.

Although some of the great Christian mystical saints—like Teresa and John—did subscribe to this form of meditation, they tempered it and never took it to its logical extreme. Instead, they related to the external world, ministering to others in the name of Christ.

A crucial problem arising from this type of meditation is the emphasis on detachment to the point of disengaging oneself from one's emotions and will and becoming acceptant of whatever happens to one. This particular mystical attitude frequently takes root where external misery is so rampant and overwhelming that one feels the only way to deal with it is to turn inward, ignoring the outer situation. The medieval world of danger and hardship which many of the saints lived in was certainly conducive to this point of view just as the present conditions of such countries as India may lead one to turn away from seemingly insurmountable outer situations.

The Use of Images in Meditation

The third type of mystical experience is that which makes use of the imagination to relate to spiritual reality. By means of this type of experience one can contact all sorts of psychic images—good *and* evil—that arise out of both a personal unconscious level and a universal or archetypal collective level. By relating to these figures, we can become more whole, more conscious and more connected to divine reality.

Early Christians like Gregory of Nyssa and Augustine employed this type of meditational practice and later Ignatius of Loyola emphasized the use of New Testament images in *The Spiritual Exercises*. Use of images in meditation can allow the stories or parables of the gospels to become real and alive to us as we participate in them imaginatively.

The Purpose of Meditating in Images

The purpose of this type of meditation is the establishment of a loving relationship to God and then, as a result, loving relationships with others. Whereas the proponents of imageless meditation usually see the universe as a cosmic mind into which we should be absorbed, the meditation through images see God as a person—a lover to whom we can relate.

Being Aware of the Dangers of Turning Inward

Certainly there are dangers that must be considered if we are embarking on a journey into the inner world. Jung warned of the powers we may set loose when we start to deal with psychic reality:

"The opening up of the unconscious always means the outbreak of intense spiritual suffering; it is as when a flourishing civilization is abandoned to invading hordes of barbarians, or when fertile fields are exposed by the bursting of a dam to a raging torrent. The World War was such an invasion which showed, as nothing else could, how thin are the walls which separate a well-ordered world from lurking chaos. But it is the same with the individual and his rationally ordered world. Seeking revenge for the violence his reason has done to her, outraged Nature only awaits the moment when the partition falls so as to overwhelm the conscious life with destruction." (C. G. Jung, *Collected Works*, Vol. II, *Psychology and Religion, West and East*, Pantheon Books, 1958, p. 344.)

The Zen and Hindu religions have also warned that one may encounter makyō, or the world of the devil when he or she deals with inner images. Both St. Teresa and St. John of the Cross felt that one ought not to pay much attention to inner images in one's meditation, for the imagination was a distraction in one's attempt to focus on the divine.

Despite his contentions, however, St. John did listen to his inner voices and used a great deal of sensual imagery in his superb poetry.

Another contributor to the belief that paying attention to images was a fallacious practice was John Calvin, who maintained that images led Christians to err. Thus much in our Christian background has not been encouraging of meditation through images.

Making Sense of Religious Experience

There are two main factors that determine or shape one's religious experience—one's worldview and one's psychological development. As we have noted, our worldview often determines what it is that we observe and experience, for if we have no place for a certain occurrence, generally we will tune it out or not perceive it at all.

So we have all sorts of ways of describing spiritual experiences and rationalizing away the occurrence of phenomena that don't fit into our preconceptions of the nature of the universe. One particularly good example of this type of thinking is seen in most people's reaction to Madame Curie's atomic discovery. It was generally dismissed until Hiroshima demonstrated the accuracy of her theory.

Secondly, one's psychological development figures importantly here, for many persons today have learned to fear the inner world. They are afraid that developing one's inner reality will lead to an inability to distinguish between inner and outer reality and will result in absorption with the psychic world, resulting in psychosis or madness. A normal person, however, is usually able to distinguish between the two worlds and to form a healthy relationship between the two so that they mutually benefit each other and provide wholeness and health to an individual.

One of the values of sacramental, ritualistic religious experience is that it enables us to concretize or project outward onto external religious containers our inner images, experiences, and longings. Meditation through images with a resulting externalization of these images in art, writing, weaving, sculpture, dance, etc., is a form of worship and celebration without which modern persons, with all of their rational sophistication, often cannot exist as integrated, joyful individuals. Unfortunately, however, the Western world has basically arrived at the conclusion that modern individuals have outgrown their need for images and that we ought to discard any elements outside the external, temporal, spatial world we live in.

If we are willing to change our worldview and recognize the psychological importance of dealing with images, we can then open ourselves up to the healing, transforming power of the numinous of which the mystics speak. Let's take a look at some of the experiences of several great saints.

Catherine of Siena

Catherine, daughter of a wealthy lawyer, Giacomo Benincasa, was born on the feast of the Annunciation in 1347. At the age of six, she saw a vision which was evidently instrumental in her choice of vocation. While walking down a road with her brother, Catherine became entranced by a vision of Christ seated in heaven with Peter, Paul and John. The Lord smiled at Catherine and reached out to bless her.

From this time forward Catherine had no interest in the usual concerns of girls at that time. In vain her parents tried to change her pastimes and her personal appearance. Catherine, however, insisted she would never marry and then cut off her beautiful hair. Her family responded to her by harassing her, giving her no solitude and saddling her with all the chores of the house. Catherine responded with unruffled calm and goodwill, for God, as she later said, gave her such refuge that no external circumstance could upset her.

Eventually her family realized she was impossible to sway, and gave her a room alone where she spent her time in prayer and fasting, sleeping on boards. Catherine became a Dominican tertiary and although she continued to have visions, she also underwent intense temptations and periods of feeling God had deserted her altogether. She cried out to the Lord, who responded that he had been at work through his grace all along, but that her time of testing was not yet over. Shortly after this event, Catherine again had a sublime vision of Christ, the Virgin, and a heavenly host. In the vision the Lord placed a betrothal ring upon Catherine's finger.

Soon after this vision Catherine was told to go forth into the world to minister to her fellow human beings. Thus Catherine became a nurse and undertook to care for those individuals in the worst physical condition. A woman with cancer and a leper named Tecca, who at first heaped abuse upon her, eventually responded to her beautiful spirit.

Evidently as a result of Catherine's willingness to make Christ's love concrete by nursing the sick, she began to have visions in public, whereas her previous solitary inclinations fostered only private visions. Many persons also claimed to have seen Catherine uplifted from the ground. She began to attract a number of friends and disciples who called her "Mamma" and felt great affection for her.

During an epidemic of plague in Siena, Catherine nursed many stricken persons to recovery and also was able to lead many to a conversion experience. In addition to caring for the sick, Catherine regularly visited condemned prisoners to assist them in coming to a knowledge of Christ before their execution.

Catherine, who became lovingly known as "La Beata Popolana" to her fellow citizens, started a religious revival in 1375 in Pisa. From there she worked as a mediator trying to establish peace between the people of Florence and Perugia on the one hand, and the Holy See and its French legates on the other.

Catherine died in 1380 at the age of 33 as a result of a seizure and a subsequent attack of paralysis.

Teresa of Avila

Born into a large family on March 28, 1515, Teresa early loved to learn about the lives of the saints and resolved, at the age of seven, with her little brother, Rodrigo, to set out to fight the Moors and become Christian martyrs. Returned to their homes by an uncle who caught them on the road, Teresa and Rodrigo attempted to build religious hermitages for themselves in the garden which were never completed.

Placed in a convent by her father at the age of fifteen to be educated, Teresa eventually decided to become a nun. Because her father wouldn't hear of it, Teresa left secretly at the age of twenty for the Carmelite convent of the Incarnation outside Avila. Later stricken there with an unknown malady, Teresa used insights received from a book entitled the *Third Spiritual Alphabet* to pray constantly for her health, which she regained three years later.

As Teresa began spending more time with people from the secular world who visited the monastery, she neglected her meditation. At the advice of a Dominican friar, however, she began again her private prayer life, never to forsake it. In her attempt to focus her will upon God, Teresa found Augustine's *Confessions* of great help. In addition, she recorded an experience of feeling Mary Magdalen coming to her aid in her attempt to be more centered upon the will of God.

Eventually as Teresa's prayer life was practiced with greater intensity and frequency, she began to have visions and inner communications. Considerably troubled by some of these visions, Teresa sought out religious mentors to help her decide whether these experiences were from God or the Devil. Advised to say the *Veni Creator Spiritus* aloud each day, Teresa did so and was one day visited by a rapturous state during which she heard the Lord tell her to discourse with angels, not mortals. This was but the first of a number of such auditory experiences which filled Teresa with joy and peace.

Occasionally Teresa was also raised above the ground during some of these ecstasies. In addition to having a concrete sense of God's goodness and love during these exalted times, Teresa also lost her fear of death. Although Teresa saw many visions, the most amazing was one she described as a piercing of her heart in a sensation of both pain and joy. And after Teresa's death in 1582 she was found to have a scar-like mark upon her heart. She was canonized in 1623.

John of the Cross

John was born to Catherine Alvarez and Gonzalo De Yepes at Fontiveros in Old Castile in 1542. After the death of his father, John had to attend a poor-school and later studied at the college of the Jesuits. At the age of twenty-one he entered the Carmelite monastery at Medina and in 1567 at the age of twenty-five he became a priest. St. Teresa, impressed by John's spirit, persuaded him to enter one of the two houses she had founded for men, so John did indeed join the first of the barefooted Carmelite friars. Eventually John became the rector of the fourth such house established at Alcala.

Although he was a source of great inspiration to others, John himself went through periods of great spiritual aridity in which he lost all sense of God's presence, a desolation described in *The Dark Night of the Soul*. Though John's ministry was marked by miracles and he was regarded as a saint, he was imprisoned in Toledo and severely beaten in 1577 for refusing to follow the orders of the provincial of Castile.

Out of his intense suffering during this period of time, John had a vision of the Mother of God promising him relief from his tribulations. This vision proved prophetic, for soon afterwards John made a miraculous escape from the prison by following the directions given by the Virgin.

Subsequently John wrote the literature which has brought him renown. He maintained that contemplation was not an end in itself, but a means toward union with God and a way of experiencing love. Although political disputes among the orders caused John untold suffering throughout his life, all manner of acclaim came to him upon his death.

Conclusion

Although frequently filled with miraculous visions, insights, and an overwhelming sense of God's love, the lives of the saints were not without suffering and a sense of God's silence from time to time. Certainly this type of experience is true of the Christian journey, for there come to us beautiful moments of illumination, followed in turn by times when we see "through a glass darkly."

We never arrive in this journey; we are constantly on the way. But meditation and the mystical experiences that come to us can help us keep our feet on the pathway, continuously moving, growing, changing. As we are more and more touched by the life of Love, we are more able to minister to others with love. This love can minister to individuals, to groups or to institutions.

17

Dreams, Imagination and the Inner Child

No sane individual will embark on a journey that leads nowhere. We will not undertake a spiritual pilgrimage unless we believe in the existence of a spiritual reality. We operate out of our belief systems; thus we cannot set out upon an inner road if there is no land to be traversed.

Christopher Columbus would never have discovered America if he had believed the earth was flat, for only a fool would set out upon a venture to end in falling off the edge of the world. Although the Greeks had maintained that the earth is spherical, the belief system of the Middle Ages had excluded this theory from its view of the universe and it was left to explorers like Magellan and Columbus to prove otherwise.

Hundreds of years ago human beings used to believe in the existence of a spiritual world that was every bit as real and complex as the material world. Although this world was explored to some degree by ancient peoples, eventually most individuals came to believe that inner reality, like the outer reality posited by the people of the Middle Ages, was flat and that one transgressed the boundaries only at one's own peril, for over the edge one would encounter either an annihilating emptiness or else demon-filled chaos. Thus, one ignored the frightening possibilities beyond known reality until eventually modern religion lost all connection to the spiritual knowledge of the ancients.

All the major world religions have believed that one can communicate with the spiritual world. The New Testament writers and the church fathers wrote extensively about our relationship to non-physical reality. Jesus himself treated angels and demons as living beings. But individuals in our modern age seem to have lost the capacity to take the spiritual world seriously—and with just cause. For the present philosophical basis of

Western thought does not permit us to believe as the early church did, that God actually intervenes in our earthly lives. The philosophical basis of Plato, in which the early church could intellectually ground its beliefs, offered a worldview that provided for the coexistence and relationship of both the material and the spiritual.

Instead of using Plato's philosophical basis, however, we in the West have accepted the outlook of Aristotle, who maintained that we know reality only through our reason and our sense experience. This belief, which so thoroughly permeates our view of the world, has caused us to view life with blinders on, oblivious to the meeting of two kinds of reality.

Such encounters between outer and inner reality are mirrored in great works like the *Divine Comedy*. If we view this masterpiece only from an outer framework, however, as our culture teaches us to do, we lose half of the story, for this great religious poetry is really Dante's tale of his inner religious journey. Unfortunately, many people today view this work as a rather provincial picture of an outmoded Christianity irrelevant to our modern age.

Modern Theology's Bankruptcy

Modern theology offers no context for believing in the sort of spiritual reality of which Dante spoke, so people who are interested in this other reality usually encounter it rather than theorize about it. This encounter which can withstand all the critical analyses of modern sophisticates, is occurring for more and more individuals as they start taking their dreams seriously.

The dream provides a natural, original, individual and convincing way of encountering spiritual reality. We all know the powerful nature of the dream, for we are sometimes awakened by frightening nightmares which have all the impact of real outer occurrences. Or we may find that a pleasant dream leaves us with a sense of well-being that accompanies us through the entire day.

Current medical and psychological studies indicate that dreams often provide healing effects on the dreamer, but no one is certain how they do so. Religion seems to provide us with a better way to understand dreams than medical science does, for many Christians over the course of 1500 years viewed dreams as God's natural means of revealing himself to individuals.

As Western philosophy became increasingly Aristotelian, denying the validity of dreams as revelation, men and women began to think of dreams as insignificant, merely reflecting a physical symptomn like over-indulgence in one's favorite dessert. When Freud once again called attention to the importance of dreams, it was mostly as a means of treating hysteria, seizures, and other forms of mental illness.

As dreams were given greater credence and as the study of the psyche continued, however, researchists found that dream deprivation resulted in inability to function in a balanced, normal way. It was as a result of his own research with patients that Carl Jung came to maintain that the dream was an important way of experiencing spiritual reality—and that being unrelated to this reality caused both mental and physical illness.

Regaining Spiritual Belief through Experience

Those who experience the dynamism of this type of contact with the spiritual world do not need to resort to more calculated and sometimes dangerous ways of relating to the inner world, for access to this world comes naturally and without trauma. Several young people I have counseled have been surprised at how much more exciting and interesting their dreams were than any LSD trip they had taken. For the dream can provide us with a connection to the meaning that can only be rooted in divine reality.

Some of the students with whom I have worked in the last few years at the University of Notre Dame have regained their lost religious beliefs through recording their dreams and paying attention to the reality of which they speak. These young men and women began to realize that there really was a vital depth to the old traditional religion that they had discarded as being lifeless and outmoded.

Not everyone needs to undertake the rigorous inner journey; in fact, it is even dangerous for some persons with unstable egos to do so. But for those whose sense of order and view of the world has already been shaken up, the dream provides a concrete way of once again contacting those living realities with which our modern age has lost relationship.

Dreams from a Christian Perspective

When I was first propelled by a personal crisis, some 25 years ago, into writing down my dreams, I searched the Bible for references to dreams and visions, and found that there were hundreds of such references. I also found that every important early church father as well as subsequent saints like Thérèse of the Little Flower believed that the dream connected one to the divine. Unfortunately the institutional church eventually lost all belief in dreams as a way to relate to the numinous, for Aristotelian thought and the Enlightenment had had a profound effect on organized religion by the middle of the eighteenth century.

Once in a while in modern times some unusual person would attest to God's intervention in his or her life through a dream. John Newton, author of "Amazing Grace" and a converted slave trader, was one such man. In the nineteenth century, Baptist minister A. J. Gordon wrote a detailed account of a life-changing dream he had. In 1968 John Sanford, a close personal friend, and I each published a book on the subject of Christian dream interpretation. Then in 1974 popular writer Catherine Marshall included in her *Something More* a chapter on her dream encounters.

Almost any discussion in which people start telling of a strange dream the previous night will elicit reactions which betray rather unexamined and ill-advised points of view. Some people are convinced that their dreams regularly predict the future; others see dreams as rather amusing examples of the meaninglessness and chaos of our lives. Still others are certain that every dream symbol is a significant portent from God. Trying to invest dreams with meaning according to a predetermined system is foolhardy, for the symbols and images that fill our dream life are complex and cannot be reduced to pat meanings.

The Many Levels of our Psyches

Because the psyche is so complex, it is able to pick up information in many ways and from different levels of both material and spiritual reality. These levels are in turn reflected in the structure and symbolic nature of our dreams. After our conscious minds have gathered a variety of experiences and knowledge from the physical world around us, we can store these experiences as memories. From this storehouse, built up through accumulated memories, a part of our psyche selects some point of particular interest which emerges as a dream. Thus material from this memory bank serves as one source of our dreams.

The Personal Unconscious

Another level of the psyche which produces dreams is the personal unconscious which can be depicted as a locked compartment into which now-forgotten contents have been deposited. These repressed, hidden contents, which we don't consciously remember, or want to remember, frequently emerge in one's dreams, allowing us to confront some unintegrated part of ourselves which may well make mischief if we don't acknowledge it.

Personal Dramas

A third level from which dreams arise produces personal dramas constructed from characters both known and unknown. These personal dreams, in which we also see our *self* as it is in outer reality, are a good way for us to recognize the outer self's relationship to the other parts of us which are depicted as separate persons in the dramas. Those small plays, as it were, frequently serve as compensations for one-sided conscious attitudes.

Archetypal Dreams

Beyond these three dream levels is a still deeper layer of psychic reality which produces what we call archetypal rather than personal symbols. These dream symbols are universal, having been found the world over in the myths, fairy tales and stories of almost all peoples. Common archetypal images include the ocean, a snake, a fire or whirlwind, and an unknown man or woman. Carl Jung found in his research that the same archetypal dream symbols occurred among twentieth-century patients that had been explored by the alchemists of the Middle Ages.

Dreams Providing Sudden Insight

Yet another level of our psyche produces the sort of phenomenon we frequently experience as a sudden insight gained from having "slept on" a problem or the remembrance of a name we have been searching our memory for. This kind of clear and direct, almost logical, communication is less frequent than the other kinds of dreams we experience, for dreams generally communicate symbolically not literally.

Numinous Dreams and other Types of Dreams

Still another part of our complex psyche produces the sort of dream we characterize as numinous, because they are overwhelming, usually frightening, and awesome. The reason for this sense of awe, of course, is that this sort of dream brings us into a direct confrontation with the holy, an experience which often caused individuals in biblical accounts to fall on their faces in fear, wonder, or rapture.

The psyche also occasionally produces dreams that tell us of outer happenings that we have no way of knowing via the usual sensory means. History attests to significant facts that have been "given" to people through their dreams. The famous chemist Kekule is one such example.

In our day and age, many persons have seemingly transcended space and time, receiving knowledge of incidents involving loved ones far away.

And finally, there is a level of the psyche from which come those once-in-a-life-time dreams that alter our whole perception of reality. Jung had one such dream-vision when he was seriously ill. A minister friend of mine had a beautifully comforting dream a few weeks before he died in which he walked upon a pathway of light toward heaven.

To summarize, our psyches enable us to know reality in several ways. Outwardly we know the world through our sense experience and also through memory. Inwardly we know that world through the symbols and images of our dreams. We may, however, also have knowledge of external reality through a deep layer of the psyche that reveals things to us we have no other way of knowing.

And then we also have access to an archetypal world that we encounter through universal symbols found in myth and story. All of these means of knowing reality—be it inner or outer—can bring us in touch with creative or divine reality. There also exists a powerful destructive reality which can only be surmounted if we appropriate the power of the one who has conquered death and destruction—the Risen Christ.

The dream, of course, is the most natural and spontaneous way of encountering inner reality, but learning the art of meditation can also put us in touch with the same reality. Meditation is a process of conscious exploration of this inner territory and it can lead us to exciting adventures we could never encounter in outer reality.

A Personal Story

My own experience with dreams dates back more than 30 years when I first started recording them nightly. Although I frequently did not like what they pointed out to me, I found that I needed to hear what they were communicating. For example, one dream pictured me in my clergyman role, trying to take up an offering through the branches of a dead tree which had fallen across the church, severing it into two parts. The message concerned the chaos and confusion reigning in my life at the time, and was a much-needed communication.

Another dream showed me that I had an inner dictator who needed taming. A particularly moving dream occurred some time after I had started faithfully writing down my dreams and paying attention to their meaning. I was to celebrate the Eucharist on Pentecost, and on the night prior to this occasion I dreamed that I was clothed in a lovely red chausable and that the Holy Spirit was touching everything around me. This numinous dream needed no explanation, for its very occurrence indicated a change in my life and attitude.

Dreams often reveal the source of a problem and may even point out a clue to the solution. But is is then up to the individual to help the inner process along by learning to meditate, to use one's imagination actively and creatively, and to know when to let the process lie dormant for awhile and act as leaven for one's inner development.

Using our Imagination

One of the processes mentioned as a way to help facilitate the inner journey was active imagination. This process allows images to arise from the unconscious and then develops these images by concentrating on them, watching them, speaking to them, etc., for the inner world and its beings are alive and real just as the beings of the outer world are real.

But active imagination works with images, not concepts, for spiritual reality does not operate on a purely rational, conscious level. It is through symbols, not logical thought, that inner changes take place. Certainly logical thought is not to be discarded, scorned or belittled, but it is only one way of dealing with reality.

Images, on the other hand, offer us the power to relate to inner reality by giving us a way to deal with the emotions and sensitivities aroused by our contact with the spiritual world.

Working with the imagination can be frightening and frustrating because the symbols and images we relate to are beyond our beck and call. Because they are not produced by the ego, we cannot manipulate them at will as we can concepts.

Although may people regard the world of intuition and imagination as an interference with the much more important world of facts and business sense, many creative scientists, philosophers and others are beginning to maintain that their highly intricate system of ideas in many cases originated with an insight or image that simply emerged spontaneously from the unconscious imaginative realm. The creativity of Albert Einstein is just one case in point.

Awakening our Imagination

There are many ways to awaken imagination, and each person must find the individual techniques that suit him or her best. One way that has proved effective is to concentrate on something graphic and concrete, like a picture, a statue or a particular object. As one fixes one's gaze upon this representation, one finds it imbued with a life of its own, so that a spontaneous, creative process, quite apart from the working of one's ego, is set in motion.

This type of inner working is quite different from daydreaming, which tends to be merely a way of escaping from current harsh realities. There is no real creativity or transforming power in idle dreaming, whereas the active images which emerge from a deep level of the unconscious put us in touch with the creative spiritual forces of the universe.

Although many persons would find it strange and perhaps threatening and unhealthy to think of dealing with images in this manner, we should note that psychologists using the Rorschach or the Thematic Apperception tests are dealing with this same psychic level in order to elicit information that will allow them to help their patients. These particular tests, which give one's imagination free reign, allow one to participate in an imaginative world where ink blots, for example, are not merely dark blobs on a piece of paper, but become representations of people, animals, objects, or even monsters.

Children and the Imaginative World

Most children are completely at home in the world of imagination. They play house, act out schoolroom dramas before they even go to kindergarten, and use imaginary stethoscopes to diagnose ailments. They create imaginary playmates with whom they carry on endless animated conversations, and they endow favorite playthings with human characteristics and names.

Unfortunately, however, as we grow up into the cold, hard, rational world of adult mores and work patterns, we tend to think of the world of imagination as childish and so we neglect it in favor of "maturity." But if we reject imagination and creative play, our undernourished child within may cry out for attention and feeding. In Thomas Harris's terminology, the parent and adult portions of our personality are well developed in modern society, but it is our inner child who suffers from neglect who may then rise up in a fit of temper and cause us problems.

Another way to develop imagination and to nourish the child within is through movement or dance therapy, which encourages the participant to act out inner fantasies and to express emotions through body movement. The spontaneity and freedom of expression which this sort of movement encourages often gets one in touch with a long-repressed childlike sense of play which is cathartic.

Guided Imaginative Journeys

Sometimes one can encounter imaginative reality through working in a group that has a leader orally guiding participants on an imaginative journey. One workshop asked those in attendance to imaginatively walk through a peaceful valley, alongside a brook, where they would encounter a friend to accompany them on a climb through an alpine area leading towards a beautiful church on the summit of a hill. In this church one was to sit imaginatively feeling the warm rays of sun coming through a window.

The participants were encouraged to share their individual stories orally with the other group members, for the details of each story were different as each person's unconscious spontaneously produced material to fill in the general outlines provided by the guide. Such a guided journey can furnish the needed stimulus to touch the wellsprings of creativity in a person. This sort of creative exercise can bring renewal and release, as many participants will testify.

Creative Writing

Creative writing can also be a means of opening oneself to the imaginative realm. Some teachers stimulate their students' creative processes by asking them to write their own myths and fairy tales, then having them typed, mimeographed, and circulated among class members. The students are usually eager to read both their own and others' imaginative writings, for the creative spark inside them has been touched, resulting in contagious enthusiasm. A good teacher can also help students read great literature in an imaginative way, so that the universality and richness of great authors can be felt and internalized.

Imagination through Art

Artistic endeavors like drawing, painting, modeling in clay and drama are also marvelous avenues for developing one's imaginative potential. The spontaneous drawings of children are frequently an outward illustration of youngsters' inner lives and may provide helpful information for child psychologists. Sandplay is also used by therapists with both children and adults.

Psychodrama may help persons to come into contact with inner forces that have great potential for creativity and personality integration.

Dance, drama, art, writing, and creative play are all forms of religious expression, for these activities spring from the creative, religious center of our being which connects to divine meaning and purpose. It is our child-like capacity to play and to imagine which brings us into relationship with all that is sacred in life. It is important to take Jesus seriously when he said, "Unless you become as little children you shall in no way get into the kingdom of heaven." It would be helpful if our churches provided more opportunities for such explorations.

FOR FURTHER READING

Assagioli, Roberto, M.D. *Psychosynthesis: A Manual of Principles and Techniques,* New York: Viking Press, 1971.
Luke, Helen, *Dark Wood to White Rose,* Pecos, N.M.: Dove Publications, 1975.
McGlashan, Alan, *The Savage and Beautiful Country,* Boston: Houghton Mifflin, 1974.

18

Taking Jesus' Healing Ministry Seriously

Today Christians need a theological basis upon which to rest a ministry of healing. In this modern age we expend much energy taking care of our health, but we don't even consider that religion may be connected in some way to our well-being.

In the past, people have believed that the spiritual world could and did affect one's physical state, and that certain mediators of this reality had powers to affect health and wholeness. This view was held by Jesus and the early church, but after the Reformation it was discarded. Today there exists a diversity of opinions on the subject, but modern theology has not developed a solid rationale for believing in spiritual healing.

Some groups in our society do emphasize healing, such as New Thought, Christian Science, and the Pentecostal sects. There is also interest in psychological healing, and many psychiatrists and psychologists can attest to the physical changes that have resulted from psychic changes. In 1954 the Academy of Religion and Mental Health was established to facilitate communication between the healing and the religious professions.

Most clergy do not seem too interested or informed on the subject, but physicians have evidenced quite a great interest in the relationship between religion and health. Opposing viewpoints in the church today evidence great divisions among Christians about how God acts in our lives, with many persons expressing interest and others showing hostility.

Arguments Against Healing

Most churches maintain that there is no connection between Christianity and physical (or mental) health. Churches have built hospitals, but that is not the same as believing that sacramental acts can bring health. This point of view is quite different from that of the early church, which held services of unction for healing. In the twelfth century these healing services were transformed into extreme unction, which became the sole sacrament of this type, and it was to be performed only in conjunction with death. Much of the role of sacraments in the Roman Catholic church was eventually adopted by the emphasis on relics and shrines. The Protestant church, however, disdained what they regarded as a popish show, and so they became hostile to the Roman Catholic attitude toward healing.

Eventually four different views of healing arose in the Protestant church. First, the materialistic view maintained that only physical means can be used to cure people. Second, many persons maintained that illness comes from God as a discipline. Third, the Dispensationalists believed that healing was given by God to human beings for a certain time only. And fourth, the theology of Bultmann believed that the supernatural cannot break into the ordinary natural world. This last view is the one we find predominant among Protestants today and even popular among some Catholics.

Starting in the 1890s the materialistic viewpoint became dominant, for human beings came to be regarded as biological beings who could be made well by proper treatment of physical organs. People started to believe that sickness could be done away with and that proper medical techniques were the answer to all disease, even to mental and emotional sickness. Communicable diseases abated greatly, but heart disease and cancer became leading killers. Mortality rates went down dramatically from 1900 to 1925, but they decreased slowly from 1925 to 1950. They are now at a plateau, and further decreases will be slow.

Over the last thirty years physicians have begun to believe that mental and emotional factors are relevant to physical health, but even so, many people believe that further knowledge, not a change in religious belief, is needed. The church concurs in this belief for the most part. Thus such nebulous things as spiritual factors could not have an effect on one's body. If the church is to affirm that religious belief can alter one's physical condition, it will have to change its worldview and accept the premise that a non-material reality exists which affects our physical world.

Because of its worldview, however, the church has had to explain away or water down large portions of the Scriptures which detail the healings of Jesus and make references to evil spirits, dreams and visions, and the Pentecost experiences. Several explanations are offered to discount the New

Testament records of healing. One is that the apostles made mistakes about the facts. Another is that these miraculous stories were added later. A third view accounts for these troublesome tales by saying that the sick were psychologically rather than physically ill, and that those individuals raised from the dead were really in comas. Some critics view all the healings in a symbolic way, saying that one may be delivered from spiritual blindness, lameness, or death.

Sickness as Punishment

Unfortunately, many people view sickness as a punishment sent by God to correct his wayward children. Even the Office of Visitation in the *Book of Common Prayer* of the Church of England regards sickness as a "fatherly correction" and as a "chastisement of the Lord." Although this office in the 1928 American *Book of Common Prayer* has removed the harsh tone from the passages dealing with sickness, no mention of God's will toward healing and wholeness is mentioned.

The underlying attitude of the pervasive theology on which this Office of Visitation rests is basically that God wills sickness. The absence of serious modern belief in a devil or power of darkness means that illness must come from God, for there is no other source to be its author. In addition, the Office rests on the idea that God is the author of sickness for two reasons—to show humankind its need to repent from sin, and to increase one's faith. Thus, if God has sent sickness, what right has the pastor or priest to remove it?

Dispensationalism

The theory of sickness as punishment does not appeal, however, to certain conservative churches who read the Bible more literally than other denominations. Thus these churches have concluded that God gave healings and other miracles for a particular reason for only one period of history. Both John Calvin and Martin Luther believed in this dispensationalist view, and their thinking greatly affected Protestant theology.

Other theologians, rather than denying healing as possible in our present era, merely neglected the subject. Such authors as Dr. Wade Boggs (*Faith Healing and the Christian Faith*) maintain that healing should be viewed with skepticism, particularly since such "fringe" groups as Christian Scientists and Pentecostals have often co-opted it, sometimes embellishing it with highly emotional practices.

The Liberal Church View

The liberal church, on the other hand, resolved the matter of healing by a different route. Both Christian existentialism and the "God is dead" movement find no place in their theology for belief in healing. The existentialists, whose basis of belief lies in Husserl and Kierkegaard, exclude any possibility that the supernatural can break into human life and maintain that we arrive at meaning for our lives only as we are rooted in the present moment of existence.

Thus those thinkers who have predicated their theology on this viewpoint, such as Bonhoeffer, Tillich, Bultmann, Bishop Robinson, and Bishop Pike, believe that healings do not happen because God does not intervene in human life. Bultmann, for example, even maintained that the Christian gospel must necessarily be demythologized if it is to speak to modern human life. According to this view, such supernatural experiences as dreams and visions, healings, prophecy, and speaking in tongues never did and cannot now take place.

The logical extension of this sort of thinking has resulted in the beliefs of the "God is dead" factions, who maintain that God is no longer active in human life.

Belief in healing, then, was hit with a double whammy, for theology could find no solid ground for belief in healing, and modern medicine seemed to make divine healing increasingly dispensable. So the church was left in the awkward position of preaching a gospel devoid of power, a message that had been over-conceptualized and stripped of its foundations. In lieu of anything else to do, churches launched building programs and emphasized increasing their numbers.

Today the church has entered the arena of social action as a way of ministering since a direct encounter with God has been viewed as impossible. Fortunately, humankind has not always viewed healing the way the majority of modern Christians do. It will be helpful to look at the Hebrew and Greek views of healing, then at the Gospel message itself, and finally at certain experiences of healing in the modern world.

Healing Among the Ancients

To really appreciate the teachings and practice of Jesus of Nazareth, it is necessary to view him in context—against the backdrop of the Judaic and Hellenistic heritage that was his. For Jesus' attitudes toward the well-being of men and women differed distinctly from the attitudes of most Jews and Greeks.

The Yahweh of the Old Testament

The predominant attitude of the Old Testament is that God is the author of both good and evil. Deuteronomy 32:29 says, "It is I who deal death and life; when I have struck it is I who heal and none can deliver from my hand." Many Old Testament incidents illustrate the destructive side of Yahweh. Jacob was lamed by wrestling with the angel of God, Uzzah was struck down for steadying the ark, and all manner of sickness was visited upon individuals who displeased God. The women of Abimelech's household were made barren, and Miriam contracted leprosy for speaking against Moses. Sickness was a potent illustration of the rift between God and humankind.

In the Psalms, outcries include pleadings for deliverance from illness thought to be inflicted by Yahweh himself. The Book of Proverbs warns that illness results from sin, for "Yahweh reproves the man he loves, as a Father checks a well-loved son" (Proverbs 3:12).

The Reasons for this
Old Testament View of Illness

One reason for the seemingly unfair visitation upon individuals was that in the Old Testament men and women usually were not viewed as separate from the collective community of Israelites. Thus, if God were displeased with some aspect of Jewish life or an error on the part of a leader, individuals became indiscriminately victimized by the collective guilt. Many people, therefore, were required to pay for David's sin.

Secondly, the Hebrews, unlike the Egyptians and others of their contemporaries, did not believe in the existence of other gods or evil spirits to whom sickness might be attributed. Thus Yahweh was the author of good and evil alike. We can easily see how the *Book of Common Prayer* view of God as the source of illness arose out of this background.

Furthermore, the Old Testament rarely mentions the use of medicine and doctors by the Hebrews, but we know that the Persians and the Chaldeans used surgery and medical treatment in dealing with disease. The Hebrews, however, for the most part, associated medical healing with divination, magic, and false gods.

God as Healer

Although the Old Testament did maintain that God was the author of sickness and disease, it also viewed him as possessing the ability to heal. A number of times barren women (Sarah, for example) were granted children. Sometimes healings took place after sacrifices had been made. But by and large, instances of healing were relegated to the sidelines in the Old Testament accounts.

It is in the Book of Job that a challenge is brought to the view of sickness and affliction as just reward for sin. Job is accused by friends and family of sins of which he is innocent, for they assume that only guilty men and women suffer. Finally Job is justified in his struggle, but he had suffered profoundly.

Certainly Jesus' view of illness and his concern for sick human beings was different from these Old Testament viewpoints; so different, in fact, that he was not in accord with the official religion of his day. Could Jesus' view have been rooted in the beliefs of the Greeks?

Healing and the Greeks

Although healing cults were found among the Greeks and formal medical study probably began in the Hippocratic school, there was really little difference between the Greco-Roman and the Judaic views of illness. The Greeks believed that illness came from the gods, but they viewed it not so much as punishment for sin but rather as a matter of fate. Although the Hebrews could call upon Yahweh for healing, only a few Greek gods were considered appropriate to petition for healing. The chief cult that mediated healing was that of Aesculapius, but he was a lesser god.

Many Greeks did, however, believe that one's physical and mental health was influenced by the realm of the spirit. In fact, some Greeks stressed shamanism—a religious attitude and way of life many peoples have held that sees the healer as a mediator between individual and spiritual reality. Thus this mediator could heal both mind and body because through him or her power was transmitted to the sick person. It was into this type of healing tradition that Jesus was to step.

Jesus as Healer

Jesus of Nazareth demonstrated more interest in the physical and mental health of men and women than any other religious leader in history. Although his ministry also consisted of preaching and teaching, his healing ministry was so important that almost one-fifth of the Gospels are devoted to discussion of this particular type of miracle. The number of physical and mental healings mentioned far surpass the number of moral healings. Forty-one instances of the former are detailed in the four Gospels. Jesus also commissioned his disciples to carry out a healing ministry. The Pharisees maintained that Jesus healed because he was possessed by a demon.

The healing ministry of Jesus made concrete his teachings, for what better way is there to show love and concern than to cure physical and emotional ills? Jesus himself maintained that his healings were a sign of the kingdom of heaven, indicative that he was the Messiah who was to put evil to flight, and, as Messiah, he revealed God's compassionate attitude toward sickness.

Jesus' View of the Human Personality

Jesus' healing ministry was the result of his attitude toward and beliefs about the human personality. Most societies have endorsed the simplistic view that individuals commit evil actions because they choose to do so and that the only way to change a person's actions is by punishment and by education. Modern legal practice is based on this view as is the administration of our jails and penitentiaries.

Jesus, however, believed that although men and women do exercise conscious control of their personalities, they are also subject to spiritual powers or demons which psychiatry calls complexes. It is these powers which cause us to lose control of ourselves, and it is only through a higher power—that of love and the Holy Spirit—that we can be free from these alien powers. Thus Jesus' compassion and healing ministry was rooted in his belief that sickness and suffering originated not from humankind's own perversity, but from foreign spiritual powers which could only be defeated by God's creative loving spirit.

The Nature of the Healings Jesus Performed

According to the New Testament, Jesus healed more individuals of mental illness, called demon possession in the Gospels, than any other single ailment. Matthew 8 and 15, Mark 1, and Luke 8 specifically note this type of healing ministry. Common afflictions of that day that Jesus healed included leprosy, lameness, paralysis, fever, and blindness. The three incidences of raising from the dead are particularly difficult for many modern persons to accept.

Of the three categories of disease—organic (structural defects), functional (malfunctioning of an organ), and psychic or mental, Jesus' healings were primarily mental and organic. Today medical doctors recognize that of these three types of illness, the psychic disturbances are by far the hardest to cure. Approximately one-half of all patients in hospitals are designated as having some sort of mental disorder. Thus Jesus, who healed all disease, was able instantaneously to cure the disease which modern medicine finds most baffling. Studies conducted recently found that one out of every ten individuals in the United States has some form of psychiatric disorder.

Jesus' Means of Healing

The majority of Jesus' healings were effected through the spoken word and the touch of his hand, later to be called the laying on of hands. Sometimes Jesus commanded evil spirits to leave a person; this practice was called exorcism. Jesus also used saliva as a healing carrier of his personal power. Sometimes individuals were healed by touching Jesus' clothing. Several times Jesus spoke of an individual's faith as the healing agent: "Your faith has restored you to health" (Mark 5:34). Twice Jesus mentioned the forgiveness of sin in conjunction with healing.

The Significance of Jesus' Healings

There are four major types of healing—medical, psychological, psychic, and religious or sacramental. Modern medicine relies heavily on the first, which emphasizes techniques like X-rays and radiation or drugs and medicines to aid the body's own recuperative powers.

Psychological healing relies on the power of suggestion, which seldom cures persons suffering from acute neurosis or psychosis. Psychotherapy, however, can help an individual deal with conflicts and thus cure illness, but it is a long, slow process. Psychic healing works at the level of unconscious images and attitudes and takes place unconsciously usually as a result of a power that emanates from certain persons.

And religious healing results from a conscious relationship to God in which the creative power of love is the healing agent. Jesus used neither medical nor psychological methods in his healing ministry. He also steered away from deliberately using his personal psychic powers and cautioned people against spreading word of his healings. Rather, it was sacramental or religious healing that Jesus used. By bringing sick persons into contact with the Spirit of God, he mediated divine wholeness to men and women.

The Reasons Jesus Healed

Jesus healed primarily because he had compassion (whose root meaning is "to know suffering together") toward people. As God incarnate, his love reached out in a caring, healing ministry. Jesus also healed because he was in opposition to the evil forces that brought sickness to human beings. In fact, Jesus was so committed to healing that he even broke the Jewish laws such as keeping the Sabbath to ensure that the sick would become well.

The Question of Sin and Sickness

We have already said that Jesus did not believe that God sent sickness as a punishment for wrongdoing. If, however, sin is viewed as a deviation from following one's pathway toward wholeness, it can indeed lead to sickness, for without the protection of a creative spiritual force to guide and accompany one on life's journey, one becomes open to the destructive spiritual forces that cause illness and mental disturbance.

Because Jesus believed that sickness was the result of the force of evil at work in the world, he believed that it was not enough to heal a person of an unclean spirit. Rather, an individual must then be filled with the creative loving spirit of God or one will be possessed by even more destructive devils (Matthew 12). Thus Jesus taught that God wishes health, not sickness, for us, his sons and daughters. Christ was sent to bring wholeness, not illness, and the Christian must necessarily believe that the message of Christianity includes teaching God's will to soundness of mind, soul and body.

19

Healing, Ministry and the Church

The subject of healing has generally been ignored, theologically speaking, in the modern world. The only important study of the subject and its relationship to the church is Evelyn Frost's *Christian Healing*. There are records, however, that provide information on the history of the ministry of healing among Christians.

The Vital Ministry of Healing
Among Early Christians

The first 200 years of the church after the apostolic period were full of vitality. Despite the fact that Christians were persecuted, the numbers of the church increased rapidly. Obviously true conviction was important, for one's life was endangered by being a Christian.

Eventually Christians began to justify their faith to the alien pagan world that surrounded them. As more and more converts came into the church, a vigorous program was developed to ensure the proper preparation for the new life. Thus the church retained its vigorous, alive quality. The "apologies" written to help the pagan world understand Christianity have been preserved and in them we find records that demonstrate the continuance of a healing ministry like that of apostolic times.

The Early Apologists

The first apologists were Quadratus and Justin Martyr, Romans of the second century. The third century produced Tertullian and Cyprian, who lived in Carthage. Clement and Origen of Alexandria and Irenaeus of Gaul were also sophisticated thinkers who wrote about Christian experience. All of these apologists, who were writing for a skeptical pagan world ready to ridicule any Christian practices, refer in some way to healings and expelling of evil spirits. Cyprian in particular noted that healing sometimes accompanied the ritual of baptism. Thus we see that the early church continued Jesus' healing ministry.

As a result of its Judaic inheritance and of Jesus' attention to and respect for material reality, the early church held the physical body in high regard. This viewpoint certainly aided the ministry of healing, for it affirmed the value of the body and its health.

The church saw the interdependence of body and soul—that each is good and that each has inevitable effects upon the other. Thus illness was in opposition to the will of God, who seeks our wholeness. Jesus had shown his victory over the Evil One, author of sin and sickness, through his death and resurrection.

As members of the body of Christ, individuals in the early church sought to care for and heal the sick so that frequently Christian shrines replaced the sites of pagan healing temples. Healing was considered to be a usual occurrence among Christians. The *Shepherd of Hermas,* for example, maintained that those who did not heal the sick were in error, and Theophilus of Antioch attested to the exorcism of demons and the healings he had witnessed. Irenaeus described healings of all sorts of diseases.

In the fourth century Arnobius and Lactantius cited instances of healings as the result of laying on of hands. Most of the ante-Nicene fathers wrote of the practice of exorcism. In the third century laity were even specifically trained to practice exorcism. The sacraments were also considered a direct means of healing, as noted by Cyprian.

So, for approximately three centuries the healing ministry was integral to the life and work of Christians. The power that these men and women called upon to work miracles also gave them the ability to withstand persecution and endure martyrdom. Neither torture nor death could eradicate the loving spirit within them and their joy and conviction was often instrumental in the conversion of many pagans.

The Healing Ministry of the Victorious Church
The victory of Constantine and the resulting Edict of Milan in 313 saw the virtual end of persecution of Christians. In fact, Christianity became *the* religion of the empire. Along with the sudden increase in numbers came a flow of new theologians and writers.

If we go back and examine these writings, we will find that the healing ministry of the church continued wherever vital faith continued to work.

Because of the now official nature of the religion, however, many Christians were followers in name only. Such great Eastern bishops of this time as Athanasius, Basil the Great, Gregory of Nyssa, and Gregory of Nazianzen all recorded healings in their writings about the church. Likewise, the church doctors of the West—Ambrose, Augustine, Jerome and Gregory the Great—all detailed accounts of healings, although their viewpoints on the subject differed markedly.

Because all these early theologians and bishops held Plato's worldview—that a spiritual reality exists concurrent with a material realm—miracles presented no problem for them, either from a theological or from an experimental angle. Healing was merely one way of sharing the workings of creative spiritual reality in the lives of human beings.

The Desert Fathers, Solitude and Healing

As the church became more and more worldly, a number of men and women retreated to the desert to live a life of devotion and discipline. These desert fathers, perhaps because of their great commitment and centered inner lives, worked a number of miracles—including exorcism of evil spirits and healings. The *Historia Lausiaca,* written by Paladius, a member of the Nitrian desert community in the fourth century, recorded some miraculous healings by an old monk named Macarius.

Athanasius also detailed accounts of the healings by the desert monks in his *Life of St. Antony.*

Healing Among Church Leaders

A number of the leaders of this era of Christianity also performed healings. St. Basil was able to heal Bishop Eusebius, and Gregory of Nazianzen described the miraculous recovery of his sister Gorgonia from a burning fever by touching the sacrament to her body.

Gregory of Nyssa, younger brother of Basil the Great, authored four books on the subject of healing—one discussing the miracles of Jesus, and three describing healings he was personally familiar with. He was the only Eastern theologian to put healing into a total theological framework, viewing it as a main avenue for the knowledge of God to come to individuals.

Another great church leader, Chrysostom of Antioch, emphasized in his writings the unchanging power of God as evidenced through individuals in Acts. He also discussed the miracles he had witnessed at the shrine of St. Babylas in Antioch.

The Relationship Between Liturgy and Healing

The importance of healing in the early church can be seen in its liturgy. The celebration of the Eucharist affirmed the joining of the soul, mind, and body in wholeness. *The Apostolic Tradition of Hippolytus* demonstrated the importance of healing in the liturgy and in life. Almost all the orders of worship provide concrete directions on the use of healing practices.

Sometimes oil for the anointing of the sick was also offered to God for sanctification during the celebration of the Eucharist. The *Apostolic Constitutions* gave instructions for ordaining healers and exorcists. Frequently the holy oil was taken home to use in anointing the sick, and in the era of Hippolytus, newly converted Christians were anointed with oil on Easter Sunday.

Other service books prescribed ways of anointing and laying hands on the sick, including directions to priests to serve Communion to the sick for seven days after the anointing ritual. Later on, this service was to change from one of healing to merely a preparation for death.

Healing and the Western Church

Augustine, the major Western theological figure for almost 1000 years, although skeptical of healing in the earlier parts of his Christian life, underwent a radical change as a result of witnessing miracles and ultimately wrote the following in his famous *City of God:* "... once I realized how many miracles were occurring in our own day and which were so like the miracles of old and also how wrong it would be to allow the memory of these marvels of divine power to perish from among our people. It is only two years ago that the keeping of records was begun here in Hippo, and already, at this writing, we have nearly seventy attested miracles."

Paulinus, Augustine's secretary, also recounted a number of miracles in the *Life of St. Ambrose,* including a raising from the dead, exorcism of unclean spirits, and the healing of a cripple. St. Martin of Tours, whose biographer, Sulpicius Severus, recounted his many healings, worked many miracles similar to those described in the New Testament.

Western Theologians and the De-emphasis of Healing

Although healings and other miracles took place in both the Eastern and the Western church, such Western theologians as Jerome began to de-emphasize healing and to warn against dream interpretation and "soothsaying." Other leaders like Cassian, who maintained that the desert fathers only healed when driven by necessity to do so, warned the church of the dangers of practicing healing, lest one lose one's humility and inner purity.

In any event, this attitude toward healing took root in the monasteries and grew until Gregory the Great, Bishop of Rome from 590 to 604 and author of the *Book of Pastoral Rules,* began to maintain that illness was sent by God as a chastisement. Thus the church began to believe that God, rather than the Evil One, authored sickness and that although God had the power to heal, he chose not to exercise that power, preferring to correct his sons and daughters through disease.

This attitude of the Western church, which became prevalent in the seventh and eighth centuries, reached its culmination in the English Office of the Visitation of the Sick, which viewed illness as an expression of divine punishment.

Modern Christianity and Healing

Certainly the attitude of the modern Christian church toward healing is an about-face from the view of the New Testament and the early church. We noted the beginnings of this change in attitude in the seventh-century Western church, but what other factors caused so drastic an alteration in theology and practice?

Three Reasons for the Change in Attitude Toward a Healing Ministry

There seem to be three main reasons for the church's changing viewpoint on healing. First, the general attitude toward God and belief in his loving concern toward individuals began to deteriorate as a result of the chaos and crumbling of Western civilization. Barbarians seized the citadels of culture and brought ruin to every major societal institution except the church itself.

Secondly, an Aristotelian worldview, maintaining that material reality was the *only* reality, replaced the Platonic view that emphasized the coexistence of the material and the spiritual realms. This rationalistic philosophy, which held that God does not break through into the lives of men and women in the here and now, certainly contained no place for belief in healing.

And finally, there existed on the part of many persons a rather uncritical, superstitious belief in and acceptance of anything reported to be miraculous. With discrimination cast to the winds and a cohesive theology to give perspective to healing discarded, it became virtually impossible to distinguish actual miracles from fanciful tales.

By the arrival of the seventh and eighth centuries and the era of Charlemagne, then, the services for the healing of the sick had begun to be altered into unction in readiness for death. The ninth-century church councils in Metz and Pavia actually verbalized the idea that unction related to forgiveness of sins more than it did to healing. The service of healing changed to emphasize confession and repentance on the part of the sick person.

The records of this era of Christianity indicate no healing sacraments. In fact, the *Summa Theologica* maintains, "Extreme Unction is a spiritual remedy, since it avails for the remission of sins, according to James 5:15. Therefore it is a sacrament.... Now the effect intended in the administration of the sacraments is the healing of the disease of sin."

The Church's Attitude Toward Medical Healing

The church not only discouraged healing within its own walls; it also began in the twelfth century to discourage attempts on the part of the secular medical world to find and practice cures for disease and illness. Human dissection was forbidden and in 1215 the Catholic church decreed in the Fourth Lateran Council that physicians had to force sick persons to confess their sins to a priest; otherwise, they had to abstain from visiting patients. It is hard to believe that the church's views had changed so drastically from the early church's loving emphasis on wholeness of body *and* soul.

The Effect of Thomas Aquinas' Thought

One of the major factors contributing to this radical change in viewpoint was the thinking and writing of Thomas Aquinas, whose belief system became the exclusive basis of Catholic theology before Vatican II. Aquinas, who lived in the thirteenth century, was an Aristotelian whose naturalistic thought the church at first regarded as inconsistent with historic Christianity.

Eventually, however, as the philosophical framework of Aristotle began to permeate the universities in particular and Western thought in general, the church began to accept Aquinas' belief structure. His basic contention on the subject of miracles was that Christ used them as proof of the validity of his teachings and of his divinity.

Aquinas did maintain, however, that miracles of the soul took place, the reason being that the soul is of greater significance than the body. It is important to note that Aquinas never finished his *Summa Theologica* because on December 6, 1273, he had an experience of God during mass which so transcended all his intellectual writings that he could not return to his theorizing. Other scholars, however, undertook to finish his work, which became a cornerstone of scholastic philosophy.

Healing and the Protestant Reformation

Although the Protestant reformation brought great changes to Christianity, it did not alter the Aristotelian worldview upon which the church had come to rest. Luther believed that true miracles were inner, not outer, in nature, and Calvin maintained that healings and other gifts had been a special dispensation.

Although Luther did not accept the Aristotelian base of Christian philosophy, he was not much concerned with the means by which God broke into human life. Rather than emphasizing experimental encounters with God, Luther concentrated on faith.

The Attitude of Present-day Churches Toward Healing

Christian workers and missionaries have founded hospitals, clinics and schools all over the world to alleviate human distress. Yet the emphasis has usually been on medical healing rather than divine intervention. Although occasional prayer groups and ministers directly intercede for the sick and may practice sacramental healing, the feeling by and large today is that God heals through medicine. No theology exists which gives us a rationale for the healing ministry. Barth, Bultmann and Bonhoeffer all conceded that they were not able to encounter a God who directly intercedes in human life.

The Importance of the Saints

As the church came to see sickness as needing forgiveness rather than just healing, and as the gap between theories about God and encounters with God became ever wider, men and women began to relate to certain concrete individuals as carriers of the divine and numinous in human life. Such individuals, canonized as saints, began to be credited with miraculous healings—either through their persons or their relics.

For example, in the twelfth century, many people noted that miracles occurred when Anselm blessed the sacrament. Bread blessed by Bernard of Clairvaux was said to be responsible for numerous healings. Dominic, St. Francis of Assisi, Antony of Padua, Thomas of Hereford, Edmund of Canterbury and Richard of Chichester were all famous for their miraculous works.

Catholics, Protestants and the Healing Ministry

Despite a theology and philosophy that did not support the idea of healing, miracles have continued to occur in both the Catholic and the Protestant churches. In many cases, the healing ministry has been predominant among those who are caring for the sick and diseased, for their concrete demonstration of compassion seems to have been an apt channel for the pouring out of God's healing love.

St. Francis Xavier, St. Vincent of Paul, and St. Catherine of Siena, who were all credited with miraculous healings, devoted their lives to the service of their fellows as workers in the medical field.

Both George Fox and John Wesley, dedicated preachers with an intense social concern, detailed miracles that resulted from their prayers. Fox even wrote a "Book of Miracles," which, unfortunately, was never published.

In addition, Prince Alexander of Hohenlohe and Johann Christoph Blumhardt of Germany discovered that they were channels for incredible healings which in Blumhardt's case caused such consternation among church authorities that he was forbidden to practice healing in his ministry for a long time.

In 1905 Francis Thompson wrote *Health and Holiness* to ask the church to view soul and body in an integrated way. Shrines have also been an instrument for ministering to the sick so that such famous places as Lourdes, Fatima, and Ste. Anne de Beaupré attract multitudes of people each year. Since 1860 over two million people have gone to Lourdes yearly.

Healing and Religious Sects

Over the last one hundred years numerous sects in the United States have practiced a healing ministry. Despite the differences it has with orthodox Christianity, Christian Science and New Thought, started by Phineas P. Quimby and Mary Baker Eddy, have evidently ministered healing to a large number of people. Mrs. Eddy's methods were based primarily upon the idea that healing came from proper belief and disease came from mental error. Quimby was experienced in the use of mesmerism, clairvoyance, and hypnotism.

The Guild of Health in England and the Order of the Nazarene in the United States both encouraged healing in cooperation with medicine. In the 1930s The Camps Farthest Out and the Order of St. Luke were begun to introduce both clergy and laity to the practice of healing. The Schools of Pastoral Care, founded by Agnes Sanford, have also introduced many persons to a healing ministry. Kathryn Kuhlman, Oral Roberts, Alfred Price, Louise Eggleston, Tommy Tyson, and Olga Worrall have all touched countless people in a healing ministry.

The real emphasis on healing is not limited to Christians alone. Japan, India, Hong Kong, and other areas of the world are all experiencing a resurgence of interest in new religions which emphasize a healing ministry.

Healing in the Modern World

Despite the fact that more and more individuals are paying attention to signs, miracles, and healings today, theology has given little credence to a healing ministry. John MacQuarrie's *Twentieth Century Religious Thought,* which surveys the thought of one hundred and fifty theologians, shows that not one relates an individual's religious life to his or her mental and physical well-being.

The Reason Modern Theology Has No Place for Healing

The main reason why theology has no place for miracles is that it holds an outmoded worldview, a philosophy that maintains that experiences must fit into a purely rational framework, since there is no such thing as a spiritual reality that can be experienced.

But the most creative modern scientists, thinkers, doctors, and psychologists are far ahead of most theologians in developing a comprehensive worldview. They have discovered that we are not limited to a merely space/time world, but that in addition to living in a material world that we know through reason and sense experience, we also are citizens of a spiritual or psychic kingdom which we encounter through such means as the sacraments, myth, ritual, dreams and visions, and prophecy and healing.

It was Carl Jung who pioneered in this area and demonstrated that there is a vast psychic world which is mediated through our unconscious minds and that the psyche is really a bridge between conscious and unconscious reality.

We know that people constantly experience this psychic realm, for clairvoyant experiences, mediumship, dreams, and other supernatural phenomena abound in our day and age, as Andrew Greeley has demonstrated in his monograph *The Sociology of the Paranormal: A Reconnaissance.*

Although the Christian needs to relate to spiritual reality if he or she is to experience God and his healing effects in his or her life, it is important to remember that this realm of reality also opens us up to the Evil One. The only way we can encounter the effects of these alien spiritual powers safely is to go in the name and power of Christ, who triumphed over evil. It is in this capacity that we need to be aware of the strength and protection that the sacraments and rituals of the church can provide as we venture on our religious journey.

How the Church Can Provide a Climate Leading to a Healing Ministry

First, the church must come to a clear understanding of the issues involved in the belief in the dual nature of reality. An adequate intellectual framework must be developed, and a familiarity with developments in psychology, philosophy, and science must be encouraged.

Secondly, the church needs to promote candid discussion of the questions and experiences of its people. Small groups often provide the best way of encouraging honest and sincere wrestling with issues.

Thirdly, if it is to encourage a valid healing ministry, the church must provide a sense of loving community. Christianity must be horizontal in relationship as well as vertical.

Fourthly, an actual healing ministry on the part of both priests and pastors as well as laity must be instituted.

And finally, the church needs to provide a counseling ministry that will help individuals grapple with and come to a resolution of the pain and perplexity in their lives. The ministry of healing must be multi-faceted, for healing is mediated in many ways.

FOR FURTHER READING

Sanford, Agnes, *The Healing Light, The Art and Method of Spiritual Healing,* St. Paul: Macalester Park, 1968.
———, *The Healing Power of the Bible,* Philadelphia: Lippincott, 1969.

20

Healing, Mysticism and Meditation

T he twentieth century has seen some of humankind's most dangerous diseases conquered. It has also seen the medical profession learn to
control others and to repair the damages and disabilities caused by illness.
Increased understanding of the workings of the human body has made it
possible to perform intricate surgery inconceivable a few decades ago.

Because of the success enjoyed by the medical profession as a result of
this increased understanding, gradually it was concluded that the human
body was merely a complicated mechanism that responded to the laws of
matter as any other physical entity would respond. Frequently patients in
hospitals began to feel that they were being treated as if they were in a sterile laboratory.

Mental disturbances also came to be regarded as merely the result of
some physical aberration—brain damage or an impairment of the nervous
system. The mechanistic view of the universe held by a majority of human
beings of the modern age precluded examining any cause of human malfunctioning other than a purely materialistic one. That one's soul or psyche could affect and alter one's physical condition was not even considered—until thinkers and scientists like Freud, Jung, Teilhard de Chardin,
Einstein, and Heisenberg began to postulate some radically different hypotheses based on their evidence.

In the first half of this century, as a result of Freud's influence in the
United States and the work of Dr. Flanders Dunbar of Columbia, clinical
psychiatry began to base its work on a psychosomatic viewpoint of illness.
Dr. Dunbar's book *Emotions and Bodily Changes* and the establishment of
the journal *Psychosomatic Medicine* contributed to the study of the role of
the psyche in illness. World War II also helped to establish the importance of psychiatry, for army physicians could find no organic reason for a
great many physical ailments felt by men and women in the armed forces.

Certainly there is division within the ranks of the medical profession itself on this subject. Mental illness induced by the use of certain new drugs has enabled some physicians to cling to the more simplistic viewpoint that there is a specific physical cause for every ailment, while other medical persons like Dr. Jerome Frank, professor of psychiatry at Johns Hopkins, has written the following (in *Persuasion and Healing,* Schocken Books, 1969):

> The question of how far a physician should go to meet a patient's expectations is a thorny one. Obviously he cannot use methods in which he himself does not believe. Moreover, reliance on the healing powers of faith, if it led to neglect of proper diagnostic or treatment procedures, would clearly be irresponsible. On the other hand, faith may be a specific antidote for certain emotions such as fear or discouragement, which may constitute the essence of a patient's illness. For such patients, the mobilization of expectant trust by whatever means may be as much an etiological remedy as penicillin for pneumonia.

Examining Changing Medical Thought

One way to examine changing medical thought about the role of the psyche in illness is to take a look at the attitude toward specific diseases. Tuberculosis, for example, a communicable disease caused by the "Bacillus tuberculosis," has been controlled so successfully that few persons die of it in the United States today.

In 1900, however, tuberculosis was the leading killer. But the disease is still a leading disabler, striking more persons than any other communicable disease except measles, venereal disease, and streptococcal sore throat. Although the medical profession knows a great deal about tuberculosis and has controlled it, the reason why it still disables is not understood.

The great Sir William Osler maintained that tuberculosis was more dependent on one's mental state than his or her physical condition. Several studies and the use of X-ray have shown that almost every one is infected by TB at some time or another, but only a few people actually contract it. Why?

Dr. Allen K. Krause, author of *Environment and Resistance in Tuberculosis,* concluded that personality disturbance has an important effect on the growth and spread of germs within one's system.

Syphilis, another common communicable disease, is spontaneously cured in over one-half of the untreated cases. What causes the bodies of some persons to have the ability to cure themselves, while others fall prey to the ravage of disease? The same question can be asked about wounds that do not respond to treatment or infections that linger on. Physicians readily admit that they cannot heal; they merely enable the body to heal itself, for without its innate recuperative powers, the body cannot respond to medical treatment.

Such questions as those raised here are being asked today by the medical profession as it attempts to discover why almost two-thirds of adults who are *not* institutionalized in the United States have one or more chronic physical complaints. Many of these ailments cannot be helped by prescriptions, and surgery certainly cannot provide help in most of these cases.

Our Language as Reflector of the Relationship Between Body and Soul

The English language has a number of common expressions which, if examined, reveal something of the close connection between body and soul. "I can't stomach it," "He's a pain in the neck," "It took my breath away," and "I was scared stiff" all show physical symptoms of an internal emotional state of being. Butterflies in one's stomach and getting cold feet, for example, certainly suggest nervousness. Changes in blood pressure, glandular secretions, and heartbeat rate are all ways of documenting changes in emotional well-being.

The Will to Live and a Sense of Meaning

Indeed, one's whole will to live affects one's physical condition and length of life. For example, John Cowper Powys shows in his *The Meaning of Culture* that human beings cannot exist apart from their culture, for meaninglessness sets in and one finds no reason to continue existing. This phenomenon has been illustrated time and again by the sudden and physically unexplainable deaths of primitive peoples whose cultures were eradicated by incoming conquerors.

The Bridge Between Mind and Body

Emotions cause physical changes in one's body primarily through the autonomic nervous system, which allows the body to organize its processes without conscious direction. This nervous system consists of two parts—the parasympathetic system, which controls such processes as digesting food, slowing the heart, and generally storing energy; and the sympathetic system, which provides quick energy and enables the body to meet emergency situations. Both systems are headquartered in the section of the brain called the hypothalamus, which receives impressions from outer stimuli and, once activated, cannot be easily shut off.

Thus any outer threat or trauma that triggers off this sympathetic system automatically calls forth a "fight or flight" response. One reacts in either an aggressive way—angrily—or with withdrawal tactics—fearfully. In either case one is reacting to a threat which the nervous system immediately responds to by causing a variety of bodily changes—such as rising blood pressure, decreasing blood clotting time, increased flow of adrenalin, and numerous other changes.

The only way to eliminate these reactions is to eliminate the source of the anger or fear. And sadly enough, many of these fears, angers, resentments, and hostilities eventually, after an accumulation of outer experiences, become internalized so that they are deposited in the unconscious where they stay buried, draining us of energy, and causing disease, as they wreak havoc upon the autonomic system which is seeking for a balance between spending and conserving energy.

One can imagine, then, what might happen to a person whose continuous emotional pressures have caused physical pressures day in and day out. Is it any wonder that businessmen and women suffer from ulcers and die from heart attacks at an alarming rate?

The January, 1972 issue of *Fortune* magazine attempted to inform its executive readers about this subject in an article entitled "What Stress Can Do To You." High blood pressure, for example, can eventually cause a stroke or a heart attack, for one's body attempts to react to continuous threat by thickening its artery muscles, thus causing a pressure buildup until finally a vulnerable spot cannot hold out any longer. Likewise, fear and anger can cause a clot to form spontaneously and advance to a brain artery and suddenly cause a cerebral hemorrhage.

Illness as an Escape Mechanism

Physicians and psychiatrists have been noting for some time that sickness can be an escape or an emotional necessity for some people. Frequently the cure of an illness in a person precipitates another sickness even more serious than the previous one, for the psychological problem that incurred disease in the first place has not been dealt with. The Simontons have suggested that illness is the only form of meditation known to most Western people.

Occasionally illness may be a way of controlling other people, for if one cannot admit consciously to certain emotional needs or desires, the body is left to act out one's unconscious wishes. Thus one young woman cited in a medical case history only recovered from her severe headaches when she realized that this was her response to the news of her beloved brother's impending marriage.

Frequently people employ illness (not always consciously by any means) to avoid some unpleasant task or situation facing them.

It has been discovered, for example, that diabetes can be brought on by a personal crisis such as loss of a loved one. Sexual function can likewise be controlled by unconscious images and feelings which affect the supply of blood to the viscera.

The body's defenses against disease are directly affected by emotions, too, for the secretion of "stress" hormones can retard the creation of antibodies needed to fight off disease. Scientists working at Duke University have also been studying the increased flow of body chemicals that occurs during dreaming, and some physicians are hypothesizing that the emotions in certain dreams can actually cause heart attacks during sleep.

Another amazing hypothesis arising from recent studies indicates that chemical changes, set off by the hypothalamus, controlling children's growth can be altered drastically by conflict in the home so that an apparently dwarfed child, when removed from the charged atmosphere, has been known to grow from five to ten inches in one year!

Time and again over my thirty years of counseling I have seen emotional disturbances reflect a sense of meaninglessness in a person's life, thus opening the individual up to disease and even death. Only when one has resolved the psychic origins of the problems does one regain one's sense of meaning and then one's health.

I think specifically of one young man who was in danger of dying from ulcerative colitis. As we discovered together that he did not want to live because of his deep-seated but unfounded fear that he was a homosexual (a fear which had destroyed his marriage), we were able to recognize and alter the emotional hurts deep within him that had caused his illness.

If psychiatrists can help one deal with hurts and emotional trauma, certainly God can bring wholeness and healing to mind and body. John Sutherland Bonnell, former president of New York Theological Seminary, has written *Do You Want To Be Healed?* which discusses the healing effects of faith in God.

The Effect of Specific Diseases
Upon Particular Parts of the Body

It is unclear exactly why specific parts of the body are affected by specific diseases, although personality structure, emotional environment, and most of all, the inherited psyche seem to play parts. In any event, it is a lot easier for most of us to merely blame a malfunctioning organ for any problems we may have, than it is to face up to underlying causes. Increasingly, psychiatrists are realizing that respiratory infections, emphysema, and asthma are emotionally-induced problems in many cases.

Both the skin and eyes are vitally connected to one's emotions. Blushing and perspiration are expressions of emotional reactions, and the eye, named the window of the soul, is regarded by physicians as indicative of one's physical condition. The lysozyme found in tears is known to be a strong germ-killer, strong enough to kill the polio virus, so that weeping can be a healing process.

Digestive problems, cardiovascular ailments, and arthritis all indicate varying ways of responding to emotional problems. Insomnia, headaches, and tumors can be signals warning us to pay attention to our emotional strains. Physicians believe that both fatigue and hyperactivity result from glandular malfunctioning as a result of stress. Even tooth decay shows a correlation with anxiety.

There is currently a psychology of being accident prone. A study of fracture patients in a hospital ward some years ago revealed a high rate of emotional disturbance that had seemingly been expressed in "accidents."

Research in this field continues as scientists like Dr. W. F. G. Swann suggest that scientific investigation also ought to deal with the realm of the soul, and others maintain that all disease has some relationship to emotions and the psyche. An article in *The American Handbook of Psychiatry* has stated:

> Fortunately, effective therapeutic work with patients does not depend upon knowledge of how emotional conflicts are translated into physiologic malfunctioning or upon resolution of problems concerning specificity. The physician who orients treatment to the patient rather *than simply to the disease* and who can utilize the doctor-patient relationship therapeutically can often alleviate emotional problems and ameliorate the physical illness.

The Resolution of Conflict

Today we know that anger and hostility, fear, resentment, anxiety, guilt, and egotism all cause emotional problems and will very likely also bring physical impairment. Both external losses and occurrences as well as internalization of past emotional trauma can bring depression, despair, and other forms of psychic pain.

All of these problems can be met and dealt with by coming into contact with the divine through a vital religious life and sacramental acts that touch us at a deep level. Certainly warmth and positive regard on the part of those to whom we relate each day has inestimable value, as does a therapeutic relationship with a competent counselor who can help us explore the roots of repressed fears, hatreds, and guilts. James Lynch documents the effects of loneliness on heart disease in his superb study, *The Broken Heart*. This type of exploration frequently brings permanent and complete healing so that tranquilizers and drugs of all sorts are no longer needed by persons undergoing therapy.

The roots of anxiety can usually be traced to one or more of several types of conflict—conflict within an individual, between individuals, or between the individual and his or her world. In the latter case, if an individual perceives the world to be meaningless and mechanistic, then the only thing that can really help him or her out of the problem is a new worldview—one which allows for belief in the existence of a spiritual reality in which God does break into our lives bringing meaning and wholeness. The church has a great responsibility in this area, for it should be showing individuals in this materialistic, anxiety-ridden age how to gain access to this reality and encounter and experience the divine. Religious experience and faith are indeed important factors in the health and wholeness of the entire person—body, soul, and mind.

Research on the "Cancer Personality"

In an address delivered before the Assembly of Episcopal Hospitals and Chaplains on March 10, 1975, Dr. Carl Simonton, Director of Oncology Associates, Forth Worth, Texas, and Mrs. Stephanie Simonton, Director of Psychotherapy, discussed the relationship of personality and attitude to cancer.

Well-known among oncologists is the surveillance theory of cancer, which says that everyone develops malignancies in his or her body, but that in the majority of cases the body fights off the malignancies so that when cancer is diagnosed in individuals, it more often indicates a breakdown in the body's defense mechanisms than it does a particular strength on the part of the developing malignancy.

Dr. Simonton pondered this theory and concluded that cancer was in many ways similar to tuberculosis and to chronic degenerative diseases that overwhelmed people when their bodies' defenses broke down. About this time he was also personally working with a bio-feedback machine that demonstrated that one could control blood pressure, heart rate and temperature by controlling one's inner emotional state via relaxation and the use of mental imagery.

Dr. Simonton decided that he would apply what he was learning from the bio-feedback machine to some of his cancer patients and see what happened. In his first test Dr. Simonton taught a patient with advanced throat cancer to relax for approximately 10 minutes three times a day and imagine his body's white blood cells attacking and flushing out of his system all the cancer cells. Amazingly enough the patient completely recovered from his cancer.

Not every patient Dr. Simonton worked with was cured by any means, but enough evidence has been gathered to document the incredible effects of active imagination—or meditation—upon the person who believes in it and uses it consistently.

Mrs. Simonton stated that many of the patients who came to the clinic refused to undergo psychotherapy and did not wish to engage in mental relaxation techniques, the purpose of which is to influence the immunity system of the body, thus discouraging and retarding the disease. She also noted that frequently cancer patients experience an emotional loss six to eighteen months prior to the cancer diagnosis, but that this loss is only one incident in a long pattern of events indicative of problems with relationships. As Mrs. Simonton helps the patients in the mental relaxation procedures and active imagination techniques, she encourages them to accept responsibility for their own lives and not to see themselves as hopeless victims of a cruel fate.

Although the Simontons have encountered a great deal of discouragement in their work, they have witnessed miraculous cures and "spontaneous" remissions of cancer. Dr. Simonton heavily stresses the need to change one's belief system—an extremely difficult thing for both patients and physicians to do—so that one can allow for such relatively unorthodox techniques as active imagination and mental relaxation and for such generally unexpected occurrences as healings. The Simontons' book, *Getting Well Again,* is excellent and describes their methods of healing.

The Healing of Emotions

It was Sigmund Freud who first discovered that personality theory was not as simple as previous thinkers maintained. In working with his patients, probing them, and taking seriously their "slips" of the tongue, dreams, and free associations, he concluded that the conscious mind was only part of one's psyche, and that by paying attention to one's unconscious, he or she could discover repressed emotions, drives, and ideas.

Carl Jung, Freud's disciple and friend, eventually found it necessary to break with Freud because his theories did not offer an explanation for a number of strange experiences Jung was witnessing. Jung concluded on the basis of his experiences with and observations of patients that beyond one's conscious mind and one's personal unconscious mind, there existed a realm of unconscious contents which transcended one's own individual experiences. By touching the power and vitality inherent in this realm, one could transcend his or her own limited and finite ego consciousness and come into contact with divine reality. Jung then concluded that if one's psyche could be viewed as a bridge between this transcendent power and one's physical body, healing—that is, healing from a religious source— could be experienced.

Jung found that as persons learned to relate to the unconscious and to pay attention to dreams, symbols and archetypal myths, they were healed of both mental disturbances and physical ailments. He noted specifically a case of extreme psoriasis which almost completely disappeared after six weeks of intense psychological analysis.

Jung noted that frequently when one ignores the unconscious and pays no attention to myth, symbol, sacrament or other ways of experiencing the transcendent realm, one's body will act out what is being ignored or repressed.

Because the unconscious can open us up to contact with both creative *and* destructive powers, it behooves us to be aware that only as we take with us into this inner realm the figure of the Risen Christ, who triumphed over the destructive forces of the universe by his death and resurrection, can we navigate this territory safely and experience transformation.

Jung maintained that the real concern of religion ought to center around mediating this transcendent reality to men and women and to direct them toward the divine source of healing. The importance of a religious outlook to healing can be seen in this now famous passage from Jung's *Modern Man in Search of a Soul:*

During the past thirty years, people from all the civilized countries of the earth have consulted me. I have treated many hundreds of patients, the larger number being Protestants, a smaller number of Jews, and not more than five or six believing Catholics. Among all my patients in the second half of life—that is to say, over thirty-five—there has not been one whose problem in the last resort was not that of finding a religious outlook on life. It is safe to say that every one of them fell ill because he had lost that which the living religions of every age have given to their followers, and none of them has been really healed who did not regain his religious outlook.

FOR FURTHER READING

Dunbar, Flanders, *Emotions and Bodily Changes* (4th Edition), New York: Columbia University Press, 1954.

Frank, Jerome D., *Persuasion and Healing,* New York: Schocken Books, 1969.

Jung, C. G., *Modern Man in Search of a Soul,* New York: Harcourt Brace Jovanovich, Inc., 1955.

Lynch, James, *The Broken Heart,* New York: Basic Books, 1977.

Simonton, O. Carl, Matthews, Stephanie, and Creighton, James, *Getting Well Again,* Los Angeles: Tarcher, 1978.

21

Tongue Speaking, A Mystical Experience

Today there is tremendous interest in the strange phenomenon known as tongue speaking. Approximately two to three million Americans have had this strange experience happen to them. Termed an evidence of "spiritual baptism," glossolalia is a technical term defined as a spontaneous utterance of sounds which occur in random and incomprehensible patterns. The phenomenon usually occurs only among certain Christian sects and is performed effortlessly, not controlled by the speaker but rather happening to or through the speaker.

The meaning of the tongue-speech is interpreted after its utterance by either another person or by the tongue-speaker. This interpretation is also given spontaneously and both the original tongue-speech and the interpretation are usually accompanied by deep joy.

Where does Tongue Speaking Occur?

Glossolalia can occur in a variety of settings—by oneself in a quiet room, or in a heavily charged atmosphere with large groups of people. Frequently the experience happens to persons who never expected it and in fact have previously found the idea of such a phenomenon repugnant. One such example is that of Myer Pearlman, a well-educated linguist, who said in *The Pentecostal Evangel:*

> As I stood there, I felt some strange influence come over me, indescribable but delightful. I saw no one and heard no audible voice. But this was the turning point in my life. . . . As I knelt to pray one day not too long afterward, to my amazement I heard myself speaking words unfamiliar to me. It lifted me into a higher realm and gave me a sense of the nearness of God.

Other persons to whom this experience has happened note that it has brought them feelings of release, of ecstasy, and has been a means of transformation in their lives.

Reaction in the Churches

The recent surge of tongue speakings has caused considerable consternation among many of the more orthodox church groups which viewed it as an unrestrained emotional indulgence leading to irrationality and dangerous primitivism. Some church leaders have even forbidden the practice among members of their congregations. On the other hand, some Christian groups view the practice as being at the core of true Christian experience, finding biblical and experimental support for it.

Originally found only in Pentecostal and Protestant churches, tongue speaking is now also a frequent experience among many Roman Catholics as well as among the conservative and traditional Protestant churches in the United States. The widespread appearance of the phenomenon has even been noted by the mass media and numerous articles have appeared on the subject. Interestingly enough, those churches which have recently enjoyed the greatest growth are precisely those who advocate and experience tongue-speaking.

The Pentecostal churches are good examples of those which emphasize conformance to biblical practice and authority and a rather strict morality, in addition to a rather exuberant display of their religious beliefs. Although they have been the object of much ridicule on the subject of tongue speaking, the Pentecostals rely on the authenticity of the practice itself to refute disbelief, for from all evidence, it is impossible to physically duplicate tongue speaking at will. Its spontaneous occurrence cannot be consciously manipulated or imitated.

Although there have been numerous disputes on the subject in the churches of the Western world, it is interesting to note that tongue speaking has always been a fact of religious life in the Eastern Orthodox churches, although the practice has been chiefly in monasteries.

A Psychological Perspective

From a psychological point of view, it would seem that there is a good basis for belief in the practice of tongue speaking. Some depth psychologists maintain that the experience is but one expression of contact with the realm of the collective unconscious which surrounds each individual's personal unconscious. Through contacting this level of transcendent reality, one gains access to experiences of the supernatural or the divine that ordinary ego-consciousness never provides.

It was the Swiss psychiatrist, Carl Jung, who first hypothesized in modern times that we can experience levels of psychic reality which allow us to encounter the numinous through dreams, visions, and intuitions, and other extrasensory experiences like tongue speaking, prophecy, etc.

My Own Perspective

Brought up with a materialistic worldview which prohibited belief in the existence of a spiritual realm that can be actually encountered by human beings, I have had to change my thinking radically to make sense theologically of the genuine spiritual experience I have seen occur. One of the results of my explorations was an interest in the phenomenon of tongue speaking. So I set out to investigate it—what the Bible and church history have had to say about it, what individuals today who have experienced it have to say about it, and how it can be better understood by examining it philosophically, theologically, and psychologically.

New Testament Instances of Glossolalia

There are a number of references to speaking in tongues in the New Testament. The coming of the Holy Spirit, which Jesus promised before his ascension, was accompanied by divine gifts and powers.

There were two ways the Holy Spirit could speak through a person, according to the New Testament accounts. The first was called prophecy; i.e., the Holy Spirit speaking through a believer in his or her own language or tongue. Prophecy in this context did not necessarily connote foretelling the future; it rather dealt with the spontaneous utterances of the spirit in preaching or meditation. Sometimes hints of the future were contained in these experiences. Thus most of the sermons delivered by the apostles to which the Book of Acts refers were called prophecy.

The second way the Holy Spirit could speak through an individual was by means of glossolalia—utterances in tongues foreign to the speaker. This practice seemed to be of value in two respects. First, it expressed religious feelings in a joyful and ecstatic way which a more rational expression (i.e., an intelligible language) often cannot do. Second, it evidenced the power from which this gift came, for a person could not contrive this form of expression; it was of necessity spontaneous and genuine.

Specific New Testament References to Tongue Speaking

The New Testament contains seven direct and eight indirect references to glossolalia. The first reference, in the second chapter of Acts, describes the baptism of the Holy Spirit, which was to give the apostles the assurance and vitality to carry forth the good news into an alien and hostile world. We read:

> While the Day of Pentecost was running its course they were all together in one place, when suddenly there came from the sky a noise like that of a strong driving wind, which filled the whole house where they were sitting. And there appeared to them tongues like flames of fire, dispersed among them and resting on each one. And they were all filled with the Holy Spirit and began to talk in other tongues, as the Spirit gave them power of utterance.
>
> Now there were living in Jerusalem devout Jews drawn from every nation under heaven; and at this sound the crowd gathered, all bewildered because each one heard the apostles talking in his own language. They were amazed and in their astonishment exclaimed, "Why, they are all Galileans, are they not, these men who are speaking? How is it then that we hear them, each of us in his own native language? Parthians, Medes, Elamites; inhabitants of Mesopotamia, of Judaea and Cappadocia, of Pontus and Asia, of Phrygia and Pamphylia, of Egypt and the districts of Libya around Cyrene; visitors from Rome, both Jews and proselytes, Cretans and Arabs, we hear them telling in our own tongues the great things God has done." And they were all amazed and perplexed, saying to one another, "What can this mean?" Others said contemptuously, "They have been drinking!"

The tenth chapter of Acts also refers to the gift of tongues. Peter has been directed through a dream or vision to go to Cornelius' house in Caesarea where, during Peter's message, the Holy Spirit was poured out upon the assembled Gentiles, to the amazement of the Jews. This particular experience had a powerful impact upon Peter, for it demonstrated to him that the old law had been superseded by the coming of Christ and his Spirit, one of the evidences of which was tongue speaking.

The Gospel of Mark also noted that believers would "speak in strange tongues." In his first letter to the Corinthians, Paul says that although he would find it pleasing if the Christians at Corinth spoke in tongues, he would find it more pleasing if they prophesied, for prophecy would be more advantageous for the church.

Paul also notes that "ecstatic utterance" is one of the gifts of the Spirit, and in his famous thirteenth chapter, he says that Christians ought to earnestly seek the spiritual gifts, but that love is to be pursued above all else: "Love will never come to an end. Are there prophets? Their work will be over. Are there tongues of ecstasy? They will cease. Is there knowledge? It will vanish away; for ... the partial vanishes when wholeness comes" (Acts 13:8-10).

Indirect References to Tongues

The indirect references to tongue speaking in the New Testament include the story of the laying-on-of-hands by Peter and John in Samaria (Acts 8:9-24), the account of Peter and John's release from prison (Acts 4:23-32), and several references to the Holy Spirit on the part of Paul in Thessalonians 5, Colossians 3, Ephesians 5, Galatians 4, and Romans 8. Although the New Testament references to glossolalia are not so numerous as the references to healing, dreams or visions, there are enough allusions to it to show that it was indeed an important part of the life of the apostles and indicative of the powerful workings of the Holy Spirit.

The History of Tongue Speaking in the Church

Although specific references to glossolalia in immediate postapostolic times are not numerous, it does appear that the sophisticated writers among the early church fathers recognized tongue-speaking as an important gift of the Spirit.

According to what we can deduce from the writings of Irenaeus, glossolalia began to be included in the term "prophecy." He noted in his *Against Heresies* that contemporary Christians saw visions, could foresee events in the future, and voiced prophetic utterances. He further noted that Christians spoke in a variety of languages as a result of having received the Holy Spirit.

Allusions to glossolalia and/or prophecy can also be found in the works of Ignatius and Justin Martyr and in the *Didache* and the *Shepherd of Hermas*. The last really specific reference to speaking in tongues occurred in the writing of Tertullian, a North African Christian of the third century. St. Pachomius, a fourth-century Egyptian abbot, was reputed to have spoken in angelic language, but after his death it was to be approximately 1000 years before the Western church would note any experience of tongue speaking. Glossolalia came to be regarded as originally given only

for the purpose of evangelizing, and it was believed to be no longer necessary to spiritual life.

Tongue Speaking in the Eastern Church

With the fall of the Roman Empire, Western Christianity, the only re-
maining vestige of civilization, found itself becoming increasingly secularized. The Eastern Orthodox Church, however, was not forced to assume
secular leadership and thus remained more mystical and spiritual. The current Patriarch of Constantinople has noted that speaking in tongues has
never completely disappeared in the Greek church—as it did in the West
for a long time.

Many of the Eastern monastic practices enabled the gifts of the spirit to
be practiced throughout the ages. Some of the Orthodox Christians, for
example, have used the Jesus Prayer consistently and found that it has led
them to intense religious experiences sometimes comparable to tongue
speaking. Mystical experience seems to have been far more heavily emphasized in the Eastern church, as Ernst Benz shows in *The Eastern Orthodox
Church: Its Thought and Life*.

The Attitude of the Western Church

Somehow in the development of Western Christianity after the fall of
Rome, tongue speaking became associated with demon possession. The
section on exorcism in the *Rituale Romanum,* presumably written about
1000 A.D., maintains, for example, that one sign of demon possession is
speaking in strange tongues.

Throughout the Western church, however, every now and then there
appeared someone who was gifted with tongue speaking. Among those acknowledged in written record as having evidenced this gift of the spirit are
St. Hildegard (twelfth century), who was able to speak and interpret a
language completely unknown to her, St. Vincent Ferrer (fourteenth century), St. Francis Xavier and St. Louis Bertrand (sixteenth century), and
numerous other saints noted by Johann Joseph von Gorres in his work on
Christian mysticism.

Suddenly in the seventeenth century in France, however, there was an
occurrence of tongue speaking of massive proportions among the Hugue-
nots, who were being severely persecuted for their religious beliefs. In addition to having the gift of tongues, these French Protestants also saw visions and had auditory extrasensory experiences, all of which phenomena

they believed to be evidence that heavenly angels were coming to help them in their hour of need.

In London in 1831 a young minister named Edward Irving found that after a season of continuous prayer in his church, tongue speaking broke out in both private and public worship, but eventually Irving was charged with heresy and excommunicated by the Church of Scotland.

Soon after the revival of tongue speaking in Irving's London church, glossolalia occurred in Sweden and in North America among both the Mormons and the Shakers. In 1855 both Armenia and Russia experienced religious revivals accompanied by tongue speaking. But it wasn't until the twentieth century that glossolalia began to be a phenomenon of great significance. The origins of this glossolalian revival seem to have been in the midwest during the 1870s, during which time numerous religious revivals were occurring.

The Beginnings of Pentecostalism

In 1900 Charles F. Parham established a Bible college in Topeka, Kansas which began to emphasize study of the subject of baptism in the Holy Spirit. As a result of their study, prayer and meditation, they soon experienced the gift of tongues. This phenomenon attracted considerable attention, and eventually outreach missions from this college touched individuals throughout the midwest, west, and south—with reports of healings, tongues, and other phenomenal experiences.

Eventually this ministry spread to Los Angeles where the actual Pentecostal Church took shape on Azusa Street in an old livery stable that had been renovated to make a church. From all over the United States people came to the Azusa Mission to be filled with the Spirit, and in the next fifty years, the Pentecostal ranks swelled to two million.

Simultaneously a religious revival was occurring in Wales, in Norway, and in North Germany. A long Pentecostal revival was also noted in Zurich in 1910. Even Russia and Armenia spawned Pentecostal communities and ironically, some of these very Pentecostals who emigrated and came to the United States "accidentally" happened on the Azusa Street Mission in Los Angeles.

The Holiness Sects as the Roots of the Pentecostal Movement

In order to discuss tongue speaking in the United States today, we will have to understand something of the Pentecostal church, its history, and its beliefs. The movement centers around a theology of tongues, for Pentecostalism was not really born until glossolalia began to be viewed as one of the major components of religious experience. The belief that tongue speaking was *the* sign of the infilling of the Holy Spirit and that it heralded a return to the Pentecostal experience of the apostolic church was the major basis of the movement.

The Pentecostal movement sprang rather organically from the Holiness sects which developed after the Civil War. In reaction against increasing Protestant liberalism, the Holiness advocates affirmed the literal inspiration of the Bible and the need for a personal, individual experience of salvation. This salvation experience consisted of three parts—first, the actual conversion; second, sanctification (a process by which one was given the ability to live a life free from immorality); and three, the experience of baptism in the Holy Spirit, one sign of which was tongue speaking.

One of the first and most important of the Holiness sects was the Christian and Missionary Alliance church, which experienced a controversy on the subject of tongue speaking when some leaders began to maintain it was essential to baptism in the Holy Spirit. Dr. A. B. Simpson, in response to the controversy, eventually wrote a report that maintained, in essence, that tongues was *one* of the gifts of the Spirit and that it was not *essential* to, or *the sign* of, being filled with the Holy Spirit.

In 1910 the five basic beliefs of fundamentalism were published. They included belief in: the infallibility of the Bible, the virgin birth, the atonement, the resurrection, and the imminent return of Christ. Furthermore, Pentecostals maintained that tongue speaking was *the* evidence of the infilling of the Spirit and that glossolalia was an experience necessary to the fullness of Christian life.

Thus it is clear why tongues has become such a pervasive issue. The multitude of Pentecostal manuals and pamphlets on the subject of preparation for receiving the Spirit and the gift of tongues testifies to its key role in the beliefs of the movement. Many of the manuals, however, do stress the importance of a quiet, prayerful expectancy rather than a heavy emotional atmosphere while awaiting the gift.

The years of rapid growth for the Pentecostals, from 1907 to 1940, were sometimes marked by an excess of emotion and fanaticism, now regretted by the church leaders who recognized that this brand of enthusiasm didn't help the Pentecostal cause and sometimes labeled it a "tongues club." Today the Pentecostal movement consists of approximately twenty-six churches—the largest of which are the Assembly of God, the United Pentecostal Church, the Church of God in Christ, and the Church of God.

The Pentecostal church has also spawned a growing lay organization called the Full Gospel Business Men's Fellowship International.

The Nature of Pentecostal Worship

In an attempt to discover something of the nature of Pentecostal services, I have attended several in a variety of geographical areas and cultural milieus. I have found the services to be more vocal than those of other denominations, including tongue speaking and frequent Amens and Hallelujahs. Some services used clapping and emphasized musical rhythms, but none was emotinally out of control by any means, and all were friendly and warm. It is evident that for many persons the tongue-speaking experience has been one means of revitalizing Christian life.

The Relationship Between Tongue Speaking and Traditional Christianity

As a result of both the vitality of many of the experiences in the Pentecostal church and the failure of liberal Protestantism to meet the religious needs of many individuals, tongue speaking has spread to many major denominations. Although there is no official organization for tongue speaking, as there is for healing, the magazine *Trinity,* the Christian Advance meetings, and numerous spontaneous occurrences of glossolalia have all furthered interest in and the experience of tongue speaking.

The phenomenon has occurred in every part of the United States—from Van Nuys, California (where the Rev. Dennis Bennett became interested in tongues and has since had a tremendous impact on other Christians), to Yale University, to Jamaica, New York. In the late 1960s the movement touched the Catholic church where it has made a powerful impact. Starting at Notre Dame and Ann Arbor, the movement has spread throughout the United States and around the world. Cardinal Suenens of Belgium has been appointed by Rome to supervise the growing renewal which has developed. His book, *A New Pentecost?,* is one of the best recent discussions of the subject.

Although many ministers, priests, and lay people do find tongue speaking objectionable, numerous clergy have written about it to show its biblical foundation and its revitalizing influence on many lives. One minister friend of mine, for example, has written movingly of his experience:

"At our informal prayer group sessions the gifts of the Spirit are in evidence 'decently and in order' relative to our own group, but obviously different from the tradition of our formal worship, which we have no intention of changing. And still, when the Spirit is flowing, the formal liturgy of the church is far from 'stylized words from a book'. . . .

"About half of us are using the avenues and truths of clinical psychology as a part of our growth process, and we see this as part of the whole picture, as a religious experience in which the Spirit brings the hidden things of darkness into light and is also the one to deal with these things. . . .

"The joy is constant, even in the 'tribulation' of self discovery, because it all figures into the growth process and the becoming. . . . The needs of men are so great and only God's power can help them. . . . The exhilaration lasts, returns and changes."

Attitudes toward Glossolalia

Basically there exist several attitudes toward the phenomenon of tongue speaking. Some believe tongues has no value because it is merely a primitive, irrational and perhaps dangerous intrusion into normal reality and consciousness. Others find tongues to have been meaningful in the New Testament, but not in the present day. And still others believe that tongues can be a valuable religious experience in our modern age.

The Importance of a Worldview that
Includes Belief in Spiritual Reality

A major reason why only a minority of persons hold this last view is that the Western world has long held a materialistic, rationalistic view of the universe which maintains that the only reality is a physical and rational one. Such a view leaves no room for belief in the existence of a spiritual reality which allows us to encounter the divine creator through such supernatural means as dreams, visions, prophecy, clairvoyance, or tongue speaking. Only as we come to see that the experience of tongues allows unconscious contents to flow through us, putting us into contact with an inner spiritual world, will we be able to view the experience in a wholistic way.

When viewed in this light, tongue speaking can be seen as a transforming, revitalizing experience, for it allows us to encounter the divine in a real, experiential way that transcends normal ego consciousness. Thus those persons who have testified of its value in their lives are witnessing to the power of God to break through into their here and now experiences.

Certainly not all persons desire, receive, or benefit from the gift of tongues. And surely there is the danger that some Christians will become entranced by the emotional intensity of the phenomenon and perhaps neglect other ways of religious growth.

In any case, however, it is important to remember that tongues can indeed be the start of a spiritual life's journey and may be a vital way to become open to religious experience.

FOR FURTHER READING

Kelsey, Morton T., *Tongue Speaking,* Garden City: Doubleday, 1968.
Suenens, Leon Joseph Cardinal, *A New Pentecost?* New York: Seabury, 1975.

22

The Modern Shaman and Christian Belief

> Now as he journeyed he approached Damascus, and suddenly a light from heaven flashed about him. And he fell to the ground and heard a voice saying to him, "Saul, Saul, why do you persecute me?" . . . When his eyes were opened, he could see nothing; so they led him by the hand and brought him into Damascus. And for three days he was without sight, and neither ate nor drank. (Acts 9:3, 4, 8, 9)

For most of us, the call to go on our spiritual journey does not come as dramatically as the apostle Paul's call did. Rather, it may surface as an anxiety neurosis, a life crisis, or as just a sense of vague dissatisfaction with the state of our lives. We live in a materialistic age that has given little credence to inner values; yet we find our lives arid and one-dimensional without the richness only the spiritual side of life can provide. As this dissatisfaction has increased, more and more people have reached out for experiences of spiritual reality.

For some, this contact comes through orthodox religious means—such as prayer and meditation. For others, ecstatic religious experiences like tongue speaking or prophecy provide a means of connection with the world of the spirit. Extrasensory experiences through hypnosis convince some persons of the reality of a non-material world, while still others reach altered states of consciousness through drug experimentation.

Whatever our means of introduction to supernatural reality, we soon learn that this non-material realm is a real and powerful one that cannot be related to casually, for it can open us up to not only the divine creative forces, but also destructive demonic ones.

If we find that we are called to go on a journey inward, we will need a mentor or guide to help us on our way (for example, in Carlos Castaneda's experiences with supernatural reality, he found he needed sorcerer Don Juan to be his spiritual companion and to guide him in changing his perception of reality). For we will find that our familiar constructs of reality no longer work once we embark on a spiritual journey.

Although modern Western culture has largely ignored the existence of spiritual reality, many archaic cultures have been deeply in touch with non-material reality, maintaining contact with it through highly developed ritual and myth. These primitive cultures were well aware of the importance of the mentor, or spiritual guide, in their midst, as mediators of spiritual reality to the collective. These mentors (called shamans) had to go through intense initiation experiences which brought them into close relationship with the supernatural. After this they could become channels or mediators of this power to the rest of the group.

The power of their own contact with the spiritual often gave shamans the ability to work miracles. We read, for example, of Hosteen Klah chasing away a whirlwind by spitting into it and chanting. Or we can hear the account of Rolling Thunder causing an object to travel to him over a distance of several miles.

The Choosing of a Shaman

Primitive Indian tribes maintained that shamans were chosen by the Great Spirit to be healers and that after this supernatural selection, a spiritual crisis occurred. Only upon successful resolution of this crisis (which included undergoing ecstatic experiences like trances and dreams and also instruction in shamanic techniques) could the shaman be accorded his full status in society.

Among the Yakut Tribe, for example, the potential shaman underwent a death/rebirth experience of a three-day duration. During this period the initiate could neither eat nor drink (see Saul's three-day fast according to Acts) and experienced a paring-down process which required him to give up the trappings of his life so that he could begin anew.

In some tribes initiation into shamanism resulted from a relationship between an old shaman and a young pupil who would sit quietly rubbing stones together, waiting for a significant event to occur. Physical deprivation and intense meditation often induced a death/rebirth experience, during which the initiate envisioned himself as a skeleton, stripped bare to begin life anew as a mediator of spiritual mysteries.

Often the initiates experienced epileptic-like seizures or some form of hysteria which they had to simply endure until the seizure had spent itself.

At this point, if the young shamans had survived the ravages intact, they were considered suitable human mediators of the sacred. In a sense they were living bearers of the religious form for their culture.

Among some peoples the process of becoming a shaman often started in a frenzy and was followed by a loss of consciousness and the need to be completely alone—perhaps in a forest— and then to go through a stripping process which included exposure to the dangers of fire and water and ultimately a wounding with knives. Then an old shaman was called to aid the younger one in dealing with all the spirits that might be encountered. Often a waiting period of *several years* was needed to legitimize the initiation of the shaman.

Frequently the initiation period included manifestations of hysteria. For example, shamanic procedures among certain Arctic peoples included a cataleptic trance in which the prospective shaman's soul was said to be out of the body. Many shamans in the south Asian and Oceanic areas of the world evinced characteristics of mental unbalance. In other areas of the world epileptics have been thought to be magicians. Initiates, at the outset of their shamanism, frequently have fallen prey to great sickness and affliction but have been cured and then become mediators of healing spiritual forces.

Some cultures have reported shamans to be high-strung and nervous but able to concentrate more intensely and for longer periods of time than other persons. It has traditionally been common for shamans to be able to perform physical feats for extremely long time spans and to successfully engage in such acts as swallowing hot coals. As a result of the intensity of their initiation experiences, shamans have been found to exude certain powerful qualities of person—perhaps what has been termed by Castaneda "personal power."

Among some peoples selection to shamanism has traditionally been followed by a time of instruction by an older shaman—after which the initiate had to interpret dreams and demonstrate other qualities showing the selection to be authentic. After these demonstrations a formal initiation took place, frequently of five or more days' duration. There was much feasting and sometimes a rite of ascent to heaven also was enacted. Among some tribes a ritual purification of the candidate occurred.

The Garb of a Shaman

The garb of the shaman has always been important, for it revealed things about shamanism and had a spiritual force all its own, for it had been consecrated. Those persons about to be initiated into shamanism often bought their costumes from relatives of dead shamans. Only shamans were permitted to wear the special garb, for the spirits present in the vestments had to be controlled or they would bother the entire tribe or clan.

One Siberian costume included a caftan, a mask, a copper pectoral, and a cap that weighed from 30 to 50 pounds. Mythical representations of animals, ribbons, snakes' tails, animal pelts, and iron and copper objects often adorned the costume. The result of all the unusual ornamentation was that the wearer resembled a bird, a reindeer or a bear.

Although the term shaman often connotes magic or practices of medicine men, shamans specialize in techniques peculiar to them alone. They are, for example, able to control spirits and not be controlled or used *by* them. Marked as unique in his society and notable because of his religious crisis or "conversion" experience, the shaman could be described as mystical, intense in religious devotion. Shamans are often androgynous, combining the gifts of both the masculine and feminine.

The shaman's role, in essence, was that of intermediary between the people of his culture and the spiritual forces of the universe. He could be intermediary or guardian of the soul only because he himself had undergone his own spiritual crisis which had wounded and purged him, enabling him to understand and minister to the wounds of others. One could become a shaman by answering a "call" from the spiritual world, by falling inheritor to the tribal role, or, on occasion, by choosing it.

It is interesting to note that although drugs are sometimes mentioned in connection with initiation into knowledge of the supernatural, the practice of this artificial method of inducing altered statres of consciousness has usually been considered invalid and non-genuine.

In his quartet dealing with the Yaqui approach to knowledge, Carlos Castaneda does show Don Juan using drugs to induce altered consciousness in his pupil, but the old Indian specifies that he uses drugs only because Carlos's construct of reality is so impenetrable that it needs to be forcefully assaulted to allow him to receive spiritual insights. Thus the drug experience is a tool only—a means to an end—that would otherwise be extremely difficult to achieve.

Beliefs of Shamanism

Although the word shaman (or shamaness) is used today to describe certain persons who possess supernatural or magic powers, it has become a catchall phrase which has lost some of its original meaning. The concept of shamanism first occurred in Siberia and central parts of Asia where the supernatural or religious elements of collective life revolved around the central cultural position of the shaman.

Cultures in which a shaman or shamaness was important believed that there were three cosmic regions—the earth, sky, and underworld. Only the shaman knew the secret of breaking through from one plane to another. The three portions of the universe were thought to be connected by a central axis which rose through a hole central to each region, enabling gods, dead people, and shamans to travel back and forth. Traditionally, this sort of central area has been considered sacred and a source of connection to a superhuman presence.

Going back and forth among the three worlds can be compared to a breakthrough into other realms of consciousness, today known as altered states of consciousness. Although many persons today experience these states in a variety of ways—through such means as dreams, visions, hypnosis, speaking in tongues, and meditation, there are some persons who seem to have greater connection to spiritual reality and can mediate the creative forces of this reality to others. As mediators, then, these persons become modern-day shamans.

The central axis of the three cosmic regions is called by a variety of names—according to the mythology of the culture. For example, in Eskimo mythology the axis is called the Pillar of the Sky and is represented by the pole which is always found in the center of a traditional Eskimo home. This idea of a pillar is also represented by a cosmic mountain image. Among archaic peoples only shamans could ascend and descend via this pillar from one world to another, so only they could have a personal extrasensory-type experience. The rest of the people in the society only lived out the religious form in a collective, ritualistic, societal sort of way.

The origin of the belief that only shamans could contact other regions of the cosmos lies in the idea of the Fall. Only privileged persons could be presumed to have the ability to contact the gods, for human beings had lost this ability as a result of the Fall. The shaman, however, had more direct knowledge of the cosmic realms and could gain direct access to them and thus intercede on behalf of humankind.

Symbolism and Shamanism

Many religious and mythical symbols are found in shamanism. The horse symbol, for example, is important, for it takes deceased persons to the other world. It is also used by the shaman to reach another level of the cosmos. Certain German and Japanese riturals include eight-legged or headless horses.

The motif of magical heat is also important to shamanism. Sometimes, for example, shamans breathe flames in order to increase their sense of mystical heat. Some practitioners of sorcery eat spices to increase their body heat. Christian healers sometimes speak of feeling warmth in their hands as they practice laying on hands. The men who accompanied Christ on the walk to Emmaus spoke of their hearts "burning" within them as they listened to Jesus' words.

Many shamans also employ bird symbolism and bird images in their ministry. The image of the soul is often pictured as a bird, and both death and out-of-body experiences are depicted as birds. In Christian symbolism the Holy Spirit is represented by a dove.

The shaman's ability to move back and forth between cosmic zones is considered a magical flight. Many saints in the Roman Catholic tradition have also experienced the phenomenon of levitation. St. Joseph of Cupertino, Sister Mary of Jesus Crucified and others have detailed their "flight" experiences.

The Bridge Motif

Another motif that frequently occurs in shamanism is the bridge. Shamans must cross a symbolic bridge when they journey to the underworld. Often specific spiritual rites and rituals are thought of as concrete bridges to mystical realities. In one culture, for example, a cord is seen as a connector between heaven and earth.

Numerous initiation rites—or rites of passage— are undergone by prospective shamans. In both Christian and Islamic myths bridge images are numerous, and medieval tales such as the legend of Sir Lancelot make allusions to sword bridges. This mythical bridge is otherwise depicted as a "strait gate" or a "dangerous passage"—dangerous because it frequently represents a tension-filled situation that deals with a reconciliation of opposites—of day and night, light and dark, heaven and earth.

In a sense, the shaman's ability, via the ecstatic experience, to transcend the opposites, to unify them by bringing them into relationship, restores the wholeness that belonged to humankind before the Fall. Thus the shaman commemorates and acts out for the collective culture the mystical experience that once was the birthright of each human being according to this worldview.

The Ladder Motif

Another important shamanic symbol is the ladder. The gods were said to come down to earth via a ladder and souls of the dead ascended to heaven via a ladder. Among some primitive peoples medicine men erect a ladder in the presence of the sick in order to elicit healing spirits from heaven. Examination of ancient Egyptian tombs has revealed the presence of ladders for the dead to ascend to heaven.

In the Old Testament, Jacob had a vision of angels ascending and descending a ladder to heaven; the stone that Jacob slept on was a holy stone (called bethel—house of God) and lay at the axis point of the earth where the three cosmic lands joined. In the Islamic religion the Jerusalem temple houses a ladder whereby souls ascend to God. The motif of ladders and stairs has always been prominent among Christian mystics who often found that it symbolized certain aspects of the Christian life.

Alchemists also envisioned seven-rung ladders as representations of the spiritual growth process. Just as the bread and wine are concrete physical mediations of the death/resurrection experience of Christ, so ladders, stairs, mountains, cords, bridges, etc., become concrete material representations of the connection between the cosmic regions.

Although shamans are not the only persons who can transcend the earthly realm and reach heaven, their uniqueness lies in their ecstatic means of experiencing this transcendence. This ecstasy, which enables the shamans in primitive cultures to recover the wholeness of human beings *before* the Fall is also experienced by initiates, cultural heroes, and kings and queens of a particular culture via other means.

In Christianity, of course, Christ is seen as the means of wholeness for each believer, and concrete expressions of this wholeness and mystical experience take place through such ecstatic means as tongue-speaking, slaying in the spirit, healing, prophecy, and visions. Other experiences which may be considered similar in nature are dreams, meditation, hypnosis, and the more dangerous practices of divination, soothsaying, and taking drugs.

In any case, the shaman or shamaness, whether Christian or non-Christian, seems to be distinguished by an intense nature—a mystical inclination—which enables him or her to be the means or form by which a religious archetype is lived out and diffused throughout that particular culture. He or she is in essence the wounded healer, bearer of the mystical, through whom the lives of others in the collective culture find a greater connection to the holy. Thus the shaman is a symbol of the holy in their midst.

The primitive shamans are comparable to the mystics of both Eastern and Western religions, says Mircea Eliade in his *Shamanism: Archaic Techniques of Ecstasy*. But he notes that "Shamanism is important not only for the place that it holds in the history of mysticism. The shamans have played an essential role in the defense of the psychic integrity of the community. They are pre-eminently the antidemonic champions; they combat not only demons and disease, but also the black magicians. . . . In a general way, it can be said that shamanism defends life, health, fertility, the world of 'light', against death, diseases, sterility, disaster, and the world of 'darkness'."

Because shamans have traditionally been the defenders of light, many cultures have emphasized the sword, the lance, and other instruments of aggression against the powers of evil. So, shamans were very important in their cultures, for they served as bulwarks versus evil and demonic powers. Human beings were reminded that they were not alone in the midst of chaos and darkness; they could call on the forces of light to go with them into the darkness and then emerge, perhaps scathed, but not defeated.

A Christian Shaman

What, then, in the light of this discussion, is the role of the modern-day Christian shaman?

First of all, if we really take the spiritual world seriously, we will be aware that the forces of darkness do indeed operate in our world. The apostle Paul speaks of putting on the whole armor of God so that we may be able to stand against the demonic powers of the cosmos.

Secondly, however, Christians, more than any other religious group, have an ultimate champion of the forces of light over the forces of darkness in the person of Christ. His actual death and resurrection are symbolically acted out each time a Christian participates in the Eucharist. Christ was and is the ultimate shaman. He was the god/man who died once and for all, who restored to human beings their connection to the divine, a connection severed by the Fall. So Christ is shamanic, but he transcends the limited, mortal role of the shaman in primitive cultures.

The Christian shaman, then, has a great advantage over previous shamans, for he or she is called upon to mediate those powers of the divine which Christ ensured to human beings in a way no other great religious leader has ever been able to do. The Christian shaman must be able to channel images of healing and wholeness so as to bring the people to whom he or she ministers into contact with the spiritual reality which our culture usually denies.

Precisely because our society doesn't emphasize ways of dealing with spiritual reality, shamans are desperately needed to guide people who are searching for a way to encounter the divine that will transform their lives.

Since shamans seek to guide others on a spiritual journey, they must have undertaken their own journeys, for the blind cannot lead the blind. The modern-day shaman must also be trained in listening and be able to establish a relationship of trust with other human beings. The spiritual leader also needs an intellectually valid, broad worldview which sees beyond the rational materialism of our age. And the Christian shaman needs to have an understanding of psi phenomena and of his or her own unconscious depths, especially as revealed through dreams, meditation, and other valid approaches to spiritual reality. The Christian shaman must also know his or her own tradition in ever-increasing depth.

Shamans in religions the world over have dealt with the destructive side of spiritual reality, have gone *through* the pain and evil, and then returned as wounded healers to help others. Because it is a treacherous undertaking to traverse the byways of spiritual reality, Christians today need spiritual guides with whom to go *into* the darkness so they may emerge as whole persons.

Christian shamans can help us appropriate the powers of God's "marvelous light" and accompany us into the shadowy realms of the spiritual world where symbolic death becomes not a terror that swallows us up, but a means of passing from one attitude of life into another. Often one must die to one's old standpoint, his old ego adaptation, if he is to grow. "He who would find his life must lose it."

Because the inner world is dangerous and we need a spiritual guide who has been *through* the chaos and come out on the other side safely and with greater openness and understanding than when he entered this world, those who have not traversed the route can hardly lead others on the way.

The Christian minister, like the shaman, puts people in touch with their own holy experiences—experiences that are concrete manifestations of the divine spirit. Thus they can function as reconcilers of the opposites inside one, which one must bear in tension and often in pain, so that finally one discovers that both joy and pain have their place in life and that both are parts of the whole.

The modern shaman needs to be articulate, compassionate, and contemplative, according to Henri Nouwen, author of *The Wounded Healer*. The Christian shaman must be willing to use his or her own pain to help others who are in search of wholeness. We cannot help others unless we are willing to enter into their pain. Christ could save because he suffered.

> Surely he has borne our griefs
> and carried our sorrows;
> Yet we esteemed him stricken,
> smitten by God and afflicted.
> But he was wounded for our transgressions,
> he was bruised for our iniquities;
> Upon him was the chastisement that made us whole,
> and with his stripes we are healed. (Isaiah 53:4-5)

Out of brokenness comes wholeness. Nouwen cites the Talmud legend as picturing the Messiah as one who sits at the gate of the city among the poor, abounding in wounds, who constantly unbind and then rebind all their sores and hurts. The Messiah, however, only unbinds one wound at a time so that he may be ready in an instant if he is needed to help others.

This talmudic story depicts the attitude of the wounded healer, the shaman, who awaits those in need and can help precisely because he or she has been wounded too, but is not disabled by the wound. In a real sense, every Christian who allows the Spirit to move in him or her is a shaman. This is a unique vocation.